THE HUNTER'S GUIDE TO ACCURATE SHOOTING

BOOKS BY WAYNE VAN ZWOLL

Mastering Mule Deer
America's Great Gunmakers
Elk Rifles, Cartridges, and Hunting Tactics
Modern Sporting Rifle Cartridges
Elk and Elk Hunting
The Hunter's Guide to Ballistics
Gun Digest *Book of Shooting Optics*
The Complete Book of the .22

THE HUNTER'S GUIDE TO ACCURATE SHOOTING

WAYNE VAN ZWOLL

The Lyons Press
Guilford, Connecticut
An imprint of The Globe Pequot Press

The Lyons Press is an imprint of The Globe Pequot Press.

Printed in the United States of America

10 9 8 7 6 5 4 3 2 1

Design by Compset, Inc.

ISBN 1-59228-490-6 (paperback)

All photos by the author unless otherwise noted.

The Library of Congress has previously cataloged an earlier (hardcover) edition as follows:

Van Zwoll, Wayne.
  The hunter's guide to accurate shooting : how to hit what you're aiming at in any situation / Wayne Van Zwoll.
    p. cm.
  ISBN 1-58574-468-9 (hc. : alk. paper)
  1. Shooting. 2. Hunting rifles. I. Title.

SK38.V26 2002
799.2'028'32—dc21

2002141575

CONTENTS

ACKNOWLEDGMENTS

Some people have told me that I shoot well. Most of them haven't seen me shoot enough to render judgment. I'll take responsibility for all the bad shots (some of them have been unbelievably bad); but credit for the good shots goes mostly to Earl Wickman.

Earl was a plumber by trade, in a small town in central Michigan where I grew up. Each Tuesday evening he'd open his basement rifle range to any street urchin willing to plunk down fifty cents for ammo and knuckle under to his coaching. Earl suffered no horseplay. In the blue haze from his cigars, we didn't notice the lead dust and powder smoke that today would send an OSHA inspector scrambling for his gas mask. With Earl's big, bony frame at my elbow, I'd peer through the sights of that DCM 40X Remington and wonder if they would ever be still. Then, as the orange disc up front dived for the black spot downrange, I'd yank the trigger. It was natural.

"You won't shoot well doin' what comes easy," Earl said softly. Despite his bulk and a fiery mop of hair, he came at you easy, drifting quietly along the firing line from one adolescent to the next. We learned slowly. Earl had patience.

Later, I studied under other coaches, and fellow shooters, on the Michigan State University Rifle Team. I learned too from softspoken veterans on the rimfire circuit—shooters like Johnny Moschkau and Herb Hollister, who showed me that to control a trigger, one first had to control his mind. The USAMTU at Fort Benning salted the open prone matches with the likes of Lones Wigger, now a friend as well as a mentor. Olympian Gary Anderson has impressed me not only with his shooting, but with his modesty. Like others of his ability, he demonstrates that doing anything well requires a certain strength of character as well as a mastery of fundamentals.

For that, I'm grateful.

Friends I've made in rifle matches—Vic Fogle, Ray Wheeler, Rich McClure, among many—have not only helped me shoot better, they've enriched my life. So have hunters like Danny O'Connell, a self-taught marksman who can tumble a coyote dodging through sagebrush or drop an elk at 400 yards with his .25–06 as if neither feat were all that noteworthy. Friends in the shooting industry have shown me how rifles and ammunition are made and tested and helped me understand why bullets behave as they do. Mike Jordan, Alan Corzine, Chub Eastman, Dave Emary, Ken Oehler, Charlie Sisk, Jeff Hoffman . . . Golly, the list is just too long!

Optics guru and good friend Bill McRae has shown me better tests for scope sights—and pointed out the Andromeda constellation in a desert night sky. He and other writers who cared enough to research tirelessly and report honestly have helped me understand shooting. "You gotta understand it before you'll get it right," Earl would say. Truly. I never met Francis Sell, though for a time we both lived in Oregon. His deer hunting book is also a great treatise on practical rifle shooting. Few other men—Jack O'Connor comes to mind—have described shooting mechanics with such compelling prose. Sam Fadala, prolific writer and good friend, provided background for part of this work with his book, *Great Shooters of the World*.

Some less accomplished marksmen have passed my way with nothing to contribute except stories—stories of shooters and matches and hunts before my time. They left me pieces of history I couldn't have scrounged anywhere else, history still meaningful to anyone who shoots a rifle. You see, the best shooters aren't just technicians. They comprise a long-standing fraternity. The rifle is both tool and artform, an implement that, over the centuries, has accrued historical value. Collectors don't accumulate just accurate rifles or handsome rifles. They collect because, since the 15th century, rifles have mattered. The guided missile may win wars now, but infantries have determined the outcome of the world's greatest conflicts. Riflemen delivered the U.S. her independence and provisioned her frontier. Riflemen protected her people while they made her the greatest economic power in the world. How easy to forget that we shooters and those who rail against guns are all indebted to riflemen who learned to shoot well.

Earl had a better grasp of all that than most. "Sometimes you can't explain everything a rifle is," he admitted. But he encouraged me to pass along what I could.

PREFACE

Books about guns abound. Books about shooting do not. Gun enthusiasts are not all interested in shooting, and few indeed shoot competitively. I know collectors who hardly ever shoot. Many hunters shoot only enough to check their zeros—and some even neglect that.

This book is mainly for hunters who want to shoot better. It is also for people who are fascinated, as I am, by marksmen who do extraordinary things with ordinary guns. The day of the exhibition shooters is gone, but their wizardry has lost none of its allure. To shooters who wonder how good they can get, the standards set by Herb Parsons, Ad Topperwein, Tom Frye, and, yes, Annie Oakley remain.

You won't find much here about pistols or shotguns. Distilling the art of rifle shooting has taken as many pages as I've been allowed. Beyond the fundamentals of rifle fit, body position, trigger and breath control, and practice, you'll get strong opinions on sights and cartridges, with straight talk on recoil and the voodoo of vertical shot angles. You'll read the best advice from the best shooters around—tips that have helped win Olympic gold and kill big game under the toughest conditions. There's plenty on long shooting: doping wind and reading yardage so you can make shots others miss and know when to decline shots you'll likely miss. Moving game? Here, you'll get lessons from shooters who can hit aspirins tossed in the air.

While I've tapped some extraordinary shooters, this book is for rifle enthusiasts of ordinary talent. Its main purpose is to improve *your* shooting afield. Whether you plink or hunt or attend the occasional metallic silhouette match, you'll find information that will help you shoot as well as you can. There's nothing extraordinary about *my* shooting, but it's better because I've taken the advice you're about to read.

Almost all the hunting anecdotes are mine, collected from thirty-five years in the field. They are included because most rifle shooters are hunters, because hunting eventually tests every skill riflemen cultivate—and because I've discovered that admitting blunders in print gets less painful with age.

Wayne van Zwoll
January 2002

PART I: A Shooter's Slice of History

1

BEFORE THE RIFLE

Firearms came relatively late to shooters, who would no doubt have welcomed them sooner. Clubs, knives, and axes made self-defense truly a short-range event. Boomerangs and spears extended the hunter's reach and increased his margin of safety, but they still had limited range because they depended directly on the power of the human arm. Air, first in blowguns and later in gun barrels, rivaled the effectiveness of the bow limb.

Oranian and Caspian cultures may have had the first bows. Though simple in appearance, the bow is not an intuitive thing. Using a string to harness the power of a bent limb and send a fletched arrow at right angles to the bend was at one time the equivalent of rocket science. We take for granted not only the principle, but subsequent bow designs and the huge impact of bows and arrows on early history. Archers helped the Persians in their conquest of the civilized world. Around 5000 B.C., Egypt freed itself from Persian domination, in part because the Egyptians had skilled bowmen. By 1000 B.C. Persia was putting archers on horseback. Short recurve bows, dating hundreds of years before the time of Christ, armed both infantry and cavalry. Soon Turks were using powerful sinew-backed recurves in competition, launching arrows half a mile.

By 300 B.C., Greeks had initiated a new science: ballistics. Later, great thinkers like Isaac Newton, Leonardo da Vinci, Galileo Galilei, Francis Bacon, and Leonard Euler would try to explain the effects of drag and gravity on projectiles—just as firearms began to make ballistics interesting. Crude explosives had been used in China for 200 years before gunpowder was described by Bacon in 1249. These compounds were both unreliable and inefficient.

Archers continued to rule the battlefields in Europe long after guns appeared as both tools and objects of art. At the Battle of Hastings in 1066, the Normans tricked their English foes into an ambush, then routed them with volleys of arrows that inflicted heavy casualties. The one-piece English longbow was named not for its tip-to-tip measure, but for the archer's draw to an anchor point at the ear or cheek. The staves *were* long, to accommodate long arrows. Bowmen drawing to the center of the chest used shorter bows. The typical longbow used by the English in battle averaged six feet in length, with a flat back and a curved belly. Because English yew couldn't match wood from Mediterranean countries for purity and straightness, the best English bows were fashioned of wood from Spain, which eventually forbade the growing of yew on the premise that it might be used against Spanish troops. The English, desperate for staves, cleverly required that a certain number be included with every shipment of Mediterranean wine.

English archers used the Viking and Norman tactic of arcing a cloud of arrows toward the enemy. The Swiss had perfected the offensive line, with their pikemen; England's longbowmen presented the same formidable wall, but with long-range sting. In defense, they delivered withering barrages that intimidated even armored troops. Armor might turn arrows, but it also burdened the soldiers who wore it. English bowmen aimed for the joints in the armor and shot with deadly accuracy at troops removing their helmets to fight in hot weather. The French learned quickly to fear the hiss of the "gray

The modern recurve bow dates back to ancient Turkey. Laminated limbs are almost as old.

goose wing." At Crecy in 1346 and at Agincourt in 1415, they were trounced by English archers. In those days England's conscripts were required to practice shooting regularly. By statute, anyone earning less than 100 pence a year *had to own* a bow and arrows and submit them to periodic inspection. Though bowmen killing the King's deer were commonly hung with their own bowstrings, convicted poachers were offered pardons in exchange for their service in battle as archers. In 1333 a regiment of these outlaws wrested Halidon Hill from the Scots, their arrows killing 4,000 of the enemy. Only 14 Englishmen died.

Longbows were seldom embellished. Unlike firearms and swords, kept as ornamentation, bows had value as tools only. Wood and its utility deteriorated with age and weather. Few longbows survive, among them a handful of unfinished staves in the Tower of London and a bow salvaged in 1841 from the wreck of the *Mary Rose*, sunk nearly 300 years before.

Bows of North American Indians varied regionally in shape and construction. In the Pacific Northwest, flat, wide limbs shaved from soft woods like yew predominated. Hardwoods like ash, hickory, and Osage orange gave longer service in the slender bows, rectangular in cross-section, carried by tribes in the East and Midwest. Limbs were sometimes backed with sinew, to protect the wood at full draw. Strips of horn appeared only on the bellies of bows (unlike sinew, horn bends under compression but has no stretch). On the plains, bows averaged nearly five feet from tip to tip, almost as long as bows used by forest Indians east of the Mississippi. Arrows in the woodlands were long and elegant, with short feathers to clear the bow handle. In the hardwoods, a hunter could expect only one shot at a deer or turkey, so accuracy was important. On the plains, where the Sioux rode alongside bison and shot several arrows quickly at short range, accuracy didn't matter as much. The long fletching on their arrows helped steer them despite imperfect releases. Raised nocks made for quicker shooting. The Plains Indian pushed the bow as much as he pulled the string, getting lots of thrust from short limbs and a draw well shy of the arrowhead. This "chest draw" stacked enough thrust to drive arrows through bison.

Tribes across North America kept to the bow long after muskets became available. The blast of a flintlock frightened game, even if the shot missed. Thick smoke obscured the animal. Several arrows could be loosed in the time needed to recharge a musket once—and with equal accuracy. Powder and ball had to be bought or stolen, but arrows could be assembled from natural materials. Bows were lighter in weight and more easily maneuverable. In practiced hands, they proved as deadly as the first rifles.

After the development of self-contained cartridges, the bow might have become an anachronism, had not its potential been tapped by colorful and talented people. Will and Maurice Thompson, Floridians limping home after the Civil War, learned to shoot flying ducks with crude bows and arrows made of reeds. The Thompsons later wrote *The Witchery of Archery*, a short but inspiring book. It was followed in 1927 by *Hunting With the Bow and Arrow* by Saxton Pope, a physician who'd attended Ishi, a Yana Indian found near a California settlement in 1911. Ishi taught Pope to make and hunt with a bow and arrow. Pope and Arthur Young kept shooting the bow after Ishi succumbed to tuberculosis. The Pope and Young Club, a records-keeping group, now recognizes outstanding big game animals taken with archery equipment.

The author's recurve bow has driven arrows completely through elk. A sharp broadhead is as deadly as a rifle bullet. American Indians used bows long after muskets became readily available.

Howard Hill made the longbow newsworthy in the early days of television and cinema. He killed game as big as elephants and shot for Errol Flynn in the movie *The Adventures of Robin Hood*. Hill had extraordinary, almost uncanny skill. In exhibitions, he used ramps to glance arrows into the bullseye, skewered small aerial targets with ease, and shot from positions that would have prevented ordinary people from drawing a bow, let alone hitting a target. His bow, so stout that three fetching maidens could not budge the string, remains beautiful in its simplicity. Howard Hill set standards of marksmanship that even today remain formidable.

Fred Bear came along while Hill was still shooting. An unassuming auto worker, Fred began using, then building, bows to hunt whitetail deer in northern Michigan. His passion became a business, and the timing was right. Bear Archery, established in Grayling, promoted bowhunting and competed successfully with Shakespeare, Ben Pearson, and the other firms then marketing bows. Fred popularized the laminated fiberglass-and-maple limb in recurve bows. He used his profits to fund hunting trips, filming many of them. A practiced and deadly game shot, he killed a polar bear and a tiger and became a celebrity. Still, Fred remained a shy and humble man, openly grateful and ever marveling that "I'm paid for something that's so much fun."

By the time the Allen compound bow appeared in 1966, bowhunting had become recognized as a credible field sport. Over the next few decades, it would grow fast. Bows changed dramatically, sprouting cables, pulleys, cams, and lighted sights. Plastic fletching replaced feathers. Aluminum, then carbon fiber, supplanted wood in shafts. Overdraw bows enabled shooters to use super-short arrows that flew half again as fast as any from a longbow.

The bow, older by centuries than the firearm, has changed more since World War II than in all its previous history. The rifle had its growth spurt earlier, during the 19th century, just 600 years after Europe got gunpowder.

2

FIRST
FIREARMS

"Chinese snow" appeared in fireworks a couple of centuries before English friar Roger Bacon described gunpowder in 1249. It would be another sixty years before the compound saw wide use as propellant, following experiments by men like Berthold Schwarz. Black powder was easy to ignite in the open air. Sparking it in a chamber to launch a ball was not so easy. The first guns, developed in Europe in the early 14th century, were simply tubes with ignition holes. Many, like the Swiss culverin, were so heavy as to require two attendants. A culveriner held the tube while his partner lit the charge. Clumsy, inaccurate, and prone to misfire, culverins remained popular with soldiers because their noise and smoke could frighten an enemy. The heavy barrels were hard to steady and were often used with mechanical rests. Even when lighter versions arrived and soldiers began to carry them on horseback, a rest helped. The petronel, a hand cannon held against the breast for firing, was often used with a forked support propped on the saddle.

Smoldering ropes and burning sticks, satisfactory for firing cannons, left much to be desired in smaller guns. When either gun or target moved, long ignition time guaranteed a miss. If the gun had a fuse, the problem was even worse. A soldier needed some mechanism to cause instant ignition. The first lock was a crude lever by which a wick was lowered to the barrel's touch-hole. A spring was eventually added to keep the match from the touch-hole. A trigger came next; it made matchlocks controllable. Arquebusiers (armed with the Spanish arquebus, a type of matchlock) carried extra wicks smoldering in metal boxes on their belts.

Even the best matchlocks often failed. More reliable ignition appeared in the 16th century, in the German "monk's gun." Its spring-loaded jaw held a piece of pyrite (flint) against a serrated bar. The shooter pulled on a ring to scoot the bar across the pyrite. The resulting sparks fell on a trail of fine gunpowder leading into the touch-hole. A more sophisticated version emerged around 1515 in Nuremberg. The wheellock had a serrated disk or wheel, wound with a spanner wrench. Pulling the trigger released the latch holding the wheel under spring tension. Its teeth spun against a chunk of pyrite, generating sparks. Wheellocks were less affected by rain than were matchlocks. They were faster to set and easier to operate on horseback, but also much more costly.

Flintlocks came next, adapted from the *Lock a la Miquelet* used by Spanish *miquelitos* (marauders) in the Pyrenees. Guns of this type featured a spring-loaded cock that swung in an arc when released. At the end of its travel, the flint in the jaws of the cock struck a pan cover or hammer, knocking it back to expose a pan much like that on earlier rifles. A priming charge in the pan caught the sparks and conducted flame to the touch-hole. The cock became known as a hammer, the hammer as a frizzen. Alas, though the frizzen covered the powder until firing, flintlocks, like the more costly wheellocks, could still be rendered inoperable by moisture in the air.

Causing a spark inside the gun became possible at last with the discovery of fulminates in the 18th century by chemists like Claude Louis Berthollet. Adding saltpeter to fulminates of mercury produced an explosive called "Howard's powder," after Englishman

Smoke from both the muzzle and pan obscures the target when a flintlock is fired.

E. C. Howard, who developed it in 1799. Seven years later, Scotch clergyman Alexander John Forsythe became the first experimenter on record to ignite a spark in a gun's chamber. The next step, cheap and practical internal ignition, frustrated inventors for years. In 1818, Joseph Manton built a gun with a spring-loaded catch that held a tiny tube of fulminate over the touch-hole. The hammer crushed the fulminate, and breech pressure blew the tube off to the side. Manton's mechanism showed up on the Merrill gun. In 1821, Westley Richards married fulminate primers to a flintlock-style pan whose cover was forced open by the hammer's impact. The pan held a cup of fulminate that sprayed sparks into the touch-hole below when ignited by the hammer's sharp nose. Two years later, American physician Dr. Samuel Guthrie formed fulminate into pellets, which proved much more convenient than loose priming compound.

Credit for the copper percussion cap goes to sea captain Joshua Shaw of Philadelphia. In 1814, the British-born Shaw was denied a patent for a steel cap because he was not yet a U.S. citizen. His next projects: pewter and copper caps. In 1822 Shaw patented his own lock, later earning a Congressional honorarium for his work. Only a few of the 72 patents issued for percussion caps between 1812 and 1825 proved out, but the idea of a tubular nipple sealed by the cap itself and leading directly to the chamber won wide acceptance.

Resistance to percussion rifles was rooted partly in suspicion of chemistry. Also, flintlocks had been refined, mechanically and esthetically, so many shooters saw no need for change. Governments, typically wary of new arms developments until battle-proven, put little faith in fulminates. But while percussion ignition stalled, firearms changed in other ways. Pilgrims arriving in North America in the early 17th century carried 75-caliber, 6-foot flintlocks with smooth bores—though much more accurate rifled bores had been used in matches since 1498 in Leipzig, Germany and 1504 in Zurich, Switzerland. By

The jaws of a flintlock hammer (previously called the cock) hold a piece of flint that strikes the frizzen (previously the hammer), knocking it back and showering sparks into the priming charge in the pan. The priming charge burns into the touch-hole in the barrel, igniting the main charge.

the time percussion caps appeared, the liabilities of rifling—great expense and slow loading—were reconsidered in light of new battlefield tactics. Skirmishes between settlers and Indians did not present walls of uniforms to either side. The enemy was often alone and partly hidden. Accuracy counted. Hunters appreciated the rifle's extra precision on long shots and the efficient use of precious lead and powder.

Flintlock rifles popular in Europe early in the 18th century had what hunters and militiamen in the New World wanted. They adopted this *jaeger* (hunter) rifle, keeping barrels to less than 30 inches in length. Rifling typically comprised seven to nine deep, slow-twist grooves. Most of these rifles wore a rectangular patchbox on a stock with a wide, flat butt. Double set triggers predominated. To conserve lead, frontier gunsmiths began boring *jaegers* to 50, 45, and even 40 caliber. (A pound of lead yields 70 balls of 40 caliber, but only 15 of 70 caliber.) The sliding patchbox cover gave way to a hinged lid. A slimmer stock had a crescent butt to fit against the shooter's upper arm. As longer barrels later came into favor, they gave the rifles a distinctive grace and a new name: "Kentucky."

During the Revolutionary War, the rifle outperformed the musket. The rifle shot farther and hit harder and more accurately. But slow loading remained a problem. Pounding balls home as they engraved the rifling was not only time-consuming (and very difficult on horseback); it made noise that revealed the shooter. To speed loading, Americans learned to swath undersize balls in greased patches. After it helped the Continental Army thrash the British, the patched ball retained favor among hunters, who appreciated the cleaning action of the patch and its protection against leading in the bore.

Even with patched balls and plenty of time, loading from the muzzle wasn't ideal. The rifle had to be handled from the front, denying immediate access to the firing mechanism and putting the shooter at risk if dormant sparks in the bore ignited a new charge of powder. Loading from the breech would be a great boon—and had actually been contemplated centuries before the advent of percussion ignition. The hinged breech dates to at least 1537; but it went nowhere without the percussion cap. The cylindrical breech plug appeared as early as the 17th century on a French musket. Lowered with a turn of the trigger guard, it had to be raised carefully, as it sometimes pinched the powder, causing early detonation. The mechanism designed in 1776 by British Major Patrick Ferguson comprised a threaded breech plug that retracted when the trigger guard was rotated. The Theiss breechloader of 1804 had a sliding block that lifted for loading with a button in front of the trigger.

Breechloaders could be used with loose powder and ball; but they begged development of the self-contained cartridge. European inventors Lepage, Pauly, Potet, and Robert pioneered breechloading rounds—the first, of paper, assembled in 1586. The shooter tore off the cartridge base with his teeth to expose the powder charge. The case burned to ashes upon firing. Replacing pyrite with the percussion cap ensured delivery of a powerful spark. It penetrated the paper so the end no longer had to be torn off.

One of the first inventors to put a primer in a cartridge was Johann Nikolaus von Dreyse. The bullet in his paper cartridge held a pellet of fulminate, which was hit by a striker penetrating the charge from the rear. About 300,000 of these "needle guns" were built for the Prussian army. Experimenters struggled to build breechloaders stout enough to withstand the heavy powder charges used for hunting and reliable enough to function continuously when hot and dirty. The first U.S. breechloader to get popular acclaim was developed by John Harris Hall in 1811. Though it earned a military contract, Hall's rifle was weak, heavy, and crude, a flintlock firing paper cartridges. War with Mexico in 1845 caused munitions experts to reconsider; factories instead began producing the older, proven Harpers Ferry 1803 muzzleloading rifle.

Cartridge development in both Europe and the U.S. began well before the advent of smokeless powder. Still, much of this country's early history was written by men with muzzleloaders.

3

RIFLES BORN IN THE USA

By the time settlers began drifting into the wilderness beyond the Eastern Seaboard, smoothbore muskets had been supplanted on the frontier by the Kentucky long rifle. The archetype had its origin not in Kentucky, but in Pennsylvania, where gunsmiths of mostly German extraction fashioned elegant flintlocks with the crudest of tools. The Kentucky's relatively small bore conserved powder and lead, but delivered a lethal blow to deer and hostiles. The long, carefully rifled barrels afforded an extended sight radius and great accuracy. While the first Kentucky rifles were made one at a time to order, an enterprising young man in New York's Mohawk River Valley built his own. From it evolved a firearms empire.

It was 1816, and Eliphalet (Lite) Remington II had just moved, with his new wife Abigail, into his father's stone house on Staley Creek in Litchfield. In a hand-built forge, Lite hatched his rifle project by heating the rod he'd chosen for his barrel. When it glowed red, he hammered it square, half an inch in cross-section. Next, he wound it around an iron mandrel not quite as big in diameter as the 45-caliber bore he had in mind. Reheating the barrel until it was white-hot, he sprinkled it with borax and sand and, holding one end with his tongs, pounded it on the stone floor to seat the coils. After checking it for straightness, Lite ground and filed eight flats, true to the custom of the day. In distant Utica, a gunsmith accepted the equivalent of a dollar for two days of work rifling the octagonal barrel. Back home, Remington bored a touch-hole and forged a breech plug and lock parts, shaping them with a file. He brazed a priming pan to the lockplate, then used uric acid and iron oxide to finish and preserve the steel. With draw-knife and chisel, Lite fashioned a walnut stock from a hand-sawn blank. He smoothed it with sandstone and sealed it with beeswax.

Lite Remington took his flintlock to a local shooting match and finished second. The winner, much impressed by the new rifle, asked if Lite would build another. Lite set a price of $10. Delivery: 10 days.

The needs of hunters changed as the American frontier crept west. Bison and grizzly bears survived the light charges fired from svelte Kentucky rifles. Long barrels were unwieldy on horseback, and slim-wristed stocks broke. By the time Daniel Boone looked beyond the Cumberlands, gunmakers were already redesigning the Kentucky rifle. Utilitarian iron hardware replaced brass patchboxes; bigger bores, shorter barrels, and thicker stocks gave the new "mountain," or "Tennessee," rifle a beefier look.

By the early 1800s, the Mountain Man era had begun. General W. H. Ashley, head of the Rocky Mountain Fur Company, established the annual Rendezvous to bring trappers together and pelts to a collection point. Tons of furs funneled from the Green River and other Rendezvous sites to St. Louis, Missouri. Among the many Easterners drawn to this boomtown was Jacob Hawkins, a young gunsmith joined in 1822 by his brother Samuel. The two changed their name back to the original Dutch "Hawken" and began taking orders for rifles. Borrowing from the Youmans design that had defined the Tennessee rifle, Jake and Sam added still more weight to the barrel and

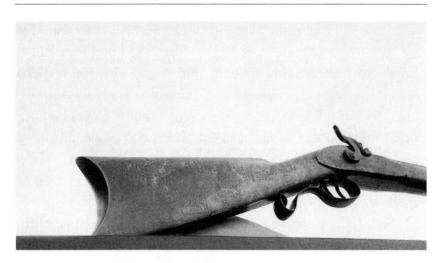

The crescent butt and unembellished stock were common on early plains rifles.

bored it out for even bigger charges. They replaced the full-length stock with a half-stock, typically maple with two keys attaching it to the barrel. The Hawken brothers used Ashmore locks as well as their own, switching to percussion ignition after about 1840. A typical Hawken weighed almost 10 pounds, with a 38-inch, slow-twist octagonal barrel of 50 caliber or larger. Charge weights typically ran 150 to 215 grains. The soft iron barrels didn't "slick up" like ordnance steel, but absorbed a trace of bullet lube and delayed the fouling that plagued contemporary English rifles. The Hawkens' slow rifling pitch controlled patched round balls better, too. Hawken rifles were noted for exceptional accuracy over a wide range of charges and reportedly even dished out less recoil than the competition. Soon, Sam and Jake were hard-pressed to keep up with the growing demand for their product. Other makers—Lehman, Henry, and Tryon, to name a few—built similar rifles, some copies of the original Hawken.

Rifle repairs kept the Hawkens busy even when orders stacked up. The frontier was hard on rifles! Fixing a lock cost between 25 and 87½ cents, according to shop records from the spring of 1826.

The brothers charged the U.S. Indian Department $1.25 for "Cutting Barrel & new brich" and 50 cents for "Repairing Rifle." Lock repair, with bullet molds, ramrod, and a rear sight, cost one customer all of two dollars. The Hawken shop also fixed miscellaneous hardware and billed 50 cents for shoeing a horse. Prices crept up during the next two decades, but in 1849, you could still buy a Hawken rifle for $22.50. That year the California Gold Rush started, and Jake Hawken died of cholera. Sam maintained the business. In 1859 he spent two months traveling in the Rockies.

Sam left his son, William Stewart Hawken, in charge of the shop. As a young man, William had ridden with Kit Carson's mounted rifles, and on September 23, 1847 had fought in the battle of Monterey. Badly outnumbered by Mexican troops, General Henderson and his small group of frontiersmen stuggled to hold a bridge over San Juan Creek. The clash left nine ambulatory men among 43 Texas Rangers. William, age 30, was one of the wounded. He made his way back to Missouri but apparently left for the West again shortly after Sam returned. Nothing more was heard of William Hawken until some years later, when a 56-caliber muzzleloader bearing his name was found in Querino Canyon, Arizona. It told nothing of the man's fate.

In his later years, Sam hired a shop hand. J. P. Gemmer, capable and industrious, had immigrated to the U.S. from Germany in 1838. In 1862 he bought Sam out. He is believed to have used the "S. Hawken" stamp on some rifles, but most of them are marked "J. P. Gemmer, St. Louis." As the bison dwindled and cartridge rifles became popular, Gemmer built other types of rifles. Sam Hawken continued to visit his shop and even built a rifle there. He outlived Bridger, Carson, and many other frontiersmen who had used Hawken rifles. Sam died at age 92—with the shop still open for business. It remained in St. Louis but was moved in 1870, 1876, 1880, and 1912. It closed for good in 1915. Mr. Gemmer died four years later.

Caribou are more challenging when you stalk close for one shot with a patched roundball.

Long before demand for Hawken rifles waned, inventors were writing the muzzleloader's epitaph. In 1847 Stephen Taylor patented a hollow-base bullet with an internal powder charge secured by a perforated end cap that admitted fire from an external primer. A year later, New York entrepreneur Walter Hunt came up with a similar bullet, its cork cap covered with paper. Hunt's "rocket balls" made news because he also designed a rifle to fire them: a repeater.

The Hunt rifle had a tubular magazine, brilliant in its simplicity, and a pillbox mechanism to advance metallic primers. But the finger lever that operated the breech often failed. With no money to promote or improve his "Volitional" repeater, Hunt sold patent rights to fellow New Yorker George A. Arrowsmith. In his machine shop, Arrowsmith huddled with talented young Lewis Jennings. Together they worked some bugs out of the Hunt rifle. Arrowsmith got patents for Jennings's work, then sold the repeater for $100,000 to railroad magnate and New York hardware merchant Courtland Palmer—who laid it in the laps of gun designers Horace Smith and Daniel Wesson. They tackled the rifle's remaining problems by investigating new cartridges. In 1852 they came up with a metallic cartridge like the Flobert, patented in 1846 and 1849. But instead of seating a ball atop a primer, Smith and Wesson modified a rocket ball to include a copper base that held the priming mix. In 1854 Palmer joined his designers in a limited partnership, advancing $10,000 to tool up a company that would become known as Smith and Wesson. But only a year later a group of forty New York and New Haven investors bought out Smith and Wesson and Palmer to form the Volcanic Repeating Arms Company.

Volcanic was to be run, oddly enough, by a shirt salesman named Oliver F. Winchester, one of the investors. Right away, Winchester moved the firm from Norwich to New Haven, but it floundered. Volcanic guns generated little interest among hunters, and bankruptcy loomed. In 1857, Oliver Winchester bought all its assets

Conical bullets in sabot sleeves are now extremely popular among black powder buffs keen to boost velocities.

for $40,000. He reorganized the company into the New Haven Arms Company.

Winchester saw a market in better ammunition; he hired Benjamin Tyler Henry to develop it. In 1860 Henry received a patent for a 15-shot rifle chambered for .44 rimfire cartridges. The Henry, a brass-frame descendant of the Hunt, was underpowered, marginally reliable, and prone to leak gas. Still, it had incredible firepower, an asset not lost on the Confederates who faced it and called it "that damned Yankee rifle you loaded on Sunday and fired all week." The Henry would spawn Winchester's Model 1866, 1873, and 1876 rifles, sealing the success of lever mechanisms and making New Haven a firearms capital.

4

RIFLES TO CLOSE A CENTURY

The 19th century delivered a bonanza in gun developments. It began with armies fielding musketeers armed with smoothbore flintlocks launching roundballs with black powder. It ended with soldiers and hunters shooting magazine rifles chambered for smokeless cartridges with jacketed bullets. In the mid-1800s, while Hunt and others raced to perfect a repeating rifle, a young machinist named Christian Sharps stood curiously alone. His goal was to build a better breechloading single-shot. A New Jersey native, Sharps apprenticed under John Hall at the Harpers Ferry Arsenal. In 1848 he received his first patent, for a rifle with a sliding breechblock. Fitted to an altered 1841 Springfield, the mechanism could handle potent hunting loads. But Sharps was no salesman; his marketing failed. Businessman J. M. McCalla and gunsmith A. S. Nippes helped underwrite production of the Sharps Model 1849, which featured a priming wheel that held 18 primers and advanced mechanically.

In August, 1851, Christian Sharps got his first rifle order: 200 carbines with 54-caliber barrels and Maynard-style locks. The good news was tempered by flooding in the new Hartford plant, built, unwisely, on a swamp. Sharps also had to deal with George Pen-field, who owned just over half the patent rights to the Model 1850 rifle, now under contract for production by Robbins and Lawrence.

The life of Christian Sharps would include a long series of failed business relationships. Many of his rifle designs were implemented by others. Robbins and Lawrence would fill fat military contracts; Christian Sharps got royalties but complained often that he'd not been treated fairly. Though his early rifles—Models 1850, 1851, and 1852—sold well, hunters better recall the later Sharps rifles. Five years before Christian Sharps died of tuberculosis, the Sharps Rifle Manufacturing Company trotted out its first dropping-block single-shot in metallic chamberings. The New Model 1869 was followed a year later (in 1870) by the New Model 1874. Its market: men killing bison for money. George Reighard was one of them. In a 1930 edition of the *Kansas City Star*, George reminisced about his 1872 expedition south of Fort Dodge. He furnished the team and wagon and did the killing, using two Sharps 50-caliber rifles with scopes. His partners furnished the supplies and did the skinning, stretching, and cooking in exchange for half the hides.

"The time I made my biggest kill I lay on a slight ridge, behind a tuft of weeds 100 yards from a bunch of a thousand buffaloes that had come a long distance to a creek, had drunk their fill and then strolled out upon the prairie to rest. . . . After I had killed about twenty-five my gun barrel became hot and began to expand. A bullet from an overheated gun does not go straight, it wobbles, so I put that gun aside and took the other. By the time that became hot the other had cooled, but then the powder smoke in front of me was so thick I could not see through it; there was not a breath of wind to carry it away, and I had to crawl backward, dragging my two guns, and work around to another position on the ridge, from which I killed fifty-four more. In one and one-half hours I had fired ninety-one shots, as a count of the empty shells showed afterwards, and had killed sev-

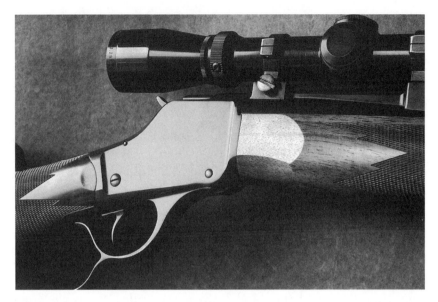

John Browning's first sale to Winchester was a single-shot mechanism that evolved into the 1885 Winchester "High Wall." This original 1885 has been expertly custom-stocked and finished.

enty-nine buffaloes. . . . On that trip I killed a few more than 3,000 buffaloes in one month. . . . "

In 1880, the Sharps Rifle Company closed its doors. The hammerless Model 1878 rifle had been received coolly by hunters who could instead choose a repeater. With the bison now gone, there was no need for cartridges too big for Winchester lever rifles, no need for the long shooting that had left more than three million tons of bones for scavengers. Sharps had not pursued a repeating mechanism. Like the bison, the company became a victim of the times.

The marriage of powerful cartridges to lever-action rifles came too late for the commercial buffalo hunter. It evolved in Ogden, Utah, where gunsmith Jonathan Browning had arrived in 1852, five years after the first of his Mormon brethren completed the trip from Nauvoo, Illinois. His son, John Moses Browning, was born in 1855, one of the family's 22 children. John showed an early interest in firearms, and at age 11 built a working gun. Later, he managed the shop. In 1878, just after his 23rd birthday, John designed a breechloading single-shot rifle, assembling the prototype by hand with files, chisels, and a foot-lathe his father had brought from Illinois. In May of 1879, John received his first patent.

In those days, Winchester Repeating Arms Company stood as the industry giant, with a net worth of $1.2 million. By 1875 it was loading a million cartridges per day. Still, declining demand for military rifles and ammo was affecting its focus. Though prescient riflemakers could see clearly that the bison would not last, prospects for recreational hunting were much brighter in the post-Civil War West. Hunters would sustain Winchester. To serve that market, the company developed the Model 1876 lever rifle, a massive, iron-frame version of the popular Model 1873, itself a descendant of Walter Hunt's Volitional repeater. But the Model 1876 lacked the strength to handle the potent .45–70 and the even bigger Sharps cartridges. The need for such a rifle, if not pressing, must have nagged at Winchester's engineers.

Company president Thomas Bennett (Oliver Winchester's son-in-law) surely thought about it, too. Then a Winchester salesman returning from the West showed him a single-shot rifle he had bought, used. The action was of clever design, and strong. The barrel inscription named the maker: Browning. Thomas Bennett had never heard of a Browning. But the rifle so intrigued—and worried—him that he immediately boarded a train to Ogden.

He found a handful of young men assembling rifles in what the storefront sign indicated was the "Largest Arms Factory Between Omaha and The Pacific." John, 28, welcomed Bennett and introduced his brothers. "I guess I'm the boss," he smiled. Bennett said he wanted to buy all rights to the single-shot. John thought for a moment, then said he could have them for $10,000—an enormous sum in 1883. Bennett offered $8,000, and John accepted, starting a 17-year business relationship that would deliver forty gun designs to Winchester.

Winchester dubbed Browning's rifle the Model 1885. It became known affectionately as the High Wall, an allusion to receiver design. A Low Wall model appeared for smaller cartridges. But by then John and his brother Matt had clinched an even bigger deal: a contract for a repeating lever-action rifle that would chamber the .45–70. Bennett bought the design, reportedly for $50,000. "More

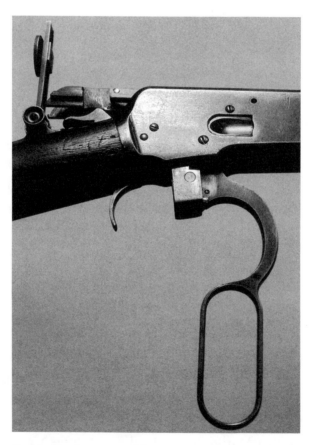

The Model 92 was one of John Browning's contributions to Winchester. Note the tang sight.

money than there was in Ogden," said John. The design, delivered faster than Bennett expected, begat Winchester's Model 1886. True to what would become a Browning trademark, it showed a genius for simplicity and reliability. John returned from his two-year Mormon mission in March 1889 and worked furiously designing new firearms. During the next four years, he garnered twenty patents. Working with only rudimentary tools, he came up with marvelous mechanisms. Those Winchester chose not to produce it bought and shelved so that its rivals wouldn't have access to their man in Utah. Among the most noteworthy of the Winchesters attributable to Browning was the Model 1892, a svelte lever-action with the Model 1886's vertical locking lugs. From the '92 would come the Model 1894, initially designed for black powder but chambered in 1895 for the .30–30, America's first centerfire smokeless cartridge. For decades, hunters would think of the '94 as the archetypal deer rifle. Winchester would sell millions.

Incidentally, the bond between John Browning and Thomas Bennett dissolved in a disagreement over a gun. Around 1900, Browning offered Winchester a self-loading shotgun. Bennett thought the price too high, and he bristled at paying a royalty, something John had not requested before. Also, the design was a radical departure from what shooters were used to, and though Bennett must have known it would function, he didn't know how the gun would sell. Finally, he was afraid a new shotgun might drain sales from other Browning-designed shotguns. Bennett didn't say yes or no at first, apparently hoping something would change to make either choice easier. But John did not appreciate the stalling. He lost patience and found a warmer reception at Fabrique Nationale (F. N.) in Belgium. Browning's Auto 5 might otherwise have been a Winchester.

While Winchester had the first lever rifles, some shooters would argue that Marlin developed the best. John Mahlon Marlin was only 18 years old in 1853, when he became an apprentice ma-

These Browning "Low Walls" in .22 Hornet and .223 derive from a John Browning design dating back to the early 1880s.

chinist in Connecticut. He agreed to work for no wages for six months, after which he'd get shop pay of $1.50. One year later, he'd qualify for a raise to $2.50—per week.

Gunmaking followed. During the 1860s, John designed and built deringer-style pistols. Alas, his own under-hammer, lever-action repeating rifle fed poorly and didn't sell.

The first successful Marlin lever-action was a side-loading, top-ejecting rifle. Named the Model 1881 for its year of introduction (but not until 1888), the 10-shot rifle featured a 28-inch octagon barrel chambered either in .45–70 or .40–60. It was initially priced at $32. Many historians name the 1881 as the first successful big-bore lever-action repeater. Its top ejection and a problematic carrier that produced jams at the rear of the magazine were dropped on later Marlins.

In 1888 Marlin announced a lever gun designed by L. L. Hepburn and chambered for short-action cartridges: the .32–20, .38–40,

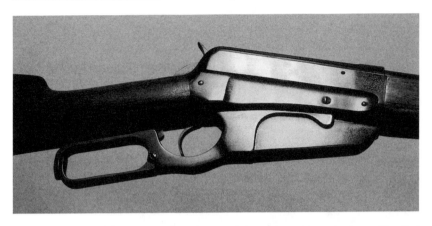

The Winchester Model 1895 was the only one of the company's popular lever rifles that had a box magazine, permitting the use of pointed bullets. Chamberings included the .30–06 and .30–40 Krag.

and .44–40. This side-loading, top-ejecting model retailed for $19.50 with a 24-inch octagon barrel. It weighed only 6½ pounds. Four years later, Hepburn came up with a better rifle, the 1889. Its solid receiver top and side ejection kept cases from bounding up through the shooter's line of sight.

In 1891 Marlin built a lever gun around the .22 rimfire cartridge. During its 25-year production run, this rifle became famous as the choice of "Little Miss Sure-Shot," Annie Oakley. It was followed in 1895 by the Model 1892 Marlin. The later Model 1897 featured Hepburn's single-screw take-down mechanism that's still used on the Marlin 39, one of the most acclaimed .22 sporting rifles of all time.

L. L. Hepburn refined the Model 1889 to handle longer cartridges than the .44–40. The Model 1893 appeared first in .32–40 and .38–55, then in .25–36, .30–30, and .32 Special. When its lever was ajar, the rear section of a two-piece firing pin would fall out of line with the front piece, preventing discharge. By the 1920s, the Model 93 had won the favor of many deer hunters. A short-action variant, the Model 1894, came on its heels. Then Marlin announced the Model 1895, essentially a large-frame Model 1893, chambered in .38–56, .40–65, .40–82, .45–70, and .45–90. The .40–70 was added in 1897, the .33 Winchester in a lightweight version in 1912. Production ceased just before the First World War but was reinstated in 1972. The 1895 gave rise more recently to the popular "Guide Gun" and "Outfitter," in .45–70 and .444 respectively, and the 1895M in .450 Marlin Magnum.

Clawing its way clear of the Depression in the 1930s, Marlin reintroduced its Model 93. Then it changed the sights, stock, and forend to come up with the Model 1936. All variations had pistol-grip stocks and listed for $32 in 1937. Eleven years later, the Model 336 replaced the 36. The most obvious difference between the two actions is the round, chrome-plated bolt of the 336. The flat mainspring of the 36 gave way to a coil mainspring. The "Marlin bullseye," deleted for a time on Model 36 stocks as a cost-saving measure, was reinstated on the 336. The 336 has since appeared in myriad variations and continues to sell well despite the shift of big game hunters to powerful bolt rifles. Marlin has managed to retain the feel and fit of early lever rifles. Pick up a 336 and marvel; its basic design predates the automobile. Throw it to your cheek and imagine a whitetail buck in the sights. Flick that lever, and you get an eager *snick, snick.* This rifle *wants* to be in the woods. It's still the quintessential deer rifle.

Firearms developments in the late 1800s left us many enduring mechanisms. But those that remained unaltered into the second half of the 20th century—like the Colt Single-Action Army—survived less as modern tools than as reminders of more romantic times. Among the few exceptions is a rifle so sophisticated that when production became too pricey 100 years after its introduction, there had been no major improvements; the Savage 99 didn't need any.

Like many of his predecessors, Arthur William Savage used one successful gun design to start a firm that would later build a variety of firearms. Born June 13, 1857, in Kingston, Jamaica, Arthur attended school in England and the United States. His father was England's Special Commissioner to the British West Indies, where he developed an educational program for newly freed slaves. But young Arthur had an adventurous streak and immediately after college sailed for Australia, where he found work on a cattle ranch. Arthur also found a wife, Annie Bryant, and fathered eight children. One of his sons was born in a wagon on a wilderness trek. An astute businessman, Arthur made lots of money in cattle. At the end of his 11-year stay in Australia he was said to own the biggest ranch on the continent.

The Outback had given him fortune and thrills (Aborigines once captured him and held him for several months), but Savage itched for new frontiers. He sold his ranch, moved back to Jamaica, and bought a coffee plantation. There he pursued an interest in firearms and explosives. With a partner he developed the Savage-Halpine torpedo, which was later sold to the Brazilian government. Savage also studied recoilless rifles. In 1892, at age 35, he came up with a repeating rifle. A less confident man may have reconsidered the hammerless lever-action design he chose, as pundits blamed the failure of the 1878 Sharps-Borchardt on its lack of a visible hammer.

The Savage rifle operated like a Winchester, though the lever admitted only one (rear) finger. Between this loop and the trigger, the guard extension lay flat against the bottom of the grip. The magazine, housed in the receiver, held eight rounds. The full-length stock, clamped by two musket bands, cradled a 29-inch barrel. Arthur Savage submitted his prototype at the 1892 ordnance trials on Governor's Island, New York. It was beaten by the Krag-Jorgensen.

Convinced his design had merit, Arthur Savage refined it for sporting use, paring magazine capacity to five for a trimmer profile and altering the lever to accommodate three fingers. He developed a new cartridge for the rifle and in 1894 formed the Savage Arms Company in Utica, New York.

The Savage 99's marvelous magazine and stout action made it suitable for modern cartridges more than a century ago. This 99 wears an Ashley rear sight.

Savage's first commercial rifle was called the Model 1895. It had a rear-locking bolt that abutted a thick steel web machined into the tail of a slim receiver milled from a forging. There were no channels rearward permitting escape of gas from a ruptured case. Side ejection kept cases from the line of sight and cleared the receiver for scope use. The coil mainspring—the first of its kind on a commercial lever-action—and a through-bolt joining buttstock to receiver added durability. But the most exciting part of this gun was its magazine, a spring-loaded brass spool tucked into the receiver, with a cartridge counter in a window in the left receiver wall. No magazine was simpler, smoother, or better protected.

Savage's spool had other advantages over the barrel-mounted tubular magazines of its day. First, it didn't affect rifle balance. Long-barreled Winchesters and Marlins became muzzle-heavy with full tubes; balance shifted rearward as the tube emptied. Secondly, the Savage magazine didn't touch the barrel and didn't affect accuracy. Most importantly, pointed, long-range bullets were safe to use in the Model 95 because the cartridges did not rest primer-to-bullet tip. The Model 95's new cartridge, the .303 Savage, drove a 190-grain bullet at 1,900 fps (feet per second). Hunter testimonials affirmed its power:

> "I have just returned from my hunting trip with one bull moose and two bull caribou, all killed stone dead in their tracks with one of your incomparable .303 rifles. I shot the moose at a distance of 350 yards."
>
> "In November [my guide] killed a very fine large mountain sheep [with] the first shot 237 yards off and in a very strong wind. [The Savage] barrel is small and [has] no long magazine to catch the wind and blow your rifle to one side."

A frugal Canadian used his first box of 20 cartridges to take eighteen big game animals, including grizzlies.

The Model 1895 came only in .303, with a straight grip, crescent butt, schnabel forend, and a barrel 22, 26, or 30 inches long. About 6,000 rifles were made between 1895 and 1899, when Savage changed the gun slightly and renamed it the Model 1899. A year later it became available in .30–30. The 99 was initially priced at $20. In 1913 Charles Newton designed for Savage a cartridge to replace the .25–35, recommending a 100-grain bullet for the new .25. Savage chose an 87-grain because it could be driven 3,000 fps. Savage called its round the .250–3000. Newton also designed the Savage .22 High-Power, or "Imp." In 1912 the firm added this chambering to its Model 99.

By 1920, Savage was offering Model 99s in five styles, with takedown and solid frames. That year the company introduced its new .300, to deliver .30–06 performance in short actions. It didn't, but hunters liked the round anyway. When, in the early 1950s, ordnance

Charles Newton developed the .250–3000 for Savage around 1912.

officers sought a cartridge to replace the .30–06 in battle rifles, they turned to the .300 Savage. Its neck proved too short for machine guns, so they lengthened it and reduced shoulder angle 10 degrees. The T-65 became the .308 Winchester in 1952. In 1955 the U.S. Army adopted it as the 7.62 NATO.

Besides managing his gun company during its early growth, Arthur Savage continued to indulge his curiosity. He invested in a citrus plantation and a tire enterprise, and even went prospecting for oil. He became the Superintendent of the Street Railway in Utica. He died in 1941, at age 84. That Model 99 rifle outlived him by 50 years, and the Savage company remains—both unusual tributes to an adventurer who once rode the Australian Outback punching cattle.

5

BEGINNINGS OF THE BOLT ACTION

Charles Newton, a contemporary of Arthur Savage, shared the man's genius but not his business acumen. Newton may also have had the worst luck of any entrepreneur in U.S. firearms history. It rode him hard.

Charles grew up in rural New York, where he worked on his father's farm until finishing school in 1886 at age 16. After a short teaching stint, he studied law and was admitted to the state bar. But he soon strayed from legal practice to experiment with rifles and wildcat cartridges. In 1911 the Savage High Power (or "Imp") appeared, the .22 centerfire Newton fashioned from the .25–35. About the same time, he necked the .30–06 to 25 caliber and called his cartridge the .25 Special. It would become the .25–06. The .250/3000 followed. Charles designed a 7mm round on the .30–06 case—matching the European 7x64 and predating the .280 Remington by nearly half a century.

A single-shot enthusiast, Charles used the .405 Winchester case to make rimmed versions of his .25 and 7mm Specials. He concocted .30, 8mm, and .35 Express rounds from the 3-1/4-inch

Sharps shell. His rimless heavyweights were decades ahead of their time. On a case the size of the .404 Jeffery, he and gunsmith Fred Adolph developed the .30 Adolph Express, or .30 Newton. Companion cartridges in .28, .35, and .40 followed. But the sharply-necked cases and small, pointed bullets struggled in markets still dominated by lever-action rounds.

Not one to brood over rejection, Charles busied himself with other projects. He necked the 7x57 case to .228 to form his .22 Newton, which drove a 90-grain bullet at 3,100 fps through fast-twist (1-in-8) rifling. His .22 Special on the Krag case pushed a 68-grain bullet at nearly 3,300. The .256 Newton (.264 bullet) outlived his two 7mms: the .276 and .280. Powders of the day limited the performance of Newton cartridges, which might also have sold better given the fuel that turned Roy Weatherby's wildcats into rockets in the 1940s. Bullets before the Great War were also ill-suited to high-velocity impact. So Charles Newton designed his own, with paper between core and jacket to keep bore friction from melting the core.

Charles started his first company on August 4, 1914, expecting a shipment of Mauser actions. Worse timing is hard to imagine. Germany declared war on August 14, *one day* before the first shipment was due in Buffalo. The company had cataloged barrels "of the best Krupp steel" for Mauser and Springfield actions. The war stopped barrel shipments, too. Charles turned to the Marlin Firearms Company to produce barrels threaded for Springfields, which he figured could be substituted for the Mausers. Unfortunately, war preparation absorbed not only existing military rifles but all the equipment needed to produce them.

Charles retrenched with his own rifle action and recruited renowned shooter and barrel maker Harry Pope as barrel shop superintendent. The first of these Newton rifles, chambered for Newton's own cartridges, were available January 1, 1917. Again, timing could hardly have been worse. On April 6, the government took

The 1917 Enfield followed the 1903 Springfield. Also chambered for the .30–06, it had the length to accommodate bigger rounds. A gunsmith has opened this one up to accept the .404 Jeffery.

over all domestic cartridge production. Without cases, a Newton rifle was worthless. To add insult to injury, the army snatched tooling from Newton Arms to augment the war effort.

In April 1919 the Chas. Newton Rifle Corporation arose, tooling to come from Eddystone Arsenal surplus. Escalating production costs in Germany soon made rifle actions prohibitively expensive. In July 1923, Charles and two partners formed the Buffalo Newton Rifle Corporation. Rifles were of Charles's own design, in .30–06 and four Newton numbers: .256, .280, .30, and .35. Chrome-vanadium receivers featured interrupted-thread lockup. With adequate capitalization and war no longer a concern, things could have gone well for Charles Newton. But as luck would have it, John Meeker, who controlled the lending group for the Buffalo Newton venture, challenged Charles for the executive spot. They went to court and Charles won, but at great expense. Now he needed more financing. After borrowing against his own life insurance, he begged Marlin to build his rifles under contract. Marlin declined.

Charles Newton was already at work on another project: the Leverbolt, a rifle derived from earlier Newtons and the Lee straight-pull. He claimed bolt-action strength and accuracy with lever-action speed. But Charles had to convince Marlin's Frank Kenna it would sell. Kenna wanted proof of demand. In mid-1929, Charles went public with a plea, asking shooters for only a $25 down payment on the $70 rifle. In October, the stock market failed. Unable to raise the capital for another venture, Charles Newton died at his New Haven home on March 9, 1932.

Newton deserved better. Many of his ideas eventually showed up on other rifles. The three-position safety he designed appears, modified, on Winchester's Model 70, which also has a Newton-style floorplate latch. He patented a compartmented bullet in 1915, decades ahead of Nosler's Partition. The voluminous rimless case with relatively small-bore bullets at high speed was Charles Newton's idea long before it was Roy Weatherby's.

Bad luck had not so plagued the bolt rifle's inventor, Peter Paul Mauser. Before Newton had finished law school—that is, while John Browning was working on Winchesters and Arthur Savage designing his lever rifle—Mauser was already refining the bolt action.

Born in 1838 in the Swabian village of Oberndorf, the youngest of thirteen children, Paul Mauser had an early interest in guns. He began working for the local government rifle factory in 1852, when he was 14. Drafted into the army in 1859, he served as an artilleryman but studied rifle actions, particularly the Dreyse needle gun. After leaving the service, Mauser improved the Dreyse with a cam that retracted the striker and eliminated the serious drawback of the first bolt actions: accidental discharge on closing. By then (1865), replacement of the paper case by metallic cartridges had all but solved the problem of gas leakage.

This modern Mauser, photographed in the shop of the late Maurice Ottmar, has the classic straight bolt handle. A drop-box magazine and side-swing safety have been added. Chambering: .404.

Paul's first gun project went nowhere, but in 1872 the single-shot 11mm Mauser Model 1871 became the official arm for Prussian troops. Its turn-bolt action derived, legend has it, from Paul's inspection of a door latch. Contrary to popular belief, the Model 1871 Mauser was not the first successful bolt gun. That distinction probably goes to the Mauser-Norris rifle designed in 1867 and patented a year later. Paul conceived the rifle; his brother Wilhelm helped build it. Paul Norris, a European representative for Remington Arms, was so taken with the rifle that he tried to finance its production. He failed, however, and the Mauser brothers sold it directly to the German Army.

History takes strange twists. Had Remington supported Norris's efforts to help the Mausers, that crude rifle and much more effective later models would have become Remington's property. In fact, the original Mauser-Norris patent was filed in the U.S. The German government's adoption of the Model 1871 Mauser, an improved

Mauser-Norris, ensured the inventor's success. This rifle had an ejector and primary extraction, both taken for granted now but big developments back then. Paul and Wilhelm got a contract to make parts, while the government initiated rifle production. By 1874, the brothers had a new factory, under the banner of Mauser Brothers & Co. Ten years later Wilhelm died, just after Paul had successfully demonstrated a tube-loading 11mm rifle. The Prussian High Command chose the new 71/84 Mauser as its infantry arm, and Serbia ordered 4,000 more of these rifles.

Following Wilhelm's premature death, Mauser became a stock company, its controlling shares purchased by Ludwig Lowe & Co. of Berlin. In 1889 Fabrique Nationale d'Armes de Guerre (F.N.) was founded near Liege to manufacture 7.65mm Mauser rifles for Belgium's army. F.N. produced 275,000 Model 1888 "Commission" rifles. They featured dual locking lugs on Mauser's one-piece bolt. By 1893, all major world powers were using or switching to smokeless cartridges. Spain adopted a 7x57 Mauser rifle with the first staggered built-in box magazine. A year later Sweden started manufacturing its 6.5x55 carbine, paying royalties for the Mauser patent. Clearly, the Mauser bolt-action was the infantry weapon of the future. Chile adopted the 7x57 Model 1895 Mauser, as did South Africa.

Over the next six years, Paul improved the action. The staggered box magazine appeared in 1893. Two years later, the Model 1895 incorporated most of the features that would make Mauser's Model 1898 Germany's choice in both world wars. By the 1930s, Mauser rifles had become available to hunters in the U.S. through A. F. Stoeger of New York, which once listed 20 types of Mauser actions, differing not only in length (four sizes), but in magazine configuration. The rifles weren't cheap. In 1939 retail prices ranged from $110 to $250.

The 1898 Mauser is still by some measures the finest bolt-action yet developed. Every bolt rifle since has some features of the

This Mauser, stocked in maple by Fred Zeglin of Casper, Wyoming, is chambered in .411 Hawk. It wears Ashley iron sights.

famous 98. Most celebrated is its claw extractor, which controls the cartridge from magazine to chamber and prevents double loading. The Mauser claw is also easily replaceable in the field—though to break one, you must all but destroy the rifle. (In fact, the only Mauser extractor I've seen fail was blown off the rifle after the shooter fired a .308 cartridge in a .270 chamber. The case melted, the bolt face cracked, and gas blew the stock into three pieces.)

In a Ruger 77, Remington 700, and Winchester Model 70, you'll find the two husky, integral locking lugs Mauser used to give 98s their great strength. Cock-on-opening cams differ in placement but derive directly from the 98. Even the Weatherby Mark V, with its low bolt lift and multiple, bolt-diameter lugs, follows the Mauser pattern. Weatherby's first rifles were pure Mauser. Even now, many crack rifle-makers prefer the Mauser 98 to other actions for custom work. The original 98, designed for military use, featured a sturdy two-stage trigger. As foolproof as a tire iron, it had a mushy release. Timney, Canjar, Sako, Dayton-Traister, and other after-market triggers came to the rescue. If you can tap a pin punch, you can re-place a Mauser trigger. Not so the top-swing safety. Paul Mauser could not have imagined that hunters would one day shoot exclu-sively with scopes. But a gunsmith can install a side-swing or three-position wing safety.

When I was a lad, converting military rifles to sporters was not only fun but economical. I'd come along after the Savage 99 had risen in price to $89. A Model 81 Remington autoloader listed at a whop-ping $120. But if you had thirty bucks, you could choose from stacks of battle-scarred Mausers. Blissfully unaware that the Gun Control Act of 1968 would one day shackle shooters who cut their teeth on ri-fles from Sears, Klein's, and other mail-order houses, I dreamed of owning a 7x57. Alas, there are no more $30 surplus Mausers in NRA "very good" condition. But the rifles have not worn out.

If you hunt with a bolt-action rifle, you're using a design that dates to before the days of black powder, before John Browning had to shave. The 98 Mauser has been refined, all right. But not all rifle-men would say that it's been improved. Sometimes old is good enough, and sometimes old is better.

6

RIFLES HUNTERS LIKE BEST

The advent of smokeless powder had a lot to do with converting both soldiers and hunters to bolt-action rifles. In the stout bolt gun, they could use all the energy of smokeless fuel without fretting about pressures. Stronger even than the lever-action, exposed-hammer rifles designed by Browning for Winchester, the turn-bolt mechanism suggested precision at long range. But bolt rifles had to earn their place at market. Winchester's first, the Hotchkiss, failed so miserably that it was dropped before 1900, shortly after its introduction. The Lee straight pull, circa 1897, lasted just six years. Then, during World War I, Winchester manufactured Pattern 14 and Model 1917 Enfield rifles for British and American troops, work that would catalyze efforts to develop a new bolt-action hunting rifle. By 1922, Winchester had identified the problems with the Lee and Hotchkiss and had critically reviewed the Enfield. Soon blueprints for a new Winchester bolt rifle appeared. The Model 54 came three years later.

The 54's coned breech derived from the 1903 Springfield, but its receiver, bolt, extractor, and safety mirrored Mauser design. The ejector, patterned after Newton's, eliminated the need for a slot in one locking lug. The barrel was of nickel steel. Continental in appearance, the 54's stock was slender, with sharp comb and schnabel forend tip. It had a "shotgun" (not a crescent) butt.

The 54 sold well. It cost more than a surplus military rifle, but much less than a Sedgley or Griffin & Howe sporter. The action cocked on opening and was strong enough for the powerful .30–06 cartridge. While the safety proved awkward to use under a scope, few shooters of that day owned scopes.

Intelligent design and the Winchester name combined to make the Model 54 attractive to American hunters. But just as important to this rifle's success was its new Winchester cartridge. The .270 was essentially a necked down .30–06. It fired a 130-grain bullet at over 3,100 fps.

The October 1929 Wall Street crash sent Winchester Repeating Arms into a tailspin. By 1931 the firm was in receivership. On December 22 of that year, it was bought by Western Cartridge Company. Western kept the 54 alive, allowing T. C. Johnson and his staff to refine the rifle they had engineered. Ten configurations evolved, with ten chamberings. Prices in 1936 ranged from $59.75 for the basic Model 54 to $111.00 for the Sniper's Match.

The Model 54's main weakness was its trigger. Fashioned after military triggers of the day, it also served as a bolt stop. Competitive shooters grumbled. Hunters content to fight a mushy trigger balked at the high-swing safety, which precluded low scope mounting. Bill Weaver's affordable Model 330 scope had shown shooters what optical sights could do. Rifles that wouldn't accommodate them had a dim future.

The Model 54 was cataloged and available through 1941, but production became a trickle during the last five years. Beginning December 29, 1934, Winchester started work on a stronger, better-looking rifle—the Model 70. It came to market slowly. The 54 was still viable, and changes were given close scrutiny. Also, lots of men were still eating in soup kitchens; there was no screaming demand for a new hunting rifle. On January 20, 1936 the first M70 receivers got serial numbers. On its official release date (January 1, 1937), 2,238 rifles were awaiting shipment.

The 70's barrel and receiver looked a lot like the Model 54's. But the trigger was much better, a separate sear allowing for adjustment in take-up, weight, and overtravel. The bolt stop was also

Winchester's current "Classic" M70 action (this one in stainless steel) features the Mauser claw extractor that helped make the pre-64 version a favorite.

separate. To eliminate misfires—too common with the Model 54's speed lock—striker travel on the Model 70 was increased 1/16-inch. The first Model 70 safety was a tab on top of the bolt shroud. It swung horizontally; four years later it would be redesigned as a side-swing tab, a middle detent blocking the striker while permitting bolt manipulation. Like the Model 54, the Model 70 had three guard screws, but instead of a stamped, fixed magazine cover and guard, the 70 wore a hinged floorplate secured by a spring-loaded plunger in the separate trigger guard. A low bolt handle acted as a safety lug. The square bolt shoulder precluded low scope mounting and was later eliminated.

Model 70 barrels (with the same contours and threads as Model 54 barrels) were drop-forged, straightened by hand with a 15-pound hammer, then turned true on a lathe. They were deep-hole-drilled, then straightened again. Next, each bore was reamed to proper diameter and hook-rifled by a cutter slicing progressively deeper on several passes, one groove at a time. Rifling took about eleven minutes per barrel. After lapping, barrels were threaded and slotted for rear sights and front sight hoods. Forged, hand-stippled ramps appeared on the first 70s; later, ramps were soldered on and machine-matted. Just before chambering, each barrel was inspected, then stamped underneath with caliber designation and the last two digits of the year of manufacture. The last of four chambering reamers left the chamber undersized to allow for headspacing. The barrel then was roll-marked, given a caliber stamping, polished, and blued. Barrel material evolved. In 1925 stainless steel appeared; in 1932, chrome-molybdenum.

Model 70 receivers were machined from solid bar stock, each beginning as a 7½-pound chrome-moly billet. After 75 machinings, a finished receiver weighed 19.3 ounces. It was 8.77 inches long, 1.357 inches through the receiver ring. Spot-hardening the extraction cam behind the bridge preceded a full heat treatment. Next, each was immersed in a 1,200-degree salt bath for 24 hours. Hard-

The strong, simple, and adjustable Model 70 trigger is still the author's favorite on hunting rifles.

ness after cooling: 47C. The test left a dimple in the tang. Most small parts were drop-forged, then machined. The extractor was fashioned from 1095 spring steel.

The Model 70's stock was more substantial than the 54's, though similar in appearance to the late Model 54 version. Standard stocks were roughed by bandsaw from 2x36-inch American black walnut. After centerpunching, they went eight at a time to the duplicator for contouring. Final inletting was by hand. After buttplate fitting, the stock was drum-sanded, then hand-sanded. Minor flaws were repaired with stick shellac, glue, or matching wood. The first stocks got a clear nitrocellulose lacquer finish over an alcohol-based stain. Because these lacquers contained carnauba wax, they produced a soft, oil-like finish. After the war, when carnauba wax became scarce, harder lacquers appeared. Hand checkering with carbide-tipped cutters followed.

Headspacing came first in assembly, then the matching of bolt parts, trigger and sear honing, and a function check. The

Winchester Proof (WP) stamp signified firing of one "blue pill" cartridge (70,000 psi). After its serial number was etched on the bolt, each rifle was zeroed at 50 yards. List price in 1937: $61.25.

Early Model 70s were offered in .22 Hornet, .220 Swift, .250–3000 Savage, .257 Roberts, .270 WCF, 7mm Mauser, and .30–06—as well as the .300 and .375 H&H Magnums. Between 1941 and 1963, nine more chamberings were added; however, the .300 Savage was never cataloged. The rest of the stable of Model 70 cartridges (all from Winchester) appeared in the 1950s and early 1960s: the .243, .264 Magnum, .308, .300 Magnum, .338 Magnum, .358, and .458 Magnum. Eventually, "pre-64" Model 70s would come in 29 basic styles and 48 sub-configurations—not including special orders.

So successful that it earned the title of "the rifleman's rifle," Winchester's Model 70 became increasingly less profitable. In 1960 company accountants urged reducing production costs. Two years later, engineers had identified 50 changes. These were implemented in 1963. The most visible drew public outrage. The stock featured crude, pressed checkering and a barrel channel in which the barrel "floated" between gaps wide enough to swallow Tootsie Rolls. The recessed bolt face had a tiny hook extractor instead of the beefy Mauser claw. Machined steel bottom metal was supplanted by aluminum, solid action pins by roll-pins, and the bolt stop's coil spring by music-wire. A painted red cocking indicator stuck out like a tongue from under the bolt shroud, arrogance on top of insult. The overall effect was depressing. Prices of pre-64 Model 70s shot through the ceiling; new rifles languished on dealer racks.

Winchester improved the "new Model 70" with an anti-bind device for the bolt in 1966, a better stock in 1972, and a Feather-weight version in 1980 that looked and handled much better. A short-action Model 70 arrived in 1984. In 1987, Winchester reintro-duced the Mauser claw extractor on custom-shop 70s, and three years later, this "Classic" version with controlled-round feed entered the catalog line. Current Model 70s, while lacking the handwork of the originals, are accurate, attractive, and thoroughly dependable.

Winchester's accountants still ponder profits; but they've apparently learned that, no matter how much money you save in manufacture, you don't make any if the rifle doesn't sell. The 1964 changes gave Remington, with its new Model 700 rifle and 7mm Magnum cartridge, a big break. Since their introduction in 1948, Remington's 722 (short-action) and 721 (long-action) rifles had trailed the Winchester Model 70 at market. Plain in appearance, they lacked the 70's Mauser extractor and hinged floorplate. The Model 700, announced in 1962, was still a "push feed" rifle, but it had a checkered stock and a hinged plate. It looked classier than the 722/721—and the 1964 Model 70. The 7mm Remington Magnum was deftly promoted as an all-around big game cartridge. Winchester, about to introduce its .300 Winchester Magnum, had failed to

Remington's Model 700 came out just before Winchester changed the Model 70 and, with the new 7mm Remington Magnum, grabbed a large share of the market. This Model 78 is a version of the 700, now discontinued. The author had it barreled to .308 Norma.

load or advertise the .264 as a deer/elk round, though with proper bullets it matches the 7mm Remington. The new 700 sold like new Ford Mustangs in the 1960s, and now gets as much attention from hunters as the Model 70. In 1968, entrepreneur Bill Ruger, who'd entered the gun business nearly twenty years earlier with an autoloading pistol, announced a new bolt-action rifle. The Ruger Model 77 wore an attractive, classic-style stock. Like the Remington 700, it gained a foothold at Winchester's expense.

Among the entrepreneurs who changed the way sportsmen think about rifles and ammunition, none is better known than Roy Weatherby. Born in 1910, shortly after the .30–06 was adopted by the U.S. Army, he grew up on a Kansas farm, plowing with horses and milking cows. Roy trapped gophers, crows, and jackrabbits for the 10-cent bounty, and sold the pelts of raccoons and skunks for half a dollar. Moving to Salina at age 13, he helped his father at a one-pump filling station. The indoor plumbing was a luxury. In 1924 the family pulled stakes again and headed for Florida; "nine of us in a four-passenger Dodge that belonged to my brother-in-law." They tent-

Weatherby rifles and ammunition have been popular with hunters who shoot far.

camped along the way, dreaming of a better life. After working construction, clerking at a music store, selling refrigerators, and driving a bakery truck, Roy Weatherby studied at Wichita State. There he met and married Camilla Jackson in 1936. After graduation and two years with Bell Telephone, Roy took Camilla west. He worked briefly as a salesman for San Diego Gas & Electric, then for the Automobile Club of Southern California at $200 a month.

By this time, Roy was a wildcatter, changing cartridge design to boost bullet speed for flat trajectory and high retained energy at long range. He reshaped the .220 Swift hull to form the .220 Weatherby Rocket. He blew the shoulder out and reduced body taper of the .300 H&H case to produce the .300 Weatherby Magnum. Shortening that brass and necking it down, Roy came up with the .257, .270, and 7mm Weatherby Magnums. These delivered sizzling performance from affordable rifle actions built for .30–06 size rounds. In 1946 Roy borrowed $5,000 from the Bank of America to fund a start-up gun company. He would build or rechamber rifles for the Weatherby line of cartridges. His occasional writing—a letter to the editor in *Sports Afield* and an article in *Hunting and Fishing* at the outset—helped publicize his business. And Roy had a gift for promotion. He was especially adept at courting high-profile people in southern California. Gary Cooper, Roy Rogers, John Wayne, Andy Devine—even Jane Powell—were photographed with Roy Weatherby's rifles. He became friends with Jack O'Connor, Brigadier General Robert Scott, and the Shah of Iran. Visitors to his plant in South Gate would include astronauts Wally Schirra and Jim Lovell, Chrysler president Ed Quinn, General Nathan Twining (then Chairman of the Joint Chiefs of Staff), Los Angeles Rams quarterback Bob Waterfield, and the King of Nepal.

Still, the early years were tough. Camilla sold a 160-acre Kansas farm that she'd inherited, netting $21,000. It all went into the Weatherby machine shop and retail outlet, where Roy often worked 14 hours a day. Advertisements in three-inch magazine columns showed Weatherby cartridges in profile. Roy's business got a boost in 1948, when respected gun writer Phil Sharpe put handloading notes for Weatherby cartridges in his *Complete Guide To Handloading*. He included the .228 and .375, both soon to be dropped. At this time, riflemaker Roy was using whatever bolt actions he could scrounge, from Model 70 Winchesters to 1903 Springfields. He fitted them with barrels from Ackley and Buhmiller and sold the rifles for $150.

In 1949, Texas oil baron Herb Klein joined a small group of investors tapped to buy $70,000 of Weatherby's, Inc. (to become Weatherby, Inc.). Klein, a keen hunter and Weatherby customer, eventually put up $50,000 and got half interest in the firm. Subsequently, Roy, with friend and attorney Bill Wittman, went to Firearms International Corporation, sole importer of F.N. (Fabrique Nationale) Mauser actions, manufactured in Belgium, and for $33.50 apiece, Weatherby ordered 100 F.N. actions, stamped "Weatherby, South Gate, California." In the next few months, Roy sought suppliers of parts and equipment for his expanded enterprise and explored ammunition manufacture, so that his cartridges would shed the wildcat stigma.

Still operating at a loss in 1950, Weatherby convinced Herb Klein to loan him $35,000, plus money to cover the cost of land and a 20,000-square-foot building on nearby Firestone Boulevard. Roy moved the shop in April 1951. Soon thereafter he set up a nationwide dealer network. He was no longer depending on custom orders; Weatherbys had become "factory rifles," selling at a base price of $230.

By the mid-1950s, Roy had decided to have his rifles built overseas to reduce production costs. But visits to a number of European makers proved largely fruitless. Schultz & Larsen did build the first rifles in .378 Weatherby Magnum, and Sako contracted to assemble 1,000 of the early F.N.s. But soon Roy committed himself to a new

Roy Weatherby came up with the Mark V action in the late 1950s. It used interrupted-thread lock-up, with nine bolt-diameter lugs. Charles Newton pioneered this system.

bolt-action, one designed in-house to bottle 200,000 psi, nearly three times as much pressure as traditional rifles had to sustain. He came up with an interrupted-thread locking system, like that used on some Newton rifles. There would be nine bolt-diameter lugs in three sets of three and an enclosed bolt face. One advantage of the triple lug sets was shallow bolt lift: 54 degrees. Roy's friend Burt Munhall at H. P. White Ballistics Laboratory in Bel Air, Maryland agreed with gun guru Julian Hatcher that the design held promise. Two years and five prototypes later, Weatherby engineer Fred Jennie helped Roy finish the new Weatherby Mark V. Barreled to .300 Weatherby and proofed with a charge of IMR 4350 that generated about 100,000 psi, the rifle held fast. Deliberately lodging a bullet in the barrel, test shooters fired a standard hunting load behind it. Both bullets exited after sending pressures off the scale. Save for a pierced primer and a slight increase in headspace, no damage resulted. No dangerous condition occurred.

Roy Weatherby contracted to have his Mark V actions produced by investment casting at Precision Founders, Inc. of San

Leandro, California. Machining followed at Gardner Machine in Hollywood; Picco Industries in Sierra Madre provided some parts. Total tooling costs: $20,000. The actions cost about $40 to make, including assembly. Escalating production costs (to $65) soon drove Roy to Europe again, where he clinched a deal with J. P. Sauer & Sohn for the manufacture not only of actions but of complete rifles. By 1959 German Weatherbys were coming ashore. Later, they would be built in Japan. The latest Mark V Magnums hail from Weatherby's U.S. contractor in Maine, with the lightweight rifles being manufactured in Minnesota.

Weatherby ammunition was initially handloaded by Roy in cases he bought from Winchester and fire-formed. He made bullets by hand from copper tubing and lead wire, and sold finished cartridges for $6 a box. In 1950, Roy contracted Richard Speer to supply cases. The cases were not forthcoming, and the arrangement ended in a lawsuit. (Speer, of Lewiston, Idaho, was brother to Vernon Speer, founder of Speer Bullet Company, but he was not associated with that firm during his contract with Weatherby). For two years while trying to get cases from Richard Speer, Roy Weatherby scrambled to fill customer orders for hulls and ammunition. After exploring other options, he settled on Norma Projektilfabrik, a Swedish company. Beginning in 1953, Norma made cases for Weatherby, for 5½ cents each. In time, Norma began loading Weatherby ammunition. It still does.

By the late 1950s, Winchester had begun manufacturing its own magnum cartridges and chambering rifles for them. To retain its lead position in an increasingly competitive field, Weatherby added to its Magnum line. In 1958 the .460 emerged, a derivative of the .378, then five years old. The .340 followed in 1962, the .224 a year later. The .240 appeared in 1968, the .416 in 1989, a year after Roy Weatherby died. Roy's son, Ed, now runs the firm and has continued to develop and market Weatherby Magnums as the most potent cartridges available to hunters. The .30–378 came out in 1996, with the .338–378 on its heels. Weatherby has also begun offering ammunition in .338–06, an old but exceedingly useful wildcat round now chambered exclusively in lightweight Mark Vs.

Though long shooting at big game may not be as necessary or advisable as is often written, it has become much easier thanks to the work of Roy Weatherby, whose hard-hitting, high-velocity bullets and accurate rifles still help hunters reach far. Roy redefined "Magnum" when landmark developments in rifle scopes gave hunters the ability to aim precisely beyond the stretch of ordinary ammunition.

7

EXTRAORDINARY RIFLEMEN

Skill with a rifle is one attribute of a successful hunter. But even ordinary marksmanship has sustained hunters of extraordinary woodsmanship, courage, and resourcefulness. Hunters who've excelled as game shots and left their mark also as adventurers or explorers have earned a special place in history.

One such man was Sir Samuel Baker, born in England in 1821. He left his homeland at age 20, after training as a railroad engineer, to seek adventure in Africa, India, and Ceylon. He didn't marry until he was 41. His bride, from Hungarian nobility, apparently had the means to support his further explorations. She also joined him on a journey to the uncharted Nile. A nobleman himself, Baker spared no expense in making his wilderness camps comfortable. On one trip he shared with his brother, the cook tent included a table with fine linen and table service, while the sleeping tent boasted four beds and a dressing table. Besides ordinary backcountry provisions, Baker routinely packed sherry and brandy, hams, pickles, currant jelly, pasta, sauces, and other expensive groceries. Never in want of native help, he was purportedly a hard taskmaster, imperial in attitude and, at 6½ feet, 250 pounds, physically imposing.

His wanderlust took Baker to game fields that, in his day, were essentially virgin. There he indulged a natural curiosity by recording the performance of bullets on game. He was among the first experimenters to have test rifles built, and to examine wound channels in assessing bullets and balls. Not all his findings held up to the scrutiny of later ballisticians blessed with more sophisticated test gear and better rifles and ammunition. In *Field* magazine, 1861, Baker wrote: "I strongly vote against conical balls for dangerous game; they make too neat a wound, and are very apt to glance on striking a bone. . . ." He went on to describe a "two-groove single rifle weighing 21 pounds, carrying a 3 oz. belted ball, with a charge of 12 drachms powder" that stopped almost every animal it hit. Baker noted that when he re-

The double rifle is a curiosity now, but until Bell and Selous and others proved the effectiveness of smallbore magazine rifles on big African game, doubles with big bullets ahead of black, then Cordite, powder were the choice of professional hunters. This rest allows for the offhand testing of double rifles while mitigating the effects of heavy recoil.

placed the ball with a 4-ounce conical bullet, the rifle became less effective. ("Drachm," incidentally, was not in this case an apothecary measure, but one equivalent to "dram." A 12-dram load equated to nearly 330 grains of black powder.)

An advocate of big-bore rifles, Baker had in his battery at least one 4-bore rifle launching 4-ounce (more than 1,700 grains) balls. The single-shot weighed 22 pounds. His smallbore rifles included an 8-gauge gun firing 2-ounce balls. He correctly favored deep, slow-twist rifling, finding that one turn in 90 inches adequately stabilized round balls. An experimental rifle, built for Baker by Gibbs of Bristol, accommodated loading from the breech. Designed for a 3-ounce belted ball, the barrel had a pretty fast twist of one turn in 36 inches. But the ball did not strip because pressures and velocities were kept low. Baker liked the double-barrel rifle—a design that had become practical in Baker's day with the regulation of barrels to hit the same point of aim. "Before breechloaders were invented," wrote Baker, "we were obliged to fit out a regular battery of four double rifles for such dangerous game as elephants, buffaloes, etc., as the delay of re-loading was most annoying. . . ."

Sir Samuel White Baker wrote many books describing his journeys. Among the best known: *The Rifle and the Hound in Ceylon* (1854), *Ismalia* (1874), and *Wild Beasts and Their Ways* (1890). Baker died in England, December 1890.

As indefatigable as Baker, and even better remembered, was Frederick Courteney Selous (pronounced sel-OO). He was born into wealth in London and later schooled as a naturalist in Switzerland and Germany. An accomplished athlete with above-average intelligence, Selous had a rosy future. But he left England in 1871 with 400 English pounds, determined to become a professional elephant hunter. Like Baker, he was 20 when he began his far-flung adventures. Africa would become his home.

His career began inauspiciously when he lost his rifle. But that proved a minor problem compared to the accident that all but cost Selous his sight—a flash of loose gunpowder caused by a companion's pipe. It severely burned both men.

Like other hunters of his time, Selous began his career with a big-bore muzzleloader, a 4-bore percussion rifle that he used to shoot elephants in the heart. The animals often ran, Selous on their heels, frantically reloading. In the early years, he and his Hottentot partner, Cigar, lived on elephant meat and sudza, a cereal porridge.

Africa was an unforgiving place; the young hunter almost died of thirst once after becoming lost. Another time, on horseback, Selous was almost killed by an elephant, which caught his steed and dashed both it and its rider to the ground. The elephant then lunged, trying to pin Selous with her tusks. They imbedded themselves by his side, and he escaped between her front legs, killing her with a companion's rifle because his had been shattered. Selous hunted long enough and hard enough to tally more than 100 elephants and 175 buffalo, plus 31 lions—an impressive score by today's standards but surpassed by other hunters of his time.

After the advent of centerfire cartridges and smokeless powder, Selous still hunted with his 10-bore muzzleloader, commonly loading 164 grains of black powder behind round balls. But smallbore magazine rifles eventually won him over. He brought a .256 bolt gun on his first hunt in North America in 1897. It fired a 160-grain bullet at 2,300 fps. He also favored a rifle in .303 British, firing its 215-grain bullet at 2,000 fps, and a .375 H&H with a 275-grain bullet also at 2,000 fps. As he became used to smallbore rifles, he was all too happy to jettison the ponderous muzzleloaders that kicked so hard.

Selous fell in love with the Rockies as he had Africa, dismissing the bone-numbing cold of late-season hunting—and wading barefoot through icy streams—as part of a "charmingly novel experience for my wife and myself. . . ." Ever the naturalist, he was keenly interested in the animals he hunted, recording their weight and measure. Selous lamented the hunting pressure and settlements that had drained the Rockies of game and feared for their future. He suggested that Yellowstone Park be enlarged for more wildlife winter range.

Selous wrote several books, including A *Hunter's Wanderings in Africa.* At the age of 64, he joined the Royal Fusiliers to fight World War I in East Africa. He attained the rank of captain and earned the D.S.O. In January 1917, he led his scouts fearlessly against forces four times their strength and was killed in action.

Another elephant hunter, born nearly thirty years after Selous, also showed a penchant for adventure early on. By his 21st birthday, Walter Dalrymple Maitland Bell had been an apprentice seaman and prospected for Canadian gold. He'd hunted lions for the

During the 19th century, explorers in Africa depended on multiple hits from double-barrel black powder rifles to stop dangerous game like Cape buffalo.

Uganda railway and started a career as an ivory hunter. His work in a gunshop included the regulation of double-rifle barrels.

But W. D. M. Bell didn't like the violent recoil of big-bore doubles. Fortunately, by the time he reached Africa, the world was awash in Paul Mauser's bolt guns chambered for such rounds as the 7x57, introduced in 1893 shooting a 173-grain bullet at around 2,200 fps. Known in some circles as the .275 Rigby, it was a cartridge Bell was to make famous. Rather than shooting elephants through the ribs or depending on a slow, heavy ball to stop a charge, Bell threaded smallbore bullets through elephant brains with uncanny precision. The great sectional density of the long, pencil-like bullets ensured penetration. He even used the 6.5x54 to collect ivory. Bell counted among his pet cartridges the .318 Westley-Richards and the ubiquitous .303 British. He favored the 250-grain .318 bullet for "slanting through-the-neck shots." He called this a "four-diameter" projectile, meaning the length was four times its caliber. Other smallbore bullets he used had similar form. The popular big-bore Express rifles of the day launched bullets only 1½ to 2½ times as long as they were thick.

Bell appreciated not only light recoil but lightweight rifles. He whittled a .256 down to a trailside weight of only 5½ pounds! Though he did not recommend small bullets for elephants, he wrote glowingly about taking a new Fraser .256 afield. He killed twelve elephants with as many shots. Ammunition problems sent him back to his 7x57. Eventually, he would tally over 1,000 elephants, 700 of them taken with a 7x57.

Like other successful ivory hunters, Bell walked a lot. In one season, he wrote, he wore out 24 pairs of boots, logging 73 miles per elephant killed. His physical prowess, untiring effort, and stellar marksmanship paid off. In one day, he netted 1,643 pounds of ivory from eleven elephants. Market value: 863 British pounds.

Named "Karamojo" for the district he commonly hunted, Bell also shot other game. Small well-placed bullets proved deadly even

Bell found that magazine rifles firing smokeless loads with long roundnose bullets were deadly not only on plains game like this sable, but, with careful shooting, on elephants.

on Cape buffalo. He once killed 23 buffalo with 23 shots—from a .22 Savage High Power! That rifle firing 80-grain bullets also accounted for 25 lions and 16 leopards. Like Selous, Bell used only iron sights. Optical sight had not yet been developed that could be relied upon in the bush.

When the world went to war, Bell left the Congo in 1917 and enlisted in the Royal Flying Corps, where he won a military cross for his scouting missions. Later, he became a fighter pilot, ascending to the rank of major. After the war, the now-famous Scot wrote of his career in *Wanderings of an Elephant Hunter*, published in 1923. A second book, *Karamojo Safari*, was released in 1949, five years before his death.

A contemporary of Bell's but hunting on another continent, Jim Corbett did not leave his roots to hunt in a far-off land. Nor did he have to travel far to earn his reputation as a slayer of man-eating cats.

Jim was born in India in 1875, son of Christopher Corbett, a veteran of the First Afghan War and later the postmaster in a remote, mountainous Himalayan resort, Naini Tal. Widowed just two years after Jim was born, his mother Mary Jane held the large Corbett family together. Her gardener took Jim into the jungle for days at a time. There the boy learned to imitate the calls of birds and animals—and to hunt. He graduated from sling to longbow, then to a muzzleloader. The Naini Volunteer Rifles accepted him at age 10 and taught him to shoot a rifle. To his delight, Jim was later issued a .450 Martini and all the ammunition he could use. He wrote: ". . . now, armed with a rifle, the jungles were open to me to wander in wherever I chose to go."

One day, waiting for jungle fowl on the bank of a ravine, Jim spied a movement that instantly became a leopard coming toward him. With little time to think, Jim fired. The cat sailed over his head and vanished in the brush. Jim reloaded and followed the trail. So confident was he of his rifle and his ability that when he saw the cat's tail just ahead, he grabbed it and pulled the dead animal out of a thicket. Such cool, deliberate action would mark Jim's career.

At that time, India's jungle held many tigers and leopards. Sometimes, especially if crippled or in some other way prevented from catching wild game, they'd turn to hunting people. Between 1907 and 1911, man-eating cats took more than 1,000 humans from rural areas like that around Naini Tal. Jim was by then a railway manager, a job title he attained at age 20. His permanent posting was Mokameh Ghat, where he was also responsible for ferries that plied the Ganges River crossing carrying thousands of passengers. Among them were people who lived under the real threat of man-eaters, people from villages in which "firearms were strictly rationed," according to Corbett. One village might have use of a single muzzleloading shotgun to keep pigs and porcupines out of the crops. But a shotgun in every hand would hardly have stopped the man-eaters. They struck too quickly.

The most cunning and voracious earned names: The Muktesar man-eater began her career after a porcupine cost her an eye and left many quills in her face. She killed a woman who chanced upon her. Then, without molesting the body, she limped to find another hide. As luck would have it, a woodcutter came to work at that exact spot. The tigress killed him. Her next victim, she stalked and ate. By the time Jim Corbett missed her over a bait, the Muktesar man-eater had killed two dozen people. He got a second chance, putting a .500 bullet into her neck at a range of two yards. That was excitement enough, even for a man who'd had to dodge a cobra in a dark bath after inadvertently splashing water on the only candle.

Jim's knowledge of the jungle, and his marksmanship, made him the man to call when local cats got out of hand. Besides, he had the respect of the natives. He was a fair, compassionate employer, a man genuinely concerned with the welfare of others. (With his own money, Jim helped start a school for the sons of his workmen.) In the Kumaon district, there were plenty of man-eaters to keep Jim busy.

One of the worst was the Panar leopard, whose ghoulish ways snuffed out 400 lives, by Corbett's estimate. He hunted it at night, over goats as bait. The leopard came in and, ignoring the goats, tried to unseat Corbett. A desperate shot sent the cat away, wounded. Jim killed it the next day at close range, as it charged out of a thicket.

Then there was the Bachelor of Powalgarh, a huge tiger Corbett hunted and killed in 1910. And the Chowgarh tigress, which almost killed him. On her trail, Corbett stopped to pick up a bird egg. He still had it in his left hand when a small sound caught his attention. He turned to see the tigress crouched just a few yards away. He wrote that had he not been mindful of the egg, he might have reflexively thrown his rifle up and precipitated a charge. As it was, he lifted the rifle slowly and killed the cat before it moved.

The man-eating leopard of Rudraprayag became the title of one of his six books, all written between 1944 and 1955 (the last, *Tree Tops*, was published posthumously). His first and best-known work is *Man-eaters of Kumaon*. In true Corbett fashion, he donated all royalties from that book to St. Dundan's Hostel for Indian soldiers blinded in the Second World War. Jim hunted into old age (he shot the Rudraprayag leopard at 63) and died at 80. Corbett National Park in the Kumaon district is named for him. He'd been a gentleman and philanthropist as well as a hunter. He earned several prestigious military and conservation awards and, wielding his rifles with the quiet confidence of an extraordinary marksman, the eternal gratitude of the people of the Indian forests.

Roy Chapman Andrews was not born in the British Isles or in a jungle. A native of Beloit, Wisconsin, he grew up hunting geese in nearby marshes. Armed with a single-barreled shotgun in 1893 at age 9, Roy promptly sneaked up on three geese and shot them before finding out they were decoys. He sold the single-barrel for $3 as soon as he got a double shotgun. The marsh almost claimed Roy when a boat he was hunting in capsized. His companion drowned.

Not a particularly good student in class, Roy eagerly read about natural history and learned taxidermy. By the time he entered Beloit College, his work ethic had improved and his innate intelligence was evident. He graduated *cum laude* in 1906, then traveled to New York City and applied for a job at the American Museum of Natural History. He was hired. But instead of the custodial work he expected, he was sent on a whaling expedition to Alaska. He killed three whales himself, with a harpoon gun. Subsequently, Roy collected museum specimens all over the world, from the far north to uninhabited islands in the South Pacific. In Korea, he hunted a man-eating tiger. In Russia, he hunted with nobility for sport.

Roy Chapman Andrews favored lightweight rifles for his sport hunting and museum expeditions. He used a Model 99 Savage like this one, in .250–3000.

Back in the states, Roy met Yvette Thorpe. They were married in 1913, the year Roy earned a Ph.D. from Columbia University. Yvette, a photographer, helped Roy produce a book, *Whale Hunting with Gun and Camera*, which appeared in 1916. That year he led the Central Asiatic Expeditions for the museum, probing the Gobi Desert in search of fossils and living organisms. His entourage included forty scientists. They and their baggage traveled in eight automobiles and on the backs of 150 camels.

Roy hunted a tiger again, but as before the cat eluded him. It went on to kill 100 people. In Burma, Roy got a disabling hand infection and malaria. He didn't slow down. On a trip to China, he collected 3,100 specimens: 2,100 mammals, plus 800 birds and 200 reptiles. Yvette came away with 8,000 feet of film. Though he claimed to hunt only for science and for food, Andrews's writings show that his love for hunting as sport and a keen interest in trophies held sway throughout his career.

A smallbore advocate, Roy favored a 6.5x54 Mannlicher bolt gun and a .250–3000 Savage Model 99 for most of his big game hunting. In *Across Mongolian Plains, A Naturalist's Account of China's 'Great Northwest'*, Andrews observed that small bullets were less destructive of museum specimens, but he also had a genuine affection for lightweight rifles. Once he wrote of killing a running antelope at 400 yards with the .250. "I know how far it was, for I paced it off." He followed up with something of a disclaimer: "I may say, in passing, that I had never before killed a running animal at that range. Ninety percent of my shooting had been well within one hundred and fifty yards, but in Mongolia conditions are most extraordinary."

So was his career—and too demanding on his marriage. In 1931, after two children, he and Yvette divorced. In January 1935, Roy Chapman Andrews became director of the American Museum of Natural History, a position he held for six years. After retirement in 1941, he continued to write about his exploration and his big game hunting in both monographs and books. They included *On The Trail of Ancient Man, This Amazing Planet, Camps and Trails in China, This Business of Exploring,* and *The New Conquest of Central Asia.* Roy died in March 1960, at the age of 76.

Many other extraordinary outdoorsmen have made a living—and reputations—with the rifle. American Frank Mayer, the last of the buffalo hunters, comes to mind, as do Africa's William Cotton Oswell, George Rushby, and John Hunter. While not all of them were students of the rifle, they became quick and accurate game shots because the times demanded it. Times have changed. Adventure in unexplored places hardly ever dominates current news. But skill with a rifle still makes you a better hunter. And even more now than then, good marksmanship makes you special.

Part II:
Equipped For
The Shot

8

HUNTING WITH LIGHTWEIGHTS

An accurate shot is pivotal to the outcome of a hunt. In that instant, your marksmanship is on the line, and so is your judgment in choosing a rifle. Some rifles help you shoot accurately. Others handicap you. Rifle weight and balance are among the most important of specifications. The greater a rifle's mass, the slower its movements as you try to settle the sight on target. Weight toward the front is especially helpful in deadening the gyrations caused by a racing pulse, quivering muscles, twitching nerves, and outside influences like wind. Properly distributed in the rifle, weight is an asset. It helps you shoot better. That's why weight limits are imposed on match rifles.

On the other hand, weight can be a liability. The hardest part of hunting is not shooting; it's finding game to shoot. If you hunt like I do, walking in rugged country, a heavy rifle soon becomes a burden. It can slow you down, tire you out, and discourage you from exploring hard-to-reach places. One of those places might hold a bruiser of a buck. To stay mobile, hunters can't carry match rifles. So what is the proper weight for a big game rifle? That's not for me to say.

Standards change with time. A 10-pound Hawken or Sharps seemed sensible to the men who carried them over a century ago. Springfields and Mausers converted to sporting rifles, like the first Model 70 Winchesters and the 721 Remington, weighed between 7½ and 8 pounds. The trend to lighter rifles accelerated with Featherweight Model 70s (7 pounds) and, later, with the Remington 700 Mountain Rifle (6½ pounds) and Ruger 77 Ultra Light (6 pounds). It's been carried to extremes with the titanium Model 700 (5½ pounds). In my youth, any rifle under 7 pounds was very light. Now, 6-pound rifles are common, and I've handled several under five pounds.

Though modern metallurgy and carbon fiber stocks enable manufacturers to trim weight like never before, the sub-6-pound rifle is not new. Winchester came out with one in 1924. The Model 53, a half-magazine lever rifle, derived from the Model 92. Its most potent chambering was .44–40—hardly fearsome by today's standards, but a good match for the buckhorn sight on the 22-inch

The author shot this Coues deer with a 6½-pound 6.5x55 on a Model 70 action (gunsmithing by Lex Webernick, Rifles, Inc.).

nickel-steel barrel. Like other saddle carbines in then-new smoke-less chamberings, it was a short-range rifle built with the agility to serve a mounted marksman. The First World War changed shooters' expectations. In trenches, durability mattered more than portability. As optical sights and wildcat cartridges gave bolt rifles a boost in popularity during the 1930s and '40s, ballistic performance grabbed the spotlight. Riflemen pined for greater reach. Weight counted for little. The Mark V action Roy Weatherby designed with Fred Jennie in 1957 had 36 ounces of steel. Roy's magnum cartridges needed long barrels to reach their potential.

In 1964, Remington introduced a strange-looking carbine, the Model 600. At 6½ pounds, it was a handy deer rifle with chamber-ings in .222, .223, .243, 6mm, and .308. But dogleg bolt handles, square forends, pressed checkering, and ventilated ribs earned these rifles little respect.

During the 1980s, lightweight rifles again began attracting hunters. Morgantown, West Virginia entrepreneur Melvin Forbes designed his Ultra Light action in 1984. It looked like a Remington Model 700, but bolt and receiver diameters were smaller. Says Melvin: "While the receiver has standard wall thickness, a smaller bolt body means less steel than in actions built for magnums." Melvin designed his Model 20 around the 7x57 Mauser cartridge. "Its case is longer than that of the .308 Winchester," he points out. "So is the 6mm Remington, .257 Roberts, and .284 Winchester. In a short-action magazine, their bullets must be seated deep. You forfeit case capacity. Our magazine box is 3 inches long, not 2.85 inches as in most short-action rifles."

Melvin didn't skeletonize the metal or cut barrels shorter than 22 inches. His Model 20 owes its feathery heft to a stock that weighs just 16 ounces. "Most synthetic stocks derive from what I call boat-hull technology: they're fiberglass," says Melvin. "Mine is carbon fiber. It's actually stiffer than the barrel." The M20 stock has no pillars; an aluminum sleeve over the front guard screw prevents over-tightening. The classic lines of this stock and its tight fit to the metal are standard. So is the roughened Dupont Imron finish that gives you a sure grip. Paint pattern and color are up to the customer. Melvin also has a longer (3⅝-inch) action for the .30–06. A Model 28 for magnum cartridges is larger in diameter. A 3-inch M28 handles the 6.5mm and .350 Remington Magnums, plus Winchester and Remington Short Magnums. The 3⅝-inch version accommodates the 7mm Remington and kin. M40 Ultra Lights swallow cartridges as big as the .416 Rigby. A midget version takes .223-size rounds.

In March 1999 Melvin Forbes sold Ultra Light Arms to Colt, which had just bought Saco, a heavy weapons factory in Maine. Colt intended to build M28 rifles there while Melvin and his crew, working for Colt, produced stocks in Morgantown. But Colt got into financial trouble. Municipal lawsuits directed at the gun industry sapped money committed to debt service. Absurd though the lawsuits proved, Colt was compelled to scrap the Ultra Light project and sold Saco to General Dynamics. Melvin bought Ultra Light back, renaming it *New* Ultra Light Arms. New Ultra Light rifles mirror the originals: 4140 chrome-moly receiver, Douglas Premium barrel, Timney trigger, Sako-style extractor, and a thumb safety that, when depressed, allows bolt cycling with the firing mechanism locked.

In 1986, two years after the Ultra Light M20, Remington's 6½-pound Mountain Rifle appeared. Of mass-produced rifles, this is still the archetype, but similar models have followed. The Remington Model 7, with 20-inch barrel, is more a carbine than a light-weight rifle, but it weighs the same. Winchester offers a Compact Model 70 with 22-inch barrel and shorter stock. Ruger's Ultra Light has a 20-inch barrel, as does Browning's A-Bolt Micro-Hunter and the Savage Model 10 FM Sierra. All three scale under 6½ pounds.

Beginning with the introduction of a six-lug Mark V rifle in 1996, Weatherby has cataloged nimble versions of the husky Mark V

Weatherby's lightweight Mark V is a perfect match for slender cartridges such as the .240 Weatherby.

Magnum. The 6½-pound Lightweight was followed in 1999 by a 5¾-pound Ultra Lightweight. Both have 24-inch barrels, a thoughtful concession to ballistic performance that also ensures proper balance. The Ultra Lightweight has additional fluting and some alloy parts. In 2001 this rifle became the first from a commercial firm to chamber the .338–06. Weatherby's Super Predator Master, initially fashioned for the walking coyote hunter, sold so well in .243, 7mm-08, and .308 that Weatherby correctly assumed that many shooters were using it on deer. The response: the Super Big Game Master, a long title for a rifle of elegant simplicity. Like the Super Predator Master, it features a tan, hand-laminated stock of Aramid, graphite, and fiberglass. The 24-inch blackened, fluted stainless barrel is a Krieger, button rifled and with a contour that keeps the weight of standard SBGM rifles down to 5¾ pounds. Magnums (with the 9-lug action and a 26-inch hammer-forged tube) weigh a pound more.

Another lightweight rifle hails from Kimber. The Clackamas, Oregon company got its start in the 1980s with a Model 82, .22 rimfire. Almost as petite, the centerfire Model 84 was chambered for the .17s, .222, and .223. The still bigger Kimber 89 looked like a Winchester M70 and chambered big game rounds like the .30–06. These rifles died when Kimber folded under Chapter 7 proceedings in 1989. Les Edelman became majority stakeholder in a new company. Strong demand for handguns gave Les the idea of producing a high-quality pistol after the 1911 Colt design. He bought a factory in Yonkers, New York, projecting a run of 5,000 pistols. Now Kimber makes 44,000 M1911-style pistols *every year.*

In 1998, Kimber fielded a new rimfire designed by Nehemiah Sirkis: the Kimber 22. The firm's next rifle, a pet project for sales chiefs Dwight Van Brunt and Ryan Busse, was the 84M. Chambered in .243, .260, 7–08, and .308 (also .22–250), it weighs 5¾ pounds with a 22-inch barrel. Stockmaker Darwin Hensley shaped the trim Claro walnut stock. Checkered 20 lines per inch, it is glassed and pillar-bedded to the action; the barrel floats. The 84M has a clean-breaking trigger, a claw extractor, steel bottom metal, and M70-style wing safety with two positions.

The trend to lighter rifles owes much of its impetus to custom shops like that of Medford, Oregon gunsmith Kevin Wyatt, and Charlie Sisk, a riflemaker in Crosby, Texas. Another able Texas craftsman, Lex Webernick of Pleasanton, has long specialized in lightweight rifles. Lex mates Winchester M70 and Remington M700 receivers to stocks and barrels of the customer's choosing. His muzzle brake is pint-size. Lex's "Rifles Incorporated" shop can deliver a 5-pound .300 Magnum on a Remington titanium action.

I've used a couple of Webernick rifles afield. Both were built on M70 actions with 24-inch barrels. The first, in .260 Remington, had Lex's own stock. The ultra-slim grip is short for my hand, but its open shape makes for fast pointing. The short forend works fine because

The author used a Webernick lightweight in .260 Remington to take this caribou.

Lex had placed the front swivel stud on the forend's nose, where it won't hang up in cases or scabbards. You don't need forend beyond the swivel. This rifle carried easily for miles on a caribou hunt. I found bulls that other hunters had not seen and got in close to one with heavy beams and bezes. He dropped to a 120-grain Nosler Ballistic Tip. I've also used Lex's rifles in my women's oudoor skills program, High Country Adventures. The grips fit small hands.

One Webernick Model 70 is still in my rack. It's a 6.5x55 Lex built for a Coues deer hunt in Sonora. It wears a McMillan stock with a longer grip and weighs 6½ pounds with a Leupold 6x—about as light as feels good to me. It points like a shotgun. The straight stock and mild cartridge make recoil a non-issue.

You can't truly appreciate carrying lightweight rifles until you've learned to shoot them. The key is to take control of the rifle. Heavy rifles require less of your participation. Be a good pedestal and don't wreck the shot, and a heavy rifle will plant the bullet close to point of aim. Rifles that bob like wands, on the other hand, must be *held*, not merely supported. The shot must be *pursued*, because you may not have time to wait for the rifle to fire itself. You must do more than bear the weight; you must tame the bounce, subdue the nervous energy between your hands.

To help a light rifle settle down, I use a Brownell's Latigo sling. It is leather, cleverly designed with minimal hardware and a quickly adjustable loop. Bipods are heavier and lack versatility, though they can make a rifle rock-solid. If you anticipate long shots in open, flat country, a bipod from Harris Engineering (270–334–3633) is worth a look. Stoney Point (507–354–3360) markets collapsible shooting sticks that are less stable but better suited for high shooting positions. For best results, plant the legs well forward and pull the intersection of the sticks toward you, using your left hand to keep the forend secure on the sticks.

Lightweight rifles can be hard to shoot accurately if they have rough, heavy triggers. Unmanageable triggers are largely responsible for the myth that lightweight rifles aren't accurate. A trigger that requires muscle to trip causes rifle movement, sending the shot astray. A consistent trigger that breaks like a glass shard is invaluable. On hunting rifles, I favor a 2-pound trigger; it's stiff enough to prevent a cold, gloved finger from prematurely releasing the sear, but it's responsive enough that you can easily fire the rifle within four seconds. (Hold the rifle too long and your muscles will tire.) Not long ago, shooting what may be the lightest rifle on the market—a 3¾-pound take-down from Kifaru, International (800–222–6139)—I managed a 1¾-inch group at 100 yards. That was from the sit, with a sling. I stood up and fired three more rounds. That cluster taped 3⅞ inches. I don't shoot much better than that, sitting or offhand, and would have had trouble duplicating those groups.

Kifaru's "Rambling Rifle" take-down, incidentally, is built on Remington's Model Seven action. My sample had 18½-inch Shilen

Taming the wobbles of a lightweight rifle calls for a low position.

match-grade barrels, fluted, in .260 and .308. Changing is easy: twist one out and the other in. Thin-walled barrels get hot fast, so Patrick Smith, the rifle's designer, gave the barrels a half-length Kevlar sleeve that matches the stock. It's attractive and functional. A screw on the receiver ring enters a detent in the barrel threads so the barrel can't back out. The screw is hardly in keeping with the trim profile of the rifle; besides, how absurd to carry a screwdriver for a 4-pound rifle! I've left it loose when shooting, and neither barrel has backed out.

The receiver is shaved to minimum dimensions, with fluting and skeletonizing everywhere. The bolt knob, a mere shell, operates a bolt body light as a corncob and perforated on the underside from lugs to cocking piece. But there's a full measure of steel around the cartridge head. The receiver ring, bolt face, and locking lugs are essentially unaltered. All steel is stainless, with a bead-blasted finish.

The buttstock is traditional in shape, though slim almost to delicacy. Kevlar construction ensures strength. In place of a forend, a tapered horizontal blade extends forward. Between it and the barrel there's nothing but air. The blade has a fixed sling swivel on its end. Barrel installation is easy because there's no forend to clear; you can grip the barrel close to the receiver to align threads. Recoil is not abusive, due to the Kifaru stock's generous comb and a Decelerator pad of practical size. The forend blade offers more control than you might expect. What's noticeable is how fast this rifle recoils. There's no mass to slow it down. *Bang!* It's there and gone, seemingly before the bullet has a full head of steam.

The take-down Rambling Rifle from Kifaru stows in a compartmented soft case with sleeves for four barrels and a separate pocket for the stock-and-receiver assembly. Patrick's company had no trouble making the case; it's been manufacturing high-quality hunting backpacks for years. In my Kifaru pack, the rifle takes up no more room than a small tent or sleeping pad. So you can hunt with this rifle, then disassemble it and stow it for a two-hands-free trip down the mountain.

9

TAKE STOCK OF WOODS RIFLES

When we say they don't make 'em like they used to, we generally mean the product isn't as good as it once was. But "good"
can mean many things. Old pickups that incorporated lots of steel
don't match current models in terms of trouble-free operation—to
say nothing of driver comfort. On the other hand, while my '65 Ford
balked now and again, I could always make it run. It understood
crescent wrenches. It had no electronic brain, no software to frus-
trate backyard mechanics who grew up greasy, tuning engines with
chalk on the flywheel.

Manufacturers now turn out powerful bolt-action rifles with little hand fitting and at reasonable cost. Those that look muscular and
sinister seem to sell best. Add a scope big enough to plug a storm
drain and most hunters are as happy as ants on a Hershey bar.

Oddly enough, a lot of riflemen—even those who often shoot
far—would shoot better with trimmer, livelier rifles. Like the old
saddle rifle or woods rifle.

Woods rifles came of age with the fighter airplane. Like the
British Spitfire, the best of them had power and grace and agility.

They became nimble extensions of the hand, responding as if to thought. Their effectiveness lay in the skill of the user. Sadly, like the Spitfire and other powerful prop fighters, the woods rifle faded after World War II. Winchester's Model 71, an elegant lever gun and the last of the firm's exposed-hammer type, appeared in 1935 and died during the fifties—even as electronic controls replaced the hand of the pilot in jet-powered fighters firing missiles at enemies miles away.

Though hunters now shoot farther than ever, most big game is still killed within 200 yards. That's because most animals like to be near or in cover. Sure, some meet their end in the open, and without rifles built to kill at a quarter-mile some hunters might shoot fewer animals. But some hunters might shoot *more* game. It's tempting to take advantage of a flat-shooting rifle when a closer shot is just a belly-crawl away. And easy to miss the long shot. At short range, the nimble rifle usually has the edge.

Woods rifles aren't merely short rifles chambered for big-bore cartridges with softball trajectories. They are not just iron-sighted lever guns. In fact, several short, big-bore lever rifles wouldn't get a second glance from a seasoned woods hunter; and some bolt-actions would. To my mind, a woods rifle is any rifle that handles like a grouse gun. It is a woods rifle because it points as quick as thought. You can shoot in the woods with a rifle built for the prairie, and most of the time you won't feel handicapped.

Some years ago I borrowed a Winchester Model 94 in .30–30 to kick around in a thicket that seemed deery. As luck would have it, a buck jumped out in front of me. I fired at it several times. It ran a short distance and dropped. The little carbine had seemed to fire itself. I didn't remember aiming. The bead simply rode the deer as the sharp raps of the steel butt kept time between the smooth pulsings of the lever.

By modern standards, the 94 has a weak action and creepy trigger. Accuracy is mediocre at best and lock time is as long as a Baptist

The Marlin 336 has an agility missing in many modern bolt rifles.

sermon. You can't use pointed bullets or mount a scope low. A
.30–30 bullet runs out of steam short of the zero range of a modern
magnum. The Model 94 keeps perking along after a century on the
trail because it is a *shootable* rifle. It seems to fit almost anyone who
picks it up. And it points as naturally as your arm. So does the Marlin
336, an updated Model 36, which is in turn an updated 1893—same
vintage as the Winchester Model 94. Sako's Finnwolf and Winchester's 88 have shorter strokes and handle more potent rounds, but in
my hands they're not as lively as most exposed-hammer lever guns.
Partly, that's because they're stocked like modern bolt rifles.

Stocks on bolt-action rifles vary a great deal in dimensions.
Here are the measurements to keep in mind when you're comparing, or contemplating alterations.

Length of pull is measured from the dish of the trigger to the dish
of the butt in a line parallel to the bore. Standard length of pull for rifles is about 13½ inches, which is supposed to fit shooters of average

build and 32- or 33-inch arms. My arms are longer (36-inch sleeve), but I like the rifle's center of gravity as close as I can get it to mine. A lot of shooters use stocks that, by the numbers, are either too long or too short. The stocks work because they're familiar or comfortable.

Drop at comb and **drop at heel** are measured from an extension of the bore line on rifles. A rifle stocked for scope use should have a fairly straight stock—that is, drop at comb and heel should be about the same. Stocks with lots of drop at heel can also be functionally straight if the cheek piece is high and falls off in a step at the heel. For example, Remington's straight-combed Model 700 Mountain Rifle has equal drop at comb and heel. But with the "monte carlo" profile of the 700 BDL, heel drop is about an inch greater. There's really no difference in the way the stocks support your cheek. Given a straight comb, drop at comb and heel should be minimal (say, ½- to ¾-inch) to support your face when your eye is in line with the scope's axis. Early lever-rifle stocks had excessive drop that prevented a good "cheek weld" and accentuated recoil. Winchester's Model 1895 had a 2⅞-inch drop at comb and a 3⅝-inch drop at heel.

Comb thickness is seldom mentioned as a stock dimension because comb radius and taper also matter and vary widely among commercial stocks. But when you shoulder the rifle quickly, your eye should come directly to center above the bore. A comb too thick will force you to mash your cheek into the stock, while a thin comb offers little support and hits you like a hatchet on recoil.

Cast-off, hardly ever available on factory rifles, describes an offset buttstock, one that angles to the right of bore axis from grip to butt. Cast-off helps put your eye squarely behind the scope. Measured in inches at the butt, cast-off at toe can differ from cast-off at heel if the stockmaker puts a "twist" in the stock. Stocks that "bend" to the left are said to have cast-on, a very rare feature in rifles.

Pitch is the angle of the butt to the bore, measured in inches from the bore's center at the muzzle to a line perpendicular to the butt and tangent to the rear of the receiver. Pitch is critical because it determines where your muzzle will point. Too much pitch puts the barrel at a steep angle to the grip, so it naturally points low. Too little pitch can cause you to shoot high. A pitch of 2½ to 3 inches is about right for most stocks, but because pitch is measured at the muzzle, it changes with barrel length. If the rifle points at the target when you toss it to your shoulder and your eye is in line with the sight, pitch is just fine.

There are no magic formulas for **grip shape** or **radius**. I prefer long, open grips, partly because I have big hands and partly because, in any hands, they make a rifle quicker to point than tight grips favored by competitive shooters. I also like slim grips, again because they're quick and easy to control. The grip is best tapered so it swells a bit at the back (bottom). Deep, broad fluting of the comb nose on the right side positions the heel of your hand.

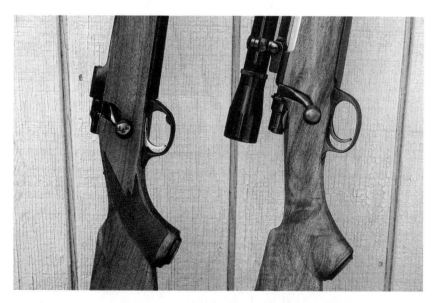

The slim, open grip on the author's custom-stocked .358 Norma (right) contrasts with a standard grip on a Ruger 77. Different hands and shooting styles mandate different grips.

The **forend** should be slender and slightly pear-shaped, not square in cross-section. A gradual taper from back to front not only looks good but gives your left hand quick purchase. That taper also helps your trigger hand bring the rifle back toward you and makes the rifle easier to swing.

Stock fit and feel can't be described by numbers alone: You know it's the stock you want when the rifle flies to your shoulder and you open your eyes and the sights are quivering on the bullseye.

The buttstock on a traditional woods rifle is short. It has lots of drop at comb and heel. The grip is long and slender and either straight or modest in curvature. The forend is short and slim, and if it must meet a deep, broad receiver or magazine well, it has a pronounced taper. Barrels, 20 to 22 inches long, are not heavy; but there's a pronounced tip toward the muzzle even in rifles without tube magazines. The archetypal Model 99 Savage, for instance, has a light barrel and thin schnabel forend. But its receiver and magazine reach well forward of the trigger. In fact, if you place a 99 on top of a Winchester 94, you'll see the center of the 99 action meets the forward edge of the 94's receiver. The Model 99's barrel emerges at about the same place (relative to the trigger) as the barrel on a Winchester 70, whose action is much longer.

The main reason stocks on early lever rifles are judged inferior to those on modern bolt guns is that our standards have changed. We've been taught that short, slim, crooked stocks accentuate kick. They do. But the recoil of a .300 Savage in a trim woods rifle is no more brutal than the recoil of a .300 Ultra Mag in a beefy bolt gun. We've also been told that low combs offer insufficient cheek support and that slender grips and forends deny our hands the control needed for accurate shooting. That's true too—if by accurate shooting you mean deliberate shooting. Fast shooting in thickets is easier with slender stocks that can slide and twist easily in your hand. Point a broomstick at a bird darting between trees. Now point a 2x6 piece of lumber. . . .

You aim with your eye, but your hands point the rifle. The sight doesn't help you point. It only shows where you're pointing. Rifles these days are mainly for shooters who rest them on flat places. Forends are thick and have flat bottoms. Grips are stout and steep. Not that long ago, forends were skinny and had round bottoms, while grips were slender as a maiden's wrist. Both ends of the stock felt alive in your hand. A little pressure here or there and the rifle would twist and tilt ever so slightly. With practice, you got on target instantly, subconsciously nudging the rifle to sightline even as it leapt to your shoulder, like a skilled cowboy works a cutting horse, or a race car driver deftly maneuvers through the corners. You should be able to *flick* a rifle to your shoulder instead of *lifting* it there.

Try it. Borrow an early Winchester 94 or a Savage 99 carbine. Starting at waist level, aim as quickly as you can. If you're like me, you'll find the rifle comes free of your grasp as it jumps to follow your eye and hands. That's OK, because the rifle is essentially pointing itself. Appreciate the help!

A wide, square forend and a steep, thick grip glue themselves to your hands because they're too big to let go. Your hands steer the rifle as it travels to your shoulder. But the rifle is also a load, and your hands are affected by that load. Instead of pointing as you'd point your finger, you move the rifle as if it were a length of pipe, battling its inertia from start to finish. Result: a slow shot.

Quick shooting with rifles is all but a lost art. We venerate little groups from the bench and long-range kills afield. Many of us have closets full of rifles that shoot accurately. Their bullets trace chalk-line paths and dump enough energy to decommission a Bradley fighting vehicle. Few of us, however, own a really good woods rifle. It needn't be a lever-action or a pump. Early Mannlicher-Schoenauer bolt rifles feel almost alive; my Dakota Model 10 single-shot in .280 Remington is as nimble a smokepole as you can imagine. Alas, few modern bolt rifles are engineered for quick handling.

I remember a friend's 20-bore Italian shotgun that one day found its way to my shoulder. The effect was all but magical: the little double seemed to hop up there by itself and pull my gaze down the rib. I couldn't slow that gun down or make it point where I wasn't looking. A handful of scatterguns have seduced me like that one. None were affordable. But they all had grips common to woods rifles, with a Spartan slimness that left the gun free to swim in my hands. I became particularly aware of grip length—how the heel of my trigger hand had no interference from the combs on those shotguns, and how the first joint of my finger settled naturally on the trigger. The steep, clubby grips of rifles designed for deliberate shooting, the forend thick enough to chock a truck parked on a steep hill; these are poor designs for the woods. You want a straight grip so the muscles of your forearm tighten as you shoulder the rifle. You want a grip not much bigger around than a broomstick up front but one that flares a bit to the rear and (if a pistol grip) down to the cap. It should be oval in cross-section, not so broad as it is tall. The comb nose has no business anywhere near your hand. If you have a very big hand, you may have to settle for deep, broad fluting on the right side rather than insisting on a comb nose so short that it looks stubbed off.

A long forend is no liability, but if it's long and slender it looks odd. And it must be slender. Don't worry about what to do with left-hand fingers and thumb. They'll find a place to relax. No matter that they touch the barrel. A forend beefy enough to keep your fingers off steel works OK on sandbags, but it's as awkward as a bridge girder to swing on running animals. A deep forend keeps the rifle from cradling in your hand.

Curious as to the measurements of grips and forends on fast-handling rifles, I took a tape to a Marlin 1894 (.357) and a Savage 99A (.250), then to a Remington 700 (.30–06) and a Model 70 Winchester (7mm Remington Magnum). Here are the comparisons, in inches:

A slim grip and forend help put traditional saddle guns on target with lightning quickness.

	Marlin 94	Savage 99	Rem. 700	Win.70
Top grip length to point of comb nose	4½	4¾	3½	3¾
Grip girth at smallest point (with lever)	5	5¼	5	4¾
Forend girth at mid-point	5½	5¼	6	6
Balance point, inches from trigger	3¼–4*	5	5½	6½
Forend length, inches from trigger	14¼	16½	17½	18¼
Barrel length	18½	20	22	26

*The balance point of the tube-fed 1894 moves only ¾-inch forward when the rifle is loaded with eight rounds.

    This comparison delivered some surprises. While "saddle rifle" grips seem slender, they're no more so at the choke point than grips of standard bolt rifles. The main difference is in grip length. The two lever-actions measured have grips that are longer by an inch over the top. The comb nose is well out of the way, giving room for the hand's heel to rotate. I was astonished to find that the slim schnabel forend on my 99 is only an inch shy of matching trigger-to-tip length of an M700 forend. But grip girth (including the barrel) on the lever-actions is smaller than on the bolt rifles. Half an inch makes a colossal difference. (The upland guns I can't afford also have petite forends.)

Balance point depends largely on barrel length and weight. It's easy to put forward tilt in a rifle, but doing it without adding unnecessary steel isn't so easy. The Savage balances at about the same point as the Remington 700, despite its shorter barrel. One thing that makes the Savage so quick is the compression of so much of its weight into a short section halfway between the hands.

Proper comb height depends on the sights. Some early woods rifles had combs too low even for iron sights, and a scope usually mandates a higher comb. Comb thickness matters too, because it also affects the placement of your eye relative to sightline. A sharp

This coyote rifle, gunsmithed by Fred Zeglin of Casper, Wyoming, is chambered in .240 Hawk. Heavy and accurate, with a forward balance, it is best for long, deliberate shooting.

comb is hard on your face and will likely put your eye to the right of center, while a thick comb feels clubby and can force you to press your face too hard against the stock to aim.

Stocks on woods rifles should be short, not only for quick mounting but to pull the rifle's center of gravity into you so you're not stretching forward trying to support that weight at arm's length. Barrels should be short, partly to keep from hanging up on tree limbs, partly to speed your swing on moving game, and partly to keep rifle weight close to your body.

You don't need minute-of-angle accuracy in thickets. If you get 3-inch groups at 100 yards, you'll have all the precision you can handle. Few hunters can keep offhand shots inside a 3-inch circle at even 50 yards, where most tube-fed lever guns will easily make an inch and a half. Any centerfire rifle will shoot accurately enough for woods hunting. The trick is to get one that helps *you* shoot accurately.

A scope on a woods rifle is a blessing because the sight picture appears in a single plane. An open-country rifle with woods rifle proportions can also use the scope's magnification. In both cases, you're best served with a trim, lightweight scope mounted low. A receiver sight with a big aperture makes sense too, especially if you combine it with a flat-faced front bead angled to catch the sun.

Despite the handwork that went into early woods rifles, they weren't perfect. Some could use more wood in the comb, and pre-war open sights leave me cold. But I'm not about to modify the woods rifles in my rack. I'm not sure I've identified everything that gives them life. And I don't want to tinker that out of them.

10

RIFLES GONE BALLISTIC

The new cartridge had a huge case for its 7mm bullet, and blistering speed limited bullet drop at long range to only a third of what shooters were used to. Then along came a 30-caliber cartridge with an even bigger case to give the same zip to heavier bullets. Soon followed a .33 that pushed 200-grain softpoints as fast as contemporary varmint bullets.

I'm talking, of course, about the 7x57 Mauser, .30–40 Krag, and .33 Winchester.

In 1892, the 7x57 was brand new, a smallbore cartridge that used smokeless powder to launch a 175-grain roundnose bullet at a sensational 2,300 fps. Given a 100-yard zero, the bullet fell about 2 feet from line of sight at 300 yards—flat-shooting indeed compared to the 6-foot drop of a 405-grain, .45–70 bullet. The .30–40 Krag, also one of the first smokeless military cartridges, powered a 220-grain bullet at just under 2,000 fps. Drop at 300 yards (100-yard zero) was nearly a foot greater than that of the 7x57 bullet, but the .30 delivered more weight. And its full-jacketed military bullet would penetrate an astonishing 58⅞-inch pine boards at 15 feet.

Compared to the .45–70, it was a brickload of lightning. Winchester didn't announce its .33 for another decade. In the Model 1886 rifle, it offered a flat-shooting, hard-hitting alternative to the .45–70, with 40 percent more energy (2,300 foot-pounds). Out to 300 yards, it shot as flat as the .30–40 Krag. The .33 Winchester bullet was 60 grains heavier than that of a .30–30 (original load) and flew 400 fps faster—about the same speed as a small game bullet in the .25–20.

Our standard big game cartridge is no longer the .45–70. Nor is it the 7x57, which survives as a curmudgeon too beloved to either leave or ignore. The .30–40 Krag, a good cartridge, knuckled under to the superior .30–06 and was all but obsolete before the First World War. The .33 Winchester *is* obsolete, an anachronism like the lever guns that chambered it. For awhile, the Krag's successor, the .30–06, remained the darling of big game hunters—and you might say it will never be replaced. But during the middle of the 20th century, hunters came to expect more out of their cartridges.

A detailed history of post-war cartridge evolution is beyond the scope of this book. But a synopsis would put rimless rounds like the .30–06 and .270 in the shadow of belted magnums based on the .375 Holland & Holland case, circa 1912. The .300 H&H, a necked-down .375, had been around since 1925, the year Winchester announced its .270. But the leggy .300 had so much more power and recoil than the lever-rifle cartridges still in common use that few hunters thought it necessary. It also required a longer rifle action than the .30–06. A Magnum Mauser or the alterations necessary on standard-length actions made a .300 an expensive project. The Depression certainly didn't boost sales of expensive rifles or costly high-performance ammunition. Riflemen who wanted a flatter-shooting big game round than the .30–06 turned to the .270.

Then Roy Weatherby began changing the shape of the .300 H&H, and cutting it down so it would fit handily in standard actions. Winchester followed in the 1950s with similar magnums, and

Remington hit pay dirt in 1962 with the 7mm Remington Magnum. Since then, longer, more powerful cartridges have surfaced, while rimless rounds of more modest (some would say more practical) dimensions have filled every conceivable gap in ballistics charts. The 7x57 Mauser, .30–40 Krag, and .33 Winchester have become grandfathers several times over. Here are some of their descendants:

Introduced in 1893, the 7x57 was at one time considered a high-velocity cartridge; it's still useful.

Cartridge, bullet weight	muzzle velocity (fps)	bullet path (inches)				
	range, yards	100	200	300	400	500
7mm-08 Rem., 140-grain	2860	+1.8	0	-7.8	-22.9	-46.8
.280 Rem., 140-grain	3060	+1.5	0	-7.0	-20.9	-43.3
7mm Rem. Mag., 140-grain	3175	+2.2	+1.9	-3.2	-14.2	-32.0
7STW, 140-grain	3325	+2.0	+1.7	-2.9	-12.8	-28.8
7mm Rem. Ultra Mag, 140-grain	3425	+1.7	+1.6	-2.6	-11.4	-25.7
.308 Win., 180-grain	2620	+2.3	0	-9.7	-28.3	-57.8
.30–06 Sprgfld., 180-grain	2700	+2.1	0	-9.0	-26.3	-54.0
.300 Win. Mag., 180-grain	2960	+2.7	+2.2	-3.7	-15.9	-35.6
.300 Rem. Ultra Mag, 180-grain	3250	+2.4	+1.8	-3.0	-12.7	-28.5
.30–378 Wby. Mag., 180-grain	3450	+2.4	+3.1	0	-7.4	-19.6
.338–06 A-Square, 210-grain	2750	+2.0	0	-8.5	-24.7	-50.7
.338 Win. Mag., 210-grain	2830	+1.8	0	-7.9	-23.2	-47.4
.338 Rem. Ultra Mag., 250-grain	2860	+1.7	0	-7.6	-22.0	-44.7
.340 Wby. Mag., 210-grain	3211	+3.2	+3.9	0	-9.5	-25.7
.338–378 Wby. Mag., 250-grain	3060	+3.5	+4.2	0	-9.8	-26.4

Note: Neither the .338 Remington Ultra Mag or the .338–378 Weatherby Mag is currently factory loaded with 210-grain bullets; any comparisons must take into account the greater energy of the heavier 250-grain bullets, not just speed and trajectory.

Making cartridges bigger doesn't absolve them of the rules of physics. If you boost bullet weight, you must reduce velocity; and velocity sells. A bullet heavier than 140 grains would make the big 7mms more useful in some types of hunting, but they could not be driven nearly as fast as the 140, and to date Remington has limited both the 7 STW and 7mm Ultra Mag to 140-grain bullets. The 7mm Remington Magnum is an example of how an increase in weight affects bullet velocity. This round launches a 140-grain soft-point at 3,175 fps. Substitute a 160-grain bullet, and velocity drops to 2,950 fps. Now, given a streamlined shape, the heavier bullet begins to catch up as soon as it leaves the muzzle, and downrange its higher ballistic coefficient will eventually bring it even with its light-weight counterpart. At 500 yards, the 140-grain and 160-grain 7mm

Magnum bullets are both traveling about 2,040 fps, and the 160 has an edge in energy: 180 ft-lbs. But marketers have learned the retail value of high *muzzle* velocity.

Bigger bores accommodate any given weight change more easily. That is, you can add 20 grains to a 30-caliber bullet without sacrificing quite so much speed. The additional weight has less effect on the bullet's length and bearing surface than does the same 20-grain increase in a smaller bore. So pressures are not as sharply affected. Nonetheless, a heavy-game bullet would make sense in the 7 STW and 7mm Ultra Mag. Remington already loads the 160-grain Swift and the more aerodynamic 160 Nosler Partition in its 7mm Magnum ammunition. The bigger STW case would seem even better suited to these bullets and would boost the versatility of the cartridge. Of course, handloaders have myriad options.

While the 7mm bore delivers both high sectional density and speed in cases of ordinary size, the 30-caliber bore shines with big cases. Magnum .30s can drive 180-grain bullets as fast as 7mm cartridges with the same powder capacity can hurl 160s. A 180-grain bullet at 2,650 fps is surely adequate for all North American big game, as thousands of .30–06 shooters can attest. A .30 magnum that drives it 3,000 fps doubles the range at which you can deliver a ton of energy to a tough animal. The '06 carries a ton to 200 yards; the .300 Winchester Magnum takes it to 400. The .300 Winchester's 180-grain bullet flies as flat as a .270 shoots its 130.

So it's surprising that American ammunition firms have sometimes been tardy with .30 magnums. When Roy Weatherby trotted out his line of sleek long-range cartridges in the early 1940s, the .270 and 7mm predated the .300—though the parent case was a .300 that had been in the country since 1925. In the 1950s, when Winchester announced its first belted magnums, the .458 led, with the .338 and .264 to follow. There was no .300. In 1962 Remington chose to bring out a 7mm Magnum, ignoring the .30. By this time, the .300

The 7mm STW (Shooting Times Westerner) derived from an 8mm Remington Magnum case. It's been eclipsed by the 7mm Remington Ultra Mag.

Weatherby Magnum had become a hunting legend, and wildcatters busied themselves necking the .338 Winchester to form the .30–338. Winchester at last heeded the signals with its .300 magnum in 1963.

The .300 Weatherby Magnum remained on top of the heap, ballistically, until upstaged by another Weatherby round, the .30–378, introduced in late 1996. Remington's search for a high-performance .30 was rumored long before the .300 Ultra Mag appeared in 1999. Based on the .404 Jeffery, a rimless British round dating to 1910, the Ultra Mag is not just a necked-down version. Ilion engineers fashioned the new cartridge specifically for the long-action Model 700 receiver. The rim is slightly rebated to fit magnum bolt faces (eliminating the need for more tooling or another shellholder on the loading bench). Though the case is long, it is just short enough to permit ordinary seating depth without jamming bullet noses against the front of the magazine.

The Ultra Mag has 13 percent more case capacity than the .300 Weatherby. But you won't get 13 percent more velocity. As case volume grows, cartridges become less efficient. You need more space and more powder per increment of performance than you did for the last increment. In fact, there's negligible difference between the .300 Ultra Mag and the .300 Weatherby Magnum as factory loaded—provided you compare Remington's Ultra Mag load with the Norma ammo that has for decades defined .300 Weatherby performance. The Ultra Mag launches a 180-grain Nosler Partition or Swift Scirocco at 3,250 fps, while the Norma-loaded Weatherby Magnum gives a 180-grain Partition or a pointed softpoint bullet 3,240 fps. A 200-grain Nosler in the .300 Ultra Mag leaves the rifle at 3,025 fps, compared to 3,060 for the same bullet in a .300 Weatherby cartridge from the Norma plant.

The picture changes when you exclude Norma. Remington stokes the .300 Weatherby cartridge to only 3,120 fps, or 130 fps off the Ultra Mag's speed. Hornady's catalog shows 3,120 for the Weatherby, too. Federal now loads both the Ultra Mag and the .300 Weatherby, at 3,250 fps and 3,190 fps, respectively (with 180-grain bullets). So in the Federal stable there's not as much difference between these two racehorses. Federal's heavy-bullet load for the .300 Weatherby is less ambitious. Its 200-grain Trophy Bonded bullet at 2,900 fps doesn't match even the 200-grain Remington load for the Weatherby. Still, there's one .300 Weatherby load from Federal that outperforms the Ultra Mag: the High Energy 180-grain Trophy Bonded. It clocks 3,330 fps at the muzzle, handily beating even Norma's speed for that round.

In handloading potential, though, the Ultra Mag has the edge on the Weatherby. It's bigger. Purists also like the rimless case that headspaces on the shoulder. In sum, the .300 Ultra Mag amounts to a .300 Weatherby Magnum with improvements. I doubt it will ever match the Weatherby's field record.

Incidentally, it's not fair to compare the .300 Ultra Mag to the gargantuan .30–378. The .30–378 requires a bigger action and bolt face, limiting it to the likes of the Weatherby Mark V rifle (designed for the .378 Weatherby in 1958). The .378 fathered the .460, and much later the .416 Weatherby Magnum. Until the debut of the .30–378 in 1996, no other commercial rounds have shared this hull. The .30–378 is factory loaded with 165-grain Nosler Ballistic Tips at an advertised 3,500 fps; 180-grain Barnes X bullets at 3,450; and 200-grain Nosler Partitions at 3,160. Given a 300-yard zero, these bullets strike less than 4 inches high at 200 yards. The 165- and 180-grain bullets hit a mere 7½ inches low at 400, while the 200-grain Noslers drop 9 inches. All three bullets carry well over a ton of energy to 500 yards and land as close to the line of sight as bullets from a .270 with 200-yard zero do at 400.

Anyone in touch with the industry could have predicted commercial production of the .338–378. It launches the biggest bullets that can be considered long-range hunting bullets faster than any

From left, the .338–06, .338 Winchester, and .338–378 Weatherby. Before the Second World War, the .30–06 was as powerful a cartridge as you'd find in elk camps. Now, some hunters dismiss it as marginal for elk.

other round. I first saw a .338–378 in action years ago, when it was still a wildcat. Between stages at a smallbore prone match in rural Oregon, one of the riflemen broke out a long-barreled bolt gun not quite heavy enough for an artillery carriage. He bellied into a sandy hillock and proceeded to demolish rocks on a hillside hundreds of yards away. They were big rocks, but they splintered when struck by those heavy bullets, sending dust and chips into the air. The blast, I remember, rattled the clubhouse windows. Without a muzzle brake, I expect that rifle would have plowed furrows with the toes of the shooter's boots.

As soon as the .338–378 became available in the Weatherby Mark V in 1999, I borrowed one of these hyper-.33s from Weatherby and benched it on a rainy day in western Washington. The 250-grain Noslers from Weatherby ammo averaged 3,005 fps from the Accumark's 26-inch fluted barrel. That's 55 fps lower than advertised — close enough, especially on a cold day. I was mightily impressed by the accuracy: about a minute of angle. At 300 yards one 3-shot group measured 2½ inches. A friend fired the rifle and beat my best 200-yard group with one that crowded 1½ inches. Our bullets seemed to arrive at distant backstops with lightning suddenness.

This rifle behaved itself with the factory-installed brake, though under the tin roof even double ear protection didn't tame the blast. Thoughtfully, Weatherby provides a small rod with which to remove the brake, and a knurled cap to replace it. I had to feel the .338–378 unshackled, so I fired one offhand shot without the brake at a 300-yard target. The kick was not only hard, but quick. I've fired many big-bore rifles, including a .700 Nitro Express. The .338–378's recoil is as brutal as any. It lifted the heavy rifle almost out of my hands (I confess to holding the forend too lightly) and spun it so the scope banged into my skull. Enough of that fun, I thought, but I was pleased to find the bullet hole just 5 inches to five o'clock of center on the 300-yard target.

The .338–378 has no close rivals. At 200 yards it delivers a crushing two tons of energy, as much as the .338 Winchester Magnum can claim at the muzzle and about equal to the payload of a .340 Weatherby Magnum at 100 yards. The .338–378 dumps more energy at 500 yards than the .33 Winchester does at the muzzle (and more than the .30–06 at 100 steps!).

Does anyone need cartridges this big—or even as big as the .300 Ultra Mag or 7mm STW? Well, no. Much smaller cartridges will kill reliably. A lot of moose have been shot with the .303 British,

When hunters see antlers like these, they want long reach and bone-smashing power.

a lot of elk with the .30–30 and .300 Savage. In his ivory-hunting days, W. D. M. Bell downed many elephants with the 7x57. What big cases give you is room for more fuel, which translates to higher bullet speed. There are three good reasons for wanting more powder capacity, and for choosing higher speed over more weight as a way to use that fuel.

1. Fast bullets shoot flatter. They're fully as susceptible to gravity as slow bullets, but over a given distance, gravity has more time to act on the slow ones. So the bullet sinks more steeply from your sightline. At long range, you must accurately estimate distance if you are to place a slow bullet precisely. A flat-shooting bullet offers you some latitude for error. Example: A 140-grain bullet from a 7mm STW (starting speed 3,325 fps) remains within 3 vertical inches of sightline out to 300 yards (250-yard zero). That bullet from a 7x57 Mauser (starting speed 2,660 fps), hits 3 inches low before it reaches 240 yards (200-yard zero). At 300 steps it strikes more than 9 inches low.

2. Fast bullets buck wind better. This is an even bigger advantage than flat flight because gravity is constant, whereas wind speed and direction are not. Even a light breeze can push a bullet far off course at long range, and the wind downrange may not be at all like the wind you're feeling, especially in broken country. Example: A 180-grain bullet from a .300 Remington Ultra Mag (starting speed 3,250 fps) drifts 13 inches at 400 yards in a 15-mph crosswind. The same wind blows the same bullet 20 inches when it's fired from a .30–06 (starting speed 2,650 fps).

3. Fast bullets carry more energy. This is obvious, but energy alone doesn't kill game, and kinetic energy measured in foot-pounds can be a misleading gauge of bullet effectiveness. Where extra energy counts is on far-away hits to bone and muscle, or on quartering-away shots. Then you'll want the inertia

necessary to smash through to the vitals. The high retained velocity that gives you more energy is also needed to ensure bullet expansion. Example: A 250-grain bullet from a .338–378 Weatherby Magnum (starting speed 3,060 fps) reaches 500 yards with 2,500 foot-pounds of energy, and it's still traveling at 2,125 fps. A .338–06 hurling the same bullet (starting speed 2,400 fps) delivers 1,420 foot-pounds to 500 yards; velocity has dropped to 1,600 fps, marginal to guarantee adequate expansion. (Most expanding bullets will open at impact speeds of 1,600 fps—about what a 180-grain .308 Winchester bullet is clocking at 500 steps. A lot of bullets fall below that level before they reach 600 yards, including missiles from the .270, .30–06, and .338 Winchester Magnum.)

You may not need a rifle that shoots chalk-line straight as far as you can see or hammers a deer with energy measured in tons. And there's no justification for flailing at animals farther than you can be sure of a good hit. On the other hand, the 7mm, .300, and .338 magnums that dwarf cartridges we once thought suitable for big game make errors in wind doping and range estimation less critical. That means hitting far away should come easier. And a surfeit of energy in the middle of the vitals is never a waste.

11

A STAMPEDE TO SHORT

How long should a cartridge be? Since the advent of the metallic cartridge in the late 1800s, cases have grown shorter—then longer again. Now they're shrinking once more.

Several black powder cartridges favored by big game hunters in our post-Civil War West had hulls over 3 inches long. The .38–90 and .40–110 Winchester come to mind; also the .45–120 and .50–140 Sharps. The British .450/400 and .500/450 Nitro Express rounds have 3¼-inch cases. At 3½ inches, brass for the .450 No. 2 is longer than a loaded .338 Winchester Magnum *cartridge*.

Ammunition shortened with the development of smokeless powder. The first successful smallbore military rounds, developed between 1887 and 1891, all come in under 2½ inches. The 7.65 Belgian case measures 2.09 inches, the 7.62 Russian 2.11. The .303 British case is 2.21 inches long, the 7.5x55 Swiss 2.18, and the 8x57 German Mauser 2.24. Our .30–40 Krag followed in 1892, its 2.31-inch case much like those of European rounds. The Krag's successor, the .30–06, towered at 2.49 inches.

In those days as now, infantry cartridges also doubled as sporting rounds. But hunters had shorter options as well. In 1895 the .30–30, case length 2.04 inches, was chambered in the 1894 Winchester. The .250–3000 Savage, developed around 1912 by Charles Newton, measures 1.91 inches. In 1920 Savage put an even shorter cartridge in its catalog. The .300 Savage hull is just 1.87 inches, base to mouth.

The .250 and .300 Savage were the first super-short, high-performance American big game rounds. Explorer Roy Chapman Andrews used a .250 in the world's wildest places. The .300 Savage never became a celebrity, but it has killed many thousands of deer and elk. I remember crawling up on a small herd of caribou in northern Quebec, clutching a Model 99 Savage rifle with iron sights. The cold wind brought sounds of idling caribou hooves and ruminations. On my belly, I closed to 80 yards, settling the bead high on the ribs of the biggest bull. He died in his bed. The antlers, with great scooping bez shovels, were so wide that the 44-inch rifle fell a foot short of reaching from beam to beam. I'd like to have taken that .300 home. Alas, it belonged to another hunter, who left it to his Inuit guide. No doubt it soon suffered the indoctrination of the North: salt spray and snow; scarring on canoe gunwales, sleds, and pack frames; plus the ministrations of Inuit gunsmiths skilled in the use of duct tape and brazing rod, to whom hammer and rifle merit equal care.

Though short cartridges pleased lever-rifle enthusiasts during the years between the world wars, it was clear that bolt rifles offered more reach. Scope sights and longer, flatter-shooting cartridges evolved together. By this time, British gunmakers had fashioned new cartridges for Cordite powder. Three of them would influence cartridge development across the Atlantic. In 1910, Jeffery announced a rimless .404 that shot a 300-grain bullet at 2,600 fps. A year later came Rigby's .416, pushing a 410-grain bullet at 2,370. In

1912, Holland & Holland brought out its .375 Magnum, which drove a 270-grain softpoint at 2,650.

The .404, .416, and .375, designed independently, share no common dimensions. The .404 has a slightly rebated case 2.86 inches long, with a .544 base and .537 rim. The .416 Rigby is rimless, with a .586 base and 2.90-inch overall length. The .375 H&H has a .532 belt ahead of the extractor groove and .532 rim; case diameter forward of the belt is .512. The belt serves as a headspacing device, holding the case head against the bolt face. The steeply tapered 2.85-inch case offers little shoulder when necked to .375; the belt was added as a more positive stop.

All three big British cartridges require long actions. Initially, only the Magnum Mausers were long enough. Surplus 1917 Enfields offered shooters a cheap alternative. Winchester's Model 70 handled the .375 and .300 Holland (introduced here in 1925); the Remington 721 was chambered for the .300. Then, in the early 1940s, short magnums appeared in the California shop of Roy Weatherby. He reduced the taper on the H&H case to give it greater capacity and reformed the shoulder. He shortened the case to 2½ inches and necked it down to midwife the .257, .270, and 7mm Weatherby Magnums. They'd fit any magazine designed for the .30–06. All you had to do to convert a military action or a sporter originally chambered for the '06 was ream the bolt face from .473 to .532 inside. Full-length .300 and .375 Weatherbys, essentially super-charged Holland rounds, followed. Next came Weatherby's Mark V rifle, which swallowed not only .375 H&H-length cases, but hulls with the bulk of the .416. The Mark V made Weatherby's .378 feasible.

The idea of short magnums really caught on with shooters in the late fifties. Winchester introduced its 2.50-inch .458 Magnum in 1956, and followed up two years later with the .264 and .338. The slightly longer (2.62-inch) .300 Winchester Magnum appeared in 1963. Remington announced its first short belted magnum, a 7mm,

The .300 Winchester Short Magnum (left) and .300 Remington Short Ultra Mag (center) deliver about the same performance as the .300 Winchester Magnum (right).

in 1962, a couple of years after Sweden sent us the .308 and .358 Norma Magnums—all sized to fit '06 actions.

But "short" is a relative term, and the standard changed in 1974. It was then that Lou Palmisano, a benchrest shooter, came up with a new cartridge by reshaping the obscure .220 Russian hull. He and Ferris Pindell called this wildcat the .22 PPC. The 6mm PPC followed. Measuring just over an inch from base to 30-degree shoulder, these cartridges were considerably shorter than any common hunting or target round of the day. Dr. Palmisano surmised that a short powder column would improve accuracy. On the benchrest circuit, where every worthy competitor shot one-hole groups, PPCs got a real test. The "triple deuce" (.222 Remington) and 6x47 (a necked-up .222 Magnum) held most of the records—and the allegiance of top competitors. Getting shooters to rebarrel rifles and try the new rounds in matches took some talking.

Fortunately, Palmisano and Pindell were both accomplished shooters. They soon proved the PPCs under fire. Once the squat little rounds started winning, converts flocked to them. In five years, from 1975 to 1980, the number of PPC rifles used by the top 20 Sporter-class competitors rose from 2 to 15. By 1989 the 20 best scores were *all* shot with PPCs. Even more impressive: the short cartridges were used by every entrant in the demanding Unlimited class; and 18 of the 20 best marksmen went PPC in Light Varmint and Heavy Varmint categories. Sako eventually chambered rifles for PPCs and began manufacturing cases (with their small-rifle primer pockets) in Finland.

While benchrest cartridges got shorter, hunters chased high velocities with bigger powder charges in longer hulls. Roy Weatherby had used the .416 Rigby case as a model for his .378 belted magnum in 1953. Five years later he necked it up to produce the .460. In 1989 he fashioned a .416. Remington's 8mm Magnum and its more popular offspring, the 7 STW, were based on the .375 H&H hull. Later came the Remington Ultra Mag series, full-length rounds grafted not from the .375 H&H but from .404 Jeffery cases.

The shift back to rimless rounds began in 1992, with Don Allen's Dakota line. The 7mm, .300, .330, and .375 Dakotas are based on the .404 Jeffery. They measure 2.50 to 2.57 inches in length, but have more capacity than the belted short magnums. For example, the .300 Dakota hull holds 97 grains of water, compared to 89 grains for the .300 H&H. The full-length .300 Weatherby holds 100, Remington's .300 Ultra Mag 110. Big-bore Dakotas include a short .404 (.423 bullet). There's also a long .416 on the .404 Jeffery case, and a .450 on the .416 Rigby.

During the 1990s, Tucson entrepreneur John Lazzeroni designed a line of rimless magnums, calibers .257 to .416, with head dimensions close to the .416 Rigby's. The performance of the 7.82 (.308) Warbird and 8.59 (.338) Titan is about like that of the .30/378 and .338/378 Weatherbys. Next John chopped .750 off these cases to come up with a stable of rounds better adapted to lightweight rifles and easier to control in recoil. The .532 bases for his .243 and .264 short

John Lazzeroni holds a Savage rifle chambered for his short-action .300, the Patriot.

cartridges are identical to those on ordinary belted magnums like the 7mm Remington (and on John Lazzeroni's long .257 Scramjet). The short 7mm, .300, .338, and .416 Lazzeronis have .580-diameter heads.

Short Lazzeronis deliver belted magnum ballistics from actions designed around Winchester's .308. To date, commercial Lazzeroni ammo has been hand-loaded at John's shop. Here's what you can expect:

- 6.17 (.243) Spitfire: 85-grain bullet at 3,618 fps
- 6.71 (.264) Phantom: 120-grain bullet at 3,312 fps
- 7.21 (.284) Tomahawk: 140-grain bullet at 3,379 fps
- 7.82 (.308) Patriot: 180-grain bullet at 3,184 fps
- 8.59 (.338) Galaxy: 225-grain bullet at 2,968 fps
- 10.57 (.416) Maverick: 400-grain bullet at 2,454 fps

These rounds are factory-chambered in Lazzeroni's own L2000SA Mountain Rifle. The McMillan action features an oversized Sako extractor, three-position safety, Jewell trigger, and fluted Schneider cut-rifled barrel. It wears a classic-style synthetic stock. A super-tough, rustproof NP3 electroless nickel finish gives the stainless rifle a platinum hue. The L2000SA Mountain Rifle weighs about 7 pounds with a 24-inch barrel.

The Lazzeroni and Dakota lines demonstrate what happens when mainstream cartridges suddenly slip off the popularity charts. Many belted magnums were—and still are—useful cartridges; but revival of the rimless case and the promotion of short powder columns have started another trend. It's apparently time. No sense lamenting the fate of Charles Newton's rimless high-octane cartridges of the 1920s, or wondering why the wildcats fashioned by Ralph Payne (Payne Express) and Harold Johnson (Kenai Rifles) from the .348 case after the Second World War remained wildcats. Or insisting that Winchester's .284 and the 6.5 and .350 Remington Magnums were abandoned too soon.

Winchester announced the .284 in 1963. Its fat case had a rebated rim to fit standard bolt faces. Essentially a short-action .280 Remington, the .284 was first chambered in Winchester's Model 88 lever-action and Model 100 autoloading rifles. Savage offered it briefly in the 99. Browning and Ruger have also cataloged the chambering, but it's about as dead as the Ford Pinto now. The .284 worked fine in short actions, and better in long ones that allowed you to seat the bullets out. Competitive shooters are still sweet on the 6.5/284 wildcat, and a few hunters use .30 and .35 wildcats on the .284 case.

Remington's first super-short magnums were belted. The .350 and 6.5 Magnums came out in 1965 and 1966, in the 600-series carbines. Neither the squat cartridges nor the ugly carbines sold well. In 1968 Remington offered a 660 model with a 20-inch barrel, 1½ inches longer than on the original 600s. Still, shooters turned a cold shoulder. The dogleg bolt, squarish forend, and crude, pressed checkering had no appeal to riflemen with fresh memories of pre-64 Model 70 Winchesters. And what was a ventilated rib doing on a rifle? Still, the cartridges (especially the .350) made some sense. Had they been offered in a rifle with the profile of the current Model Seven, they might have taken root. And they might not have. Shooters were still looking for more speed in those days, not efficiency.

No doubt remembering the .284 and the Model 600 carbines, Winchester and Remington did not leap to join Lazzeroni. But both have now committed to the super-short rimless magnums. The .300 Winchester Short Magnum was announced late in the year 2000. Based on the .404 Jeffery case, the .300 WSM measures just 2.76 inches long, *loaded*. In comparison, a .300 Winchester Magnum cartridge is 3.31 inches from base to mouth, a .300 Weatherby 3.56. Web diameter of the WSM roughly matches *belt* diameter on traditional short magnums.

The .300 WSM is more efficient than a .300 Winchester Magnum. Shooters like the rimless case because it headspaces on the shoulder and fits short actions.

The .300 WSM was apparently Browning's idea. According to Travis Hall at Browning's Utah headquarters, company engineers approached Winchester with the idea of a super-short magnum "early in 1999." A joint effort resulted. Despite its squat stature, the .300 WSM carries all the authority of the .300 Winchester Magnum, moving a 180-grain bullet at 2,970 fps. It delivers 3,526 ft-lbs at the muzzle, and with a 200-yard zero hits 7 inches low at 300, 20 inches low at 400. WSM factory loads include two in Winchester's Supreme line: a 150-grain Ballistic Silvertip and a 180-grain Fail Safe. The 150 gets away at 3,300 fps. Sleek form ensures flat flight (16 inches of drop at 400 yards) and high energy retention (1,940 ft-lbs at 400 steps, 140 more than the 180 Fail Safe). The other .300 WSM load is a Super-X with 180-grain Power-Point bullet. It turns up slightly more energy downrange than the Fail Safe, and Super-X ammo is less expensive than Supreme. Only Supreme cases are nickeled. Winchester's Mike Jordan tells me the company loads its own W760 powder in the .300 WSM. "We're using less propellant and getting more out of it," he notes.

John Lazzeroni said the same thing about RL-15 in the 8.59 Galaxie. The short, thick powder column puts the center of the fuel body closer to the primer than is the case in .30–06-length cases. Theoretically, there's more combustion inside the case, and less powder moving out the neck as ejecta. A combination of faster powder (less fuel weight) and more efficient burn (less ejecta) reduces recoil. Felt recoil isn't a lot less than a .300 Winchester Magnum delivers at the same performance level. But the WSM delights shooters enamored of cartridge efficiency.

The .300 WSM is currently chambered in Winchester's Model 70 Classic Featherweight. At 7¼ pounds with 24-inch barrel and a tastefully designed stock, it appeals to me more than the Browning A-Bolt in Hunter, Stainless Stalker, Composite Stalker, and Medallion versions. These WSMs have 23-inch barrels and weigh under 7 pounds.

The .270 Winchester Short Magnum (WSM) arrived in 2001, though rifles and ammo didn't reach the market until the spring of 2002. With a case just 2.10 inches long and a 35-degree shoulder, the .270 WSM is simply a necked-down .300. The .535 base diameter fits magnum bolt faces accepting the standard .532 bases of most belted rounds. The 7mm WSM, slated for introduction after this book goes to press, is being revamped so the case won't chamber in a .270 WSM.

I was treated to one of the first .270 WSM prototype rifles, a Browning A-Bolt with 23-inch barrel. Factory-loaded 130 Ballistic Silvertips crossed my Oehler sky screens at 3,290 fps, matching Winchester's chart speed, even from the relatively short barrel. The 140 Fail Safes left at 3,115, also right on target. Accuracy? The A-Bolt turned out to be one of the most accurate hunting rifles I've ever handled. After boresighting with a Kahles 3–9x variable, I zeroed the .270 WSM A-Bolt from prone. An advantage of living in a

Browning recontoured the A-Bolt's box magazine to handle the short magnums. It works fine all the time.

small rural town is the availability of places to shoot. A disadvantage is the lack of a developed range. I've come to trust, even prefer, zeroes established from field positions. This day, I loosed my final two shots prone at 200 yards. Both hit the target's 1-inch center ring. A good omen. But repeatable?

My chance to bench this marvel came at Browning's range near Mountain Green, Utah. Two Fail Safes went into a single oblong hole at 200 yards. With no need to shred that target (or press my luck), I posted another at 300 yards. Three shots later, a 1½-inch triangle, dead center in the bullseye, grinned back through the spotting scope. I later shot an elk with this rifle, sneaking in on the bull as a storm brewed over the Wyoming Range. The 140-grain Fail Safe drilled through both lungs. The elk dashed 50 yards and collapsed in a clump of alders.

I've had a chance to do some handloading with the .270 WSM. These relatively mild loads were clocked from a twenty-four-inch barrel.

.270 WSM

charge, powder	bullet weight, type	velocity (fps)	notes
62 H4350	130 Nosler Ball. Tip	3250	
65 RL-19	130 Nosler Ball. Tip	3140	
62 N-160	130 Nosler Ball. Tip	3080	1 moa
54 IMR 4064	130 Nosler Ball. Tip	3075	1 moa
66 H4831	130 Swift Scirocco	3235	1 moa
61 W760	130 Swift Scirocco	3185	
65 AA 3100	130 Swift Scirocco	3230	½ moa
65 H450	130 Swift Scirocco	3245	

NOTE: MOA = minute of angle

Remington's announcement of .300 and 7mm Short Ultra Mags was both surprising and expected. Surprising on the heels of the .300 WSM; expected because while new cartridges demand no response from a competitor, new cartridge *designs* must either be taken up or rejected. Remington chose to get in the game. Before it goes to market commercially, any new cartridge must be approved by SAAMI (Sporting Arms and Ammunition Manufacturers' Institute). Winchester earned SAAMI's stamp while Remington fleshed out its full-length Ultra Mag series with the 7mm and .375. But Remington was also busy with blueprints for a shorter version. The two companies eventually consulted and, with SAAMI, agreed that the WSM and SUM cases were different enough in name and dimensions to proceed with both.

Like the Lazzeronis and WSMs, the .300 and 7mm Short Ultra Mags fit .308-length actions. Rim diameter is almost the same on Winchester and Remington rounds, about .043 less than the .577 heads diameter of the Lazzeroni line and essentially equal to that of the .404 Jeffery. Winchester's hull is longest to the shoulder but has about the same capacity as the shorter, broader Lazzeroni case. Remington's SUM brass is shorter from base to mouth, to fit Model

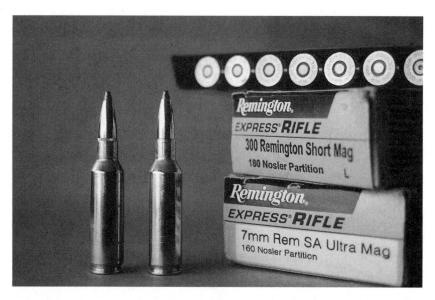

Remington's .300 and 7mm Short Ultra Mags are slightly shorter than the .300 and .270 WSMs.

Seven rifles. It holds 7.5 percent less powder than the WSM, but ballistically the two are comparable. Winchester claims 2,970 fps from the .300 WSM in a 24-inch barrel. Remington's .300 SUM with 180-grain Partitions clocks 2,940 fps from the 22-inch barrel of my Model Seven.

I fired prototype rifles in 7mm SUM and .300 SUM as soon as they were available. Accuracy varied from ½ to 2 m.o.a. (minute of angle) for three shots, depending on the rifle and load. Remington loads 180-grain Nosler Partitions and a new 180-grain Core-Lokt with thick mid-section jacket in .300 SUM ammo. You get a 140-grain or 160-grain Partition in the 7mm. W760 apparently fuels the .300 SUM—the same propellant as in the WSM. Here's how the Winchester and Remington short magnums compare ballistically.

.300 Winchester Short Magnum		Muzzle	100	200	300	400
Win. 150 Ballistic Silvertip	velocity, fps:	3300	3061	2834	2619	2414
	energy, ft-lbs:	3628	3121	2676	2285	1941
	arc, inches:	+1.1	0	-5.4	-15.9	
Win. 180 Fail Safe	velocity, fps:	2970	2741	2524	2317	2120
	energy, ft-lbs:	3526	3005	2547	2147	1797
	arc, inches:	+1.6	0	-7.0	-20.5	
Win. 180 Power-Point	velocity, fps:	2970	2755	2549	2353	2166
	energy, ft-lbs:	3526	3034	2598	2214	1875
	arc, inches:	+1.5	0	-6.9	-20.1	

.270 Winchester Short Magnum		Muzzle	100	200	300	400
130 Ballistic Silvertip	velocity, fps:	3275	3041	2820	2609	2408
	energy, ft-lbs:	3096	2669	2295	1964	1673
	arc, inches:	+1.1	0	-5.5	-16.1	
140 Fail Safe	velocity, fps:	3125	2865	2619	2386	2165
	energy, ft-lbs:	3035	2550	2132	1769	1457
	arc, inches:	+1.4	0	-6.5	-19.0	
150 Power-Point	velocity, fps:	3150	2867	2601	2350	2113
	energy, ft-lbs:	3304	2737	2252	1839	1487
	arc, inches:	+1.4	0	-6.5	-19.4	

.300 Remington Short Ultra Mag		Muzzle	100	200	300	400
Rem. 180 Partition	velocity, fps:	2960	2761	2571	2389	2214
	energy, ft-lbs:	3501	3047	2642	2280	1959
	arc, inches:	+1.5	0	-6.8	-19.7	

7mm Remington Short Ultra Mag		Muzzle	100	200	300	400
Rem. 160 Partition	velocity, fps:	2960	2762	2572	2390	2215
	energy, ft-lbs:	3112	2709	2350	2029	1744
	arc, inches:	+1.5	0	-6.8	-19.7	

These cartridges are too young to have bloodied themselves often afield. I've seen one caribou taken with the .300 WSM. It fell to multiple hits at long range. Two black bears died after single hits with 7mm and .300 SUMs. Then I took a Custom-Shop Model Seven in .300 SUM into Idaho's Frank Church River-Of-No-Return Wilderness. I climbed around this spectacular country for several days before finding a five-point bull elk in a thicket. Scooting close on the steep east face, I could place the animal by sound, but the dense conifers kept my target hidden. After a few moments, I heard the elk sneaking along the ridge above me. It paused in a small gap, showing me only head and neck. I waited briefly for a better shot, but the wind was swirling. Out of patience, I pulled down as much as I dared and touched off the shot. A follow-up round failed to penetrate the brush. As the elk wheeled away, it came clear of the limbs, and my third bullet broke its neck. Hardly exemplary shooting. And at 65 yards, I didn't need the reach and power of the .300 Short Ultra Mag. But shooting in that burned-over country *can* be long, and to my mind the nimble Model Seven in this chambering was an ideal pick for the hunt.

Truly, we have enough cases that launch hunting-weight bullets at 3,000 fps. Still, the short cartridges have advantages over traditional belted rounds. I like the rimless, headspace-on-the-shoulder design, its efficiency, and the (marginally) lighter recoil. Shorter, lighter actions and quicker bolt throws are bonuses, if overstated. None of these advantages compare with, say, the thrill shooters must have had firing their first smokeless round or first cartridge rifle. The WSMs and SUMs do for hunters now what the .300 Savage did for hunters eighty years ago: They offer impressive horsepower in a compact package. And another excuse to buy a new rifle.

12

POWER DOWN

It was thirty years ago at a camp in central Maine that Magnum Man came into my life. He was from Boston, I think. Every visiting bear hunter along the Patten Highway was from Boston or New York, and the locals treated them both the same: with courtesy. No matter how abrasive, the clients got a welcome befitting their contribution to the rural economy. I didn't have much to contribute, but farm-boy innocence must have counted for something, because in short order I was one of the family.

We checked the baits that night, bones with a scent still lingering. Woodsman's Fly Dope, our creosote-based cologne, kept the clouds of no-see-ums circling, landing gear down. Magnum Man and his pretty blonde companion got back to the lodge first. Cradling a tumbler of something amber, he was telling their guide about his .44 Magnum. "It's got thump like you wouldn't believe. And I can shoot it. Can't I, Sugar?" A dutiful nod from Blondie. "If a bear comes within 50 yards, it's one dead bear. She's seen me shoot." He sipped. "Not many people hunt with pistols. They're a tough gun to master. Took me a long time, didn't it, Sugar?" Another nod, and a smile that lit me up, though it didn't come my way. Magnum Man was as debonair as the black convertible in the drive was expensive. I slunk off to avoid any talk that might bring up my bear rifle, a war-surplus .303 SMLE.

A guide saw me and caught my arm.

"He'll miss."

"What?"

"He'll miss a bear."

"How do you know?"

He shrugged and flashed a gap-toothed grin from a field of black stubble. "They talk when they can't shoot."

The next evening, I shot a bear. It patiently hung around after it saw me, while I fought free of my mosquito netting so I could make out the sights in the failing light. The handgunner missed one bear, then crippled another. "We'll find it," he said, when they returned that night. "Won't we, Sugar?"

They didn't.

Magnum Man has since resurfaced with other artillery in other places. He's not always so good-looking or self-indulging. But he likes to flaunt firepower. Sometimes he can use it to good effect; mostly, it's a handicap. In lightweight rifles, powerful cartridges promise grenade-like violence. Magnum Man knows that. A flinch results.

Don't argue. It's true. If you think you have enough testosterone to fire a hard-kicking rifle without flinching, strike the palm of your hand against your brow. Without blinking. Try it again. Flinching isn't a sign of weakness. It's a natural defense mechanism. If you don't flinch when you expect an explosion a few inches from your face, or a sharp blow to your clavicle, something is wrong with you! The noise and muzzle jump attendant to a shot can be as unnerving as the thrust delivered to your shoulder and cheek. Powerful rifles can be fun, useful, even necessary. They are without question harder to shoot well than rifles with a mild report and little recoil.

Karen Mehall shot this black bear with a 7mm Remington Ultra Mag. In the author's view, she could have killed it just as quickly with a .243.

Sir Isaac Newton described recoil when he figured out that for every action there's an equal and opposite reaction. You can calculate the kinetic energy of recoil using this formula: KE = MV2 / GC, where M is the rifle's mass and V its velocity. GC is a gravitational constant for earth: 64.32.

Mass and weight aren't the same. Mass is really the measure of an object's inertia. The theory of relativity tells us that two objects have equal mass if the same force gives them the same acceleration. Using gravity as the force, we equate mass with weight. That is, weight is a measure of the force with which an object is drawn to earth by gravity. Because rifles respond pretty much the same to gravity, rifles of the same weight have essentially the same mass.

To get rifle velocity, we have to crunch some numbers. We already know most of them. The formula: V = bullet weight (grains) / 7,000 x bullet velocity (fps) + powder weight (grains) / 7,000 x powder gas velocity (fps). Powder and its gas figure in because like the bullet they are "ejecta" and cause recoil. You can get powder weight from factory rounds by pulling bullets and weighing charges. Gas velocity varies, but Art Alphin, whose A-Square loading manual has a fine ballistics section, says 5,200 fps is a useful average. The 7,000 denominators convert grains to pounds so units make sense in the end.

For a 180-grain bullet fired at 3,000 fps from my 8½-pound .30–338 or .308 Norma rifles I'd calculate recoil this way: 180 / 7,000 x 3,000 + 70 / 7,000 x 5,200 = 8.5 x V. That simplifies to (77.143 + 52) / 8.5 = V = 15.19 fps. Then I can calculate recoil using the first formula: KE = MV2 / GC. The result looks like this: 8.5 (15.19)2 / 64.32 = 30.49 foot-pounds of recoil.

If I reduce rifle weight to 6½ pounds, the numbers change. Skipping preliminaries, I come up with a recoil velocity of (77.143 + 52) / 6.5, or 19.87 fps. KE then equals 6.5 (19.87)2 / 64.32, or 39.90. That's essentially a 33-percent jump in recoil energy. Hard to ignore. But the same rifle chambered in .30–06 recoils much less severely. In fact, in a 6½-pound rifle it delivers less retina-plucking punch than the 8½-pound .300 magnum. Lighter bullets in smaller bores make shooting more pleasant still. An 8-pound .270 pats you with only 16.4 foot-pounds. Reduce rifle weight to 7 pounds, and recoil climbs to 19.2 foot-pounds. A 6-pound .270 delivers 22.4 foot-pounds, or about 2 foot-pounds less than an 8-pound 7mm Remington Magnum with bullets of the same weight (150 grains).

Kinetic energy is not "kick." Felt recoil can vary significantly among rifles delivering the same recoil in foot-pounds. There are a couple of reasons for this. One is that while bullet speed figures into the energy calculation, its contribution to rifle "slap" does not. Slap is my homespun term for what happens during quick recoil. Plainly put, a bullet that exits fast dumps all its energy fast, too. The rifle seems to slap you instead of shoving you. Pile enough foot-pounds behind that slap, and it becomes a punch.

Example: the .45–70 Government cartridge pushing a 405-grain bullet 1,800 fps from a long-barreled Ruger Number One (don't try that load in your Springfield!) recoils at about 17 fps. So does a .338 Winchester Magnum thrusting a 225-grain spitzer at 2,800 fps from another Number One S. You absorb about the same dose of energy from both rifles. But the .338 is apt to feel more punishing because the bullet leaves faster. All the reactive motion must be completed right away. The .45–70 leaks recoil over a longer period.

A muzzle brake can tame recoil, but it adds decibels to the blast. On the bench, given double ear protection, a brake keeps the rifle manageable and helps prevent flinching. In the field, without ear protection, you may incur ear damage. Heavy rifles not only reduce felt recoil, they come back more slowly. Their greater inertia takes some time to overcome. A soft, inch-thick recoil pad is a must on hard-kicking rifles. The popular Decelerator pad looks good on any rifle and also keeps the butt from slipping when you lean the rifle against a tree or bush. Long barrels put the blast well out in front while reducing muzzle jump. A stock that's properly proportioned can make violent recoil tolerable by distributing it equitably through hands, shoulder, and cheek. You want a straight comb with a smooth cheekrest gently curved for lots of cheek contact. Checkering on grip

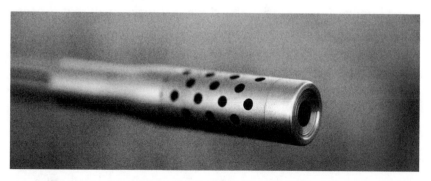

Muzzle brakes make hard-kicking rifles manageable, but the increased blast can damage your hearing.

and forend keeps your hands in control and gives them recoil that would be less comfortable elsewhere. A grip and forend shaped so you have lots of contact help too, as does a broad recoil pad.

By my total, we now have 17 domestic rimless and belted magnum cartridges—in 7mm and .300 alone. That's counting only rounds that equal or exceed the performance of the 7mm Remington Magnum and the .300 H&H Magnum. If you want to be pummeled by violent rifles, there are lots to choose from.

But the deer that we're shooting are the same as when the .25–35 was popular. Elk don't grow any tougher now than in 1939, when a survey of 2,300 Washington hunters showed the .30–06 to be most potent by far of the six most popular elk rounds, which included the .30–30, .30 Remington, .30–40 Krag, .35 Remington, and .300 Savage.

It makes sense to choose a cartridge that will shoot to the limits of your sight and your ability. Scopes now help us hit well beyond the effective range of, say, the .303 Savage. On the other hand, it's not necessary to punch animals harder than a .303 did at close range, with its 190-grain bullet loafing along at 1,940 fps. Ballistics tables show that a 180-grain .30–06 bullet delivers that much speed at 400 yards! Few riflemen can keep bullets in vitals at greater range under field conditions, no matter the rifle or scope. In fact, 250 yards is a long shot for many hunters—not only because the target looks small, but because getting closer than 250 is often an option. At 200 yards, a Barnes XLC 180 in a .30-06 Federal load dumps 2,220 foot-pounds of energy, nearly 30 percent more than a .303 Savage at the muzzle.

A .300 Winchester (Federal 180 Barnes XLC) delivers more, but less than you might suppose. Its payload at 200 yards is 2700 foot-pounds. At 400 yards, the gap narrows: 1670 for the .30–06 and 2050 for the .300 Winchester Magnum. Why? Well, the faster a bullet is launched, the greater the air resistance. Stick your hand out a car window at 30 mph, then at 70, and you'll notice the difference. Drag levels the playing field early in the game. As bullets decelerate, drag eases up. A fast bullet will always win at normal hunting ranges. But a .300 Winchester rifle has 35 percent more recoil than a .30–06 of the same weight, and you seldom need more killing energy.

Bullet arcs reflect drag, too. Zeroed at 200 yards, a .30–06 plants a 180-grain Nosler 9 inches low at 300 yards and 25 inches low at 400 yards. The same bullet sent nearly 300 fps faster from a .300 Winchester Magnum strikes 7 and 21 inches low. Not much difference. In fact, the .308 Winchester, a much smaller cartridge, hits within 2½ inches of the Magnum at 300 yards. Incidentally, that .308 bullet (Federal load) delivers more than a ton of energy to 200 yards and hits as hard at 300 as some .300 Winchester loads at 400.

You can play the same games comparing the .270 with the 7mm Remington Magnum. It's easy to find wider performance gaps between magnums and ordinary cartridges. But at some level, it makes sense to think about how much energy you need to make a

This fine Oregon ram fell to Tad Woosley's .30–06 at 310 yards.

quick kill and how flat a bullet must fly to deliver useful point-blank range. Here are factory loads that seem to me adequate for any North American big game out to 300 yards (200-yard zero).

cartridge/bullet weight, type (source)	velocity (fps) muzzle	velocity (fps) 300	energy (ft-lbs) muzzle	energy (ft-lbs) 300	drop (in.) 300
.25–06 115 Nosler Partition (Fed.)	2990	2300	2285	1350	7.0
.260 125 Nosler Partition (Rem.)	2875	2285	2294	1449	7.4
.270 140 Win. Fail Safe (Win.)	2920	2211	2651	1519	7.6
7x57 139 Hornady SP boat-tail (Hor.)	2700	2137	2251	1410	8.5
7mm-08 140 Nosler Partition (Fed.)	2800	2200	2435	1500	8.0
.280 150 Rem. PSP Core-Lokt (Rem.)	2890	2135	2781	1518	8.0
.308 165 Speer Grand Slam (Speer)	2700	2057	2670	1550	8.9
.30–06 180 CT Partition Gold (Win.)	2790	2192	3112	1920	8.0

You might include other cartridges; certainly there are other loads. In fact, you can choose from nearly 80 factory loads for the .30–06 alone. Many feature bullets once available only to handloaders. For higher velocity in some standard and magnum rounds, shop the Federal High Energy and Hornady Light and Heavy Magnum lines. This ammunition costs more but delivers a substantial boost in performance. A two-stage powder-charging process, and propellants not sold on the component market, yield higher speeds without exceeding SAAMI pressure limits.

cartridge	bullet weight	Standard muzzle velocities (fps)	Federal High Energy	Hornady Light Magnum
6mm	100	3100		3250
.25–06	117	2990		3110
.270	140	2940	3100	3100
7mm-08	140	2800	2950	3000 (139-grain)
.308	165	2700	2870	2870
.300 Wby. Mag	180	3190	3330	
.303 British	180	2460	2590	
.338 Win. Mag	225	2800	2940	2920

Not that you need more punch or a flatter flight than you get with ordinary loads in cartridges like the .308. Settlers in East Africa used the .303 British to good effect, mainly with the old 215-grain roundnose bullet that flew slightly flatter than a cinder block. Its high sectional density aided penetration in tough game at the modest ranges tough game was shot. Surplused in Canada, SMLEs have also accounted for thousands of moose.

Just as we take for granted power steering in automobiles and telephones that travel with us, our expectations of rifle cartridges are as much influenced by what's available as by what's needed.

Cartridges that treat you tenderly can still kill game. One of my friends carries a .243 for elk and kills them neatly with it. Another has used a .25–06 to take more than 20 elk. The last shot spanned over 400 yards. A single 100-grain Hornady was enough. "I don't like to shoot that far, but there was no doubt that if the bullet went through the front slats it would kill the bull. I've shot enough elk to know." More to the point, he's shot that Remington 700 year-round at enough 'chucks, coyotes, and paper targets to shoot it well. Elk may be tough, but if you can thread a bullet through the aorta, there really isn't any option for the bull but to die.

It's useful sometimes to read about the exploits of hunters using rounds like the .303 Savage when *they* were the titans. And to let a friend load (or not load) your rifle sometimes while you shoot from hunting positions, just to see if the rifle jumps when the chamber is empty. It's a good idea to decide whether you need the mayhem that caves your clavicle and mashes your molars each time you pull the trigger—before you start flinching in your sleep.

Part III: Aiming

13

SCOPES, CLEARLY

If you grew up aiming through glass, you may wonder why anyone would favor iron sights. Scopes are so popular—superior?—that many rifles are no longer factory-equipped with irons. Once kept as backups for scopes that often failed, auxiliary open sights have gone the way of spare distributor points in automobiles.

Though the switch from irons to scopes accelerated after World War II, it began long before that. Partly to recruit men for the Union Army in the early 1860s, Colonel Hiram Berdan demonstrated his own marksmanship by shooting the vest buttons out of a Jeff Davis target at over 200 yards. That caplock rifle weighed 32 pounds with a 31-inch barrel and full-length telescope. The scope was of low magnification, the glass as murky as pond water; but iron sights on battle rifles could hardly match its precision. Berdan's Sharpshooters, incidentally, were required to put 10 consecutive shots an average of 5 inches from the bullseye at 200 yards. An optical sight made sense. With it they could drop a general's horse at several hundred steps, or keep distant sentries sleepless.

Scopes have improved since the 1860s, most big changes coming in mid-20th century. Around 1940, Zeiss engineer A. Smakula found that coating a lens surface with magnesium fluoride salvaged most of the light lost to reflection and refraction (up to 4 percent on each lens surface). Nine years later Leupold became the first U.S. optics firm to fill scopes with nitrogen under vacuum to prevent fogging. About a decade after that, engineers made sure the reticle stayed in the center of the field of view.

The physical placement of reticles varies, however. Front-mounted reticles, popular in Europe, stay the same size *relative to the target* (so they can be used as rangefinders) throughout the power range of a variable scope, changing apparent dimensions as the target gets bigger and smaller. A rear-mounted reticle keeps the same apparent dimensions through power changes. Most American shooters don't like reticles that get big at high power and small at low power. They want a fine aiming point at high magnification for tiny, distant targets; a bold reticle at low power for quick, close shots. Zeiss and Swarovski court U.S. buyers with rear-plane reticles.

In the 1980s, European scope makers also began hawking 30mm scopes in the U.S. The bigger tubes increased adjustment latitude in some scopes because they gave erector assemblies more room to move. They added weight and bulk, too—which matter little in Austrian tree stands but encumber rifles built for alpine hunting. At the same time, super-size objective lenses became increasingly popular. Shooters wanted a brighter sight picture at the edge of day, and bigger front glass admits more light.

Exit pupil, the disk of light you see in the scope when you hold it at arm's length, determines how much light reaches your eye. You calculate its measure by dividing the objective lens diameter by magnification. A 6x42 has an exit of 7mm. Your eye dilates only to about 7mm, even at night. That's why military binoculars are 7x50s and 8x56s. The Pentagon can afford bigger glass, but there's no

Held by Talley rings on a .338–08 by Charlie Sisk, this 4x Kahles is the author's idea of an all-around big game scope.

sense to it until you boost magnification. A 4x32 scope delivers more light than your eye can use. A 50mm objective on a variable scope helps you only at magnifications of 8x or higher, and even then only in poor light when your eye opens up. Most of the time, a 5mm exit pupil gives you the brightest picture you need. At dawn and dusk a 6mm exit pupil can be useful. In a 2–7x32 variable you'll get that 6mm exit pupil at 5x. In my experience, 3x is enough power for big game hunting. A 21mm front gives you a 7mm exit pupil in a 3x scope. I still like simple, low-power scopes. As a lad I'd have been smart to hoard Leupold M8 4x scopes, which I believe once sold for $59.50. They appeared in 1964 with the Vari-X II 2–7x (a year after the M8 3x and Vari-X II 3–9x) and haven't changed much since. They cost a lot more now.

A big exit pupil is not all you need to pick out detail in dim light. You need power, too. One measure of low-light resolving capability is the twilight factor. Mathematically, it's the square root of [magnification multiplied by objective diameter]. So if you have a

4–12x40 scope set at 8x, TF is the square root of 320, or 17.9. Increase scope magnification to 10x, and TF becomes the square root of 400, or 20—while exit pupil shrinks from 5mm to 4mm. The extra magnification more than offsets the drop in brightness to show you more detail. If you make the objective lens 25 percent bigger (50mm) the TF at 8x is 20. At 10x it's 22.3. A 4x32 scope has a twilight factor of just 11.31.

Once again, high magnification yields a greater TF value. You need 25-percent gain in objective diameter to equal a 20-percent boost in magnification. So, while brightness is an asset, reducing magnification to make the exit pupil bigger will not necessarily give you a higher twilight factor or better resolution in dim light.

Relative brightness, another index of transmitted light, is simply the square of the exit pupil. An exit pupil of 6mm has a relative brightness of 36.

Just as important as a big exit pupil is an adequate field of view. Field is one leg of an "optical triangle" that also includes magnification and eye relief. Boost magnification or eye relief, and you diminish field. Increase field at the expense of eye relief. Crank up magnification at the expense of eye relief, field, or both. That's why high-power scopes have less eye relief and smaller fields of view than low-power scopes. A typical 4x scope has a field of about 26 feet at 100 yards. If you jump a bull elk at 20 steps, you'll see only the length of the elk. A variable scope set at 8x will show you nothing but hair at 20 yards—if you find the elk at all. To lead or simply keep the crosswire on a running elk, you need more field. For long, deliberate shooting, field is much less important. Target shooters use scopes as powerful as 80x. While the size of the ocular lens affects field of view, objective lens diameter does not. At 100 yards, you get a whopping 62 feet from a 1.5x scope with no objective bell.

Hunting scopes need generous, non-critical eye relief, the distance from the ocular lens at which your eye gets the full field of view. Most scopes are designed to provide 3 to 4 inches of eye relief, so recoil doesn't clobber you with the ocular housing. High magnification generally makes eye relief more critical; that is, your eye must be at *exactly* the right distance behind the lens or the field "blacks out." Incidentally, black-out will occur if your eye is not lined up with the scope's axis, but that is not a function of eye relief. A big exit pupil is more forgiving than a small one with regard to eye alignment.

One thing to remember when you're shopping for or mounting a variable scope: Eye relief typically decreases as you boost power. You'll want the scope positioned so your eye naturally falls the proper distance from the ocular lens at the magnification you normally use. Some variables deliver the same eye relief from low power to high. In my view, constant eye relief is a huge asset. When you mount a scope, position it a little farther forward than you think it should be. You'll aim faster if the correct eye relief comes when

Most hunters mount their scopes too far to the rear. You should find a full field of view (correct eye relief) when your cheek is as far forward as is comfortable on the comb.

your cheek is as far forward on the comb as is comfortable. Forward mounting also gives your skull protection when you're shooting from prone or aiming uphill from sitting or kneeling positions. Remember that *optical* eye relief is not *physical* eye relief. The distance between your eye and the eyepiece may be considerably shorter than the distance between eye and lens.

When scopes began replacing iron sights in quantity during the 1940s and 1950s, shooters resisting the switch pointed out that tight fields of view in scopes slowed their aim. Small ocular lenses in early scopes *did* restrict field, and uncoated glass compounded the problem with dim images. Stocks designed for iron sights offered no cheek support if you mounted a scope, so you had to move your head around in space to find a sight picture of any kind. The slender crosswire and dot reticles popular just after World War II were not only hard to see, but wandered out of center when you zeroed. Modern scopes are much brighter, with wider fields. The best-selling "plex" reticle is easy to see even in the purple light at the edge of day. It stays in the middle of the field during scope adjustment. Rifle stocks now bring your eye into the scope's axis right away. But there's one problem better optics and stocks have not solved: wobble.

You see, what *really* makes a scope slower than iron sights, for beginner and accomplished rifleman alike, is muscle tremor and your efforts to deaden it. The higher the magnification, the more furiously that reticle hops about and the more determined you become to make it behave. The longer you stall, the more weary you become. At last the reticle is jerking around with such speed and scribing such wide arcs that you cannot fire an accurate shot. We're conditioned to believe what we see and to act on what we believe. If the crosswire is bouncing on and off the target, in and out of the vitals, we lose confidence because we see that our aim is true only a fraction of the time. We try to increase the "dwell" of a reticle on target by reducing the speed and amplitude of its movement. Either that, or we try to anticipate its dips and hops so we can trigger the rifle as the reticle is diving into the target.

When I had even more to learn about shooting than I do now, I practiced the "controlled jerk" in smallbore competition. I eventually got it half right, mastering the jerk but failing any control. My scores didn't improve until I disciplined myself to crush ounces from the trigger slowly, holding pressure when the sights or reticle wandered off, increasing pressure when the picture again looked right. This a tough assignment, because you frequently run out of breath before the trigger breaks, or your muscles become fatigued and start bucking just as you've taken up the slack.

On the popular premise that knowledge is power, riflemen are demanding more and more magnification from their scopes. They

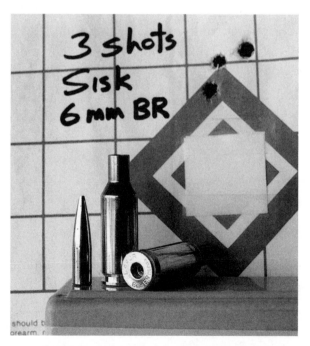

Scopes of modest magnification are best for hunting. The 6x responsible for this 100-yard group reflects a 200-yard zero.

want to see everything that's going on. After all, if they pick up more target detail and track the slightest changes in the relationship between reticle and target, won't that make them better marksmen?

Uh-uh. Knowledge isn't always helpful. If you're a pilot, you don't react to every thermal bounce or gust of wind. You try instead to guide the airplane with a steady hand on the yoke, correcting not for the individual bumps but for their collective effect on your course. You want to stay in close touch with your airplane, either through the instruments or by feel. On the other hand, you must sift the inconsequential signals from those that matter.

So it is with shooting. A rifle equipped with a coarse front bead won't allow you to hit a small target because it denies you a clear view of that target. You need more information. But mount a powerful scope, and you may get more data than you can handle. Watching all the little gyrations of your rifle causes you unnecessary angst and can scuttle your efforts to control the big bumps: the movements that matter. You can't eliminate pulse or muscle tremor any more than you can escape air currents in a Cessna. But magnifying them can be as detrimental to accuracy as pretending they aren't there.

When I started shooting at metallic silhouette targets, they'd just come across the Mexican border. The first match I fired went to a fellow shooting a .30–06 Winchester with a Weaver K4. In a sudden-death shootoff for class placing, I managed to topple a ram with a Henriksen-built Mauser in .270. It wore a 6x Pecar scope that showed me all the wobble I could handle offhand. Within a few years, however, the top-scoring metallic silhouette shooters had gone to scopes as powerful as 24x (and to specially built rifles hardly in keeping with the spirit of the game).

Small targets don't always require as much magnification as many shooters think. If you can see target in all corners that define the intersection of the crosswire, you have power enough for a hit. If you have lots of time and a steady position, you might use additional magnification to advantage—mainly to read conditions as you squeeze and to shade accordingly. If recoil isn't severe, high scope power helps you see the bullet's strike. (On the other hand, the wide field of low-power glass gives you quicker recovery after a shot. Not long ago I guided a hunter to a big mule deer, which he dropped with a fine shot at 300 yards. Because the buck still showed life, I urged that he shoot once more. He couldn't find the animal because recoil had taken it out of the small field of his high-power scope. Distance and shrubs made the buck hard to spot with the naked eye, and getting it in the scope again took time.

My Model 37 Remington pokes little groups in smallbore prone targets with a 20x Redfield 3200 scope I bought used for $100 in 1970 and mounted initially on an Anschutz 1413. I need that much magnification to shoot into bullet holes at 50 meters while reading changes in the mirage. On hunting rifles, even 8x may be too much power, as you must often shoot when breathing hard from getting into unorthodox positions, sometimes quickly and in wind, and always with a rifle light enough to carry.

Balancing sight-picture detail and wobble is easier with a variable scope, because conditions affect wobble, and conditions change. In fact, I consider wobble management the strongest argument for owning a variable scope. A variable allows you to dial up the most magnification you can handle, and trim wobble when it becomes too great. The only sensible alternative is to choose a scope low enough in power that you're never flustered by a bouncing reticle. That's better than choosing a scope that offers more precision and less control. When you must shoot fast and the crosswire won't behave, you will likely either lose the shot to delay or miss by jerking.

Most hunters overestimate the magnification they need for effective shooting. In prone competition, iron-sight scores commonly come close to matching those shot with scopes. It's no trick to shoot groups under half an inch at 50 meters with irons, and in favorable weather the better shooters punch quarter-inch one-holers. So it seems odd to me that hunters insist on setting variables at 8x to 10x to shoot animals the size of a Honda Gold Wing. If National Match shooters can lob .30–06 bullets into the V-ring at 600 yards with irons, there's no reason hunters can't center a deer's ribcage at half that distance with a 4x scope. High magnification won't necessarily prevent you from finding a target quickly, but it can make the shot a long and bumpy ride.

Powerful scopes and long shooting have brought parallax adjustments from the target range to the hunting field. Parallax is the apparent shift of the target behind the reticle as you move your eye away from the scope's optical axis. Parallax is a function of target range. Images formed by objects at varying distances fall at different points along the scope's axis. Because the reticle does not slide back and forth, it meets a focused image only when the target is at a specific distance. Most hunting-style scopes are set for zero parallax at

Turret-mounted parallax knobs let you adjust for distance without getting out of position.

100 or 150 yards, though scopes for shotguns, pistols, and rimfire rifles are commonly parallax-free at shorter ranges. Because parallax is a greater problem when you're shooting far away at small targets, many high-power scopes have parallax adjustment sleeves on the front bell. A recent and handier alternative is parallax correction in a third turret dial. Parallax can make you miss by the amount that the reticle seems displaced. It is not, however, as serious or prevalent a problem as some shooters believe. It is no problem at all if your eye is on the scope's axis.

Mounting a scope securely and in the right place without damaging the scope isn't hard. It does take time and your full attention, plus the right tools. My gunsmith screwdriver set from Brownell's has most of the screwdriver tips I need. I keep a length of 1-inch dowel handy to turn dovetail rings into battery.

Incidentally, when John Redfield designed that dovetail mount in 1916, he was onto something. Since then, it has been copied by Burris and Leupold and remains a popular design. The dovetail front attachment, combined with "windage" screws in the back, make for a secure, good-looking mount. It's not a good idea to turn the front ring with the scope tube, or to remove the ring from the base and replace it often or with a ring from another base—you might compromise the tight ring-to-base fit.

Weaver's inexpensive Tip-Off is as ubiquitous as the Redfield-style mount. Alloy bases make it lightweight. My favorite mounts are made by Conetrol and Talley. The Conetrol, perhaps the best-looking mount on the market, is not quite as easy to assemble as Talley. Mounts I like *least* include any with tunnels that let you see iron sights (at the expense of cheek support and aiming speed when you want to use the scope). Quick-Detachable mounts appeal to a lot of shooters, but not to me, because I don't take scopes off rifles in the field. Alloy mounts make sense on the lightest of rifles, but they can't be kept as trim as steel mounts. On rifles of heavy recoil, I'd as soon have steel. One ring screw per side seems sufficient except, again, on rifles that kick violently—which you might fit with 8–40 base screws instead of the 6–48s that are the standard for most mounts. One base or two? Both have their advocates.

I prefer clean, trim scope mounts that put the sight as low as the objective and ocular bells allow. Whatever your choice of mount, here are some tips to help you mount it right:

1. Secure your rifle in a work rest or vise.
2. Remove mount screw fillers. Squirt a rust-breaking, rust-inhibiting spray into the holes.
3. Wipe excess oil from around the holes with a clean cloth. Wipe all components with a clean cloth.
4. Install the bases with a tight-fitting screwdriver.
5. Mate the rings to the bases and snug but do not tighten the bottom halves.
6. Turning in dovetail rings, use a 1-inch wooden dowel, not the scope!
7. Wipe the scope with a clean cloth, then set it in the rings loosely, eyepiece well forward.
8. Wiggle the scope until it "finds bottom," then snug the rings. You don't want to force the tube to bend.
9. Pull the scope back gently until eye relief is just right. Remove the rifle and aim it if you must.
10. Looking from behind the butt, align the vertical crosswire with the butt. Then tighten the screws.

You've probably looked through scopes in which the reticle appeared tipped. A reticle or sight not square with the world is said to be canted.

A canted reticle will not cause a miss. In fact, you can rotate the scope so the crosswire looks like an "X" and use it as effectively as before. A small disadvantage is that you won't have a vertical wire to help you hold off for wind deflection or show you the line of bullet drop at long range. You also won't have a horizontal wire to help you lead running animals.

A canted *rifle*, however, is another story. Regardless of how the reticle appears, if the rifle is tipped, you'll have problems hitting beyond zero range because the bullet path won't fall along the vertical wire or directly below the intersection. If the sightline is directly over the bore, a long shot requires you only to hold high. If the sightline is forced by a canted rifle to the *side* of a vertical plane through the bore, you'll also have to hold to one side.

Here's the reason: Given a scope mounted directly above the bore, your line of sight crosses the bullet path twice. The first crossing happens at about 35 yards, the second at zero range—say 200 yards. If the rifle is rotated so the scope falls to the side of the barrel, the sightline will cross only once, because gravity sucks the bullet straight down, while the line of sight has a horizontal component. Whether the scope is on top of the rifle or to the side, the line of sight will converge with the bullet path, slice through it, then angle away. If the scope is on top of the rifle, gravity pulls the bullet in an arc back into and through the straight line of sight. If the scope is not on top, the bullet path still dips below the horizontal plane of the sightline; but the trajectory is to the side of where you're looking.

How much practical difference will canting make? Not much. A cant that escapes your notice won't cause a noticeable shift in bullet impact at normal hunting ranges. As the targets get smaller and the range longer, and when you impose stricter accuracy standards, cant starts to matter.

When I was on the Michigan State University rifle team, I marveled at a colleague who shot well but used a cant that would have spilled coffee. Standing, he looked straight ahead through sights that fell into his natural line of vision when he rotated the rifle on

Brian Schuetz has a scope level on his varmint rifle to indicate cant. A cant can make you miss.

his shoulder. The adjustable butt let him do that without changing the contact angle of the butt hook. So his rifle tilted in toward him. Not only the line of sight but the rifle's center of gravity fell closer to the centerline of his torso. From a mechanical perspective, this made perfect sense. I tried shooting that way and found it darned near impossible.

In traditional bullseye rifle competition, targets are very small and the rifles supremely accurate, so shooters must correct for cant. (Some globe sights for target rifles have tiny bubble levels that show you the slightest cant at a glance, and similar devices are now available for scopes.) On the other hand, my teammate on the MSU squad didn't have to worry about horizontal angles because his shooting was done at one precisely measured distance. It's easy to accommodate cant at a single distance. You simply move the sight to put the bullets where you look. Forget about how sightline and trajectory converge and what they do beyond the target. It doesn't matter.

Hunters don't shoot at just one distance or with adjustable stocks. So although small degrees of cant seldom affect their performance on game, it's a good idea to shoot with the sights squarely on top of the rifle. Cant is just one more thing to worry about, one more distraction, a small but thorny threat to the self-confidence that can help you shoot well. Test for cant by shouldering your rifle repeatedly with eyes closed, opening them to look through the sight. The wire should appear vertical. If it does not, you're tipping the rifle. Practice holding it with the sight at twelve o'clock, where it belongs.

Sometimes shooters slip a cant into their shooting routine without knowing it. They mount the scope carelessly and subconsciously adjust their hold on the rifle to correct for a reticle that's tilted. A culprit here is the ubiquitous Weaver Tip-Off scope ring. This inexpensive ring has been around a long time—and for good reason. It's strong and lightweight. But because the top half hooks the base on one side and its two screws take up all the slack on the opposite side, tightening a Tip-Off ring can rotate the scope tube down toward the screws. If they're installed on the right-hand side, you put a clockwise tilt into your reticle as you cinch them up. You may have aligned the reticle perfectly with the butt before installing the top part of the rings, but now the crosswire is tipped! Solution: back off on the screws and twist the scope counterclockwise about as far as you think it moved. Tighten the screws again, and check the reticle.

14

SCOPE RETICLES

Between the Great Depression and the Vietnam War, the most popular scope reticles among hunters were the crosshair and the post-and-crosshair. Some riflemen paid extra for a dot. T. K. "Tackhole" Lee made a business of installing them on very fine crosshairs made of spider web. In 1962 Leupold & Stevens introduced what has since become the overwhelming reticle of choice among hunters. The Duplex, a crosswire with heavy outer sections and slim lines in the center, makes a lot of sense. The thick shanks grab your eye, directing it to the middle of the scope, where the thin intersection allows you to aim precisely. In very poor light you can aim with the heavy wire alone. Knowing the subtention of the center wire at a given magnification, you can use the Duplex as a rangefinder. Lots of scope makers have copied this reticle, but of course they can't call it the Duplex.

Leupold's Duplex is a mechanical reticle, meaning it is suspended on a mount. Leupold uses .0012 platinum wire flattened to .0004 to make the outer sections of the wire wider ("thicker") than the middle sections. Burris plex reticles are .0035 to start; they're flattened in the middle at 90 degrees to make that section of the wire narrow. Critics object to the edge contact in the middle, claiming recoil can deform the edges to produce a thickening. I've no such objection. Premier Reticle, Ltd., a Virginia company that has supplied reticles to every major scope maker except Zeiss, employs ribbon wire, twisted in the middle, to make a plex.

The other way to fashion a plex reticle is to use a photo-etching process on metal foil, in which chemicals strip away all material around the etched pattern. The foil is only about .0007 thick and must be cemented to the mount, whereas wire reticles can be soldered. Proper tension of foil reticles is critical. Too little, and the foil will whip under recoil; too much and it won't withstand extreme variations in temperature. Allowing a scope with such a reticle to point at the sun can result in a reticle burned apart. Still, many fine scopes have foil reticles. All come from offshore companies, I'm told, because the etching process includes nasty chemicals.

The various plex reticles now include fine plex and heavy plex versions. Burris offers a fine plex in its 8–32x target/varmint scope. So does Pentax in a 6–24x. For its 1.75–6x variable and fixed-power shotgun scopes, Pentax installs a heavy plex reticle. Steiner's "Ultimate Z" hunting scopes (made in the U.S.) feature a heavy plex option. Leupold's M8 4x and Vari-X II 1–4x and 2–7x shotgun scopes also wear an extra-heavy plex reticle.

There's not much you can say against the plex as a hunting reticle. It's justifiably popular.

But other reticles are available. The crosshair is simple and still useful. I have a slender one in my Redfield 3200. I can quarter the tiny X-ring of a 50-meter smallbore target with it or, if wind and mirage warrant, "shade" by holding it tangent to that ring. Actually, a fine crosshair works well with any high-power scope. The shanks of a plex serve no purpose if you're shooting deliberately in good light at small, stationary targets at known ranges.

The 2.5x Sightron scope on this Weatherby rifle is properly fitted with a bold reticle for quick aim in timber or shadow.

Fine crosshairs used to be fashioned of spider web because stronger material couldn't be made thin enough. Dick Thomas of Premier Reticle, Ltd. says his father, Bob, who began an optics career working on the Norden bomb sight during World War II, later kept a spider in a Dixie cup to make crosshairs. "He'd pinch the spider gently with tweezers to get a defensive reaction. The spider would start releasing web, and my father would pull it to keep it coming. After he started making reticles for Lyman in the 1950s, and later for Redfield, milking spiders couldn't give him enough material. By the late 1970s we had tungsten wire. We can draw that down to a ten-thousandth of an inch, a thirtieth the diameter of a human hair."

A heavy crosshair in a low-power scope is hard to beat for deer shooting in close places. You won't need a rangefinder. A thick intersection won't hide anything important. Sadly, most crosshairs now are too fine for use on big game in thickets or when the light is poor.

Before the Duplex, hunters who wanted a prominent reticle chose a post. Some were tapered, and some had parallel sides. A post properly pokes above the horizontal wire. You zero with the tip of the post, not the intersection of post and wire. Posts have fallen on hard times because the plex is as easy to see and can help with range estimation. Very heavy posts obscure the target if you have to hold over. In failing light, there's no guide to the center from any direction except six o'clock. Posts were popular in early scopes because shooters were used to blade or post front sights, and the transition was easy. Posts are essentially dead in the U.S. now. Some European firms—Swarovski, for instance—still list a tapered post and cross-wire (#2 reticle). Post reticles can be made from stiff wire soldered to the mount ring.

I used to like dot reticles until I lost one against the shoulder of a big bull elk in the timber at dusk. With nothing to point your eye to the dot in poor light, it's a poor woods reticle. Useful in open country under bright light, dots also work for target shooting. In my view, a dot for hunting should be larger than most riflemen think, and a dot for target shooting should be smaller. You can't afford to lose a dot even momentarily on an animal or your attention will be drawn from making the shot to finding the reticle. If a dot in a target scope obscures more than a quarter of the X-ring, it's too clumsy for shading. On a rimfire rifle, it can keep you from seeing bullet holes appear. Then you'll be tempted to move the scope to see the bullets hit, ruining your shots.

Dot size is given in minutes. The right dot size depends on scope magnification and what you intend to shoot. To my eye, a 4-minute dot is about right for a 2.5x scope on a lever-action carbine in hardwoods. It would appear huge in a 6x scope you might prefer for your .25–06 pronghorn rifle. A three-minute dot works fine in a 4x scope, and a 2-minute dot looks about the same size in a 6x scope as the 4-minute dot in a 2.5x scope. *Subtention will be as listed for each dot, but because a deer appears bigger in a 6x than in a 4x scope, so a 3-minute dot will appear bigger because it must cover the same area on that deer.* A non-magnifying dot in a variable scope will vary in its coverage of the target as you change power.

The Leupold dot includes four slender pointers in lieu of crosshairs, ending just shy of the center. (Leica offers a similar reticle.) At 3x in a Vari-X II, the dot subtends 2 minutes, at 9x .8 minutes. Target dots typically subtend a quarter-minute at around 10x. The Burris 8–32x is cataloged with a quarter-minute dot. You get that coverage only at 8x. Leupold's target dot in its 36x scope covers a mere .1 inch at 100 yards. Dots were once the rage in target scopes. Dick Thomas claims that Homer Culver's world record benchrest group with a dot from Premier Reticle fueled the success of that company in the early days.

A dot combined with a standard crosshair doesn't attract me. It's like turkey gravy and sour cream: Either is enough for a potato; together they're too much. The Leupold dot is OK because the prongs are very slim.

Another dot reticle is the mil-dot. Fashioned by the U.S. Marine Corps for sniper use, the mil-dot features a series of dots emanating

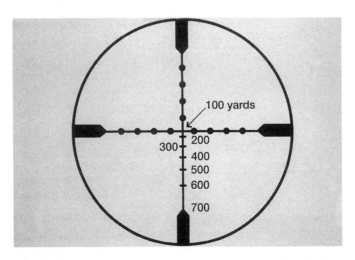

The Burris Ballistic Mil-Dot reticle combines ladder-type subtention bars with mil-dots to help you find the range.

from the center on crosswires. In some there's a thickening of the wire to the outside so the shooter can use it like a standard plex reticle in near-darkness. Mil-dots (and other complex reticles) may be etched on interior glass. Premier Reticle makes suspended (mechanical) mil-dot reticles for Leupold. The 16 dots are installed by hand.

The mil-dot reticle is not so named because it is popular in military circles but because it enables you to find proper holdover at great distances. A milliradian is part of a circle, which comprises 360 degrees or 2pi radians. So a circle has 6.28 radians, and one radian is 57.32 degrees. A minute of angle is a 60th of a degree; thus there are 3,439 minutes of angle in one radian, 3.44 minutes of angle in a milliradian. Dividing 3.44 into 60 (the number of minutes per degree) gives us 17.44. So a milliradian is about $\frac{1}{17}$th of a degree. The spaces or interstices between dots each subtend one milliradian or mil. That amounts to 3.6 inches at a hundred yards or 3 feet at 1,000 yards.

To use the mil-dot reticle as a rangefinder, you divide a target's height in mils by the number of interstices subtending the target to get range in hundreds of yards. A deer (10 mils at the shoulder) that appears in the scope to be two dots high is 500 yards away. A moose (20 mils tall) that fills two spaces would be about 1,000 yards off. Actually, the official method is to divide target size in yards by the number of mils subtended and multiply by 1,000. Naturally, scope reticles with mil-dots are calibrated for only one magnification. Most tactical scopes with mil-dot reticles are 10x fixed-powers. Variables are typically calibrated at the top end, but mil-dot reticles are sometimes set for a power below the top in variables of very high magnification.

While the mil-dot has only recently made its way into commercial scope catalogs, the principle is hardly new. Stadia wires that bracket targets of known size are an easy way to determine range. Redfield's Accu-trac provides a set of stadia wires at the top of the field. You fit a deer-size target inside by adjusting magnification, then read a range indicator at the bottom of the field. Next, you turn a dial on the turret to the appropriate number (4 for 400 yards) and hold center. Changing the magnification after setting the turret dial will not affect bullet placement.

In the Shepherd scope (Box 189, Waterloo, NE 68069) a series of circles on the lower vertical wire are sized and spaced so that if a deer's shoulder fits snugly inside one, all you have to do is keep it there and pull the trigger.

The Shepherd has two reticle systems and four dials on the turret. The rear dials, slotted in standard fashion, move the crosswire that's located in the second focal plane, behind the erector tube in the scope. That is, it's in the same place as reticles in other U.S. scopes. It stays the same size throughout the Shepherd's 3.5–10x power range.

But the other reticle, a series of circles arranged top to bottom in descending order of size on the vertical wire, is in the *first* focal plane. As you boost power, the circles get bigger, just as do the crosswires and posts in European scopes with first-plane reticles. The disadvantage of a reticle that "grows" with increasing magnification is that it covers the target you're trying to see better by turning up the power. Because the Shepherd's front reticle comprises small, open circles, they don't cover anything as they swell.

Why have a first-plane reticle at all? Its one great advantage is a constant degree of subtention throughout the power range. That is, the reticle appears the same size in relation to the target at every magnification. Each circle on the wire spans 18 inches at a specific range no matter what power you use. Thus, if you bracket the 18-inch chest of a deer with any circle, you have found the range while elevating properly to compensate for bullet drop. As the crosswire is behind the erector tube, it doesn't grow or shrink at all.

Shepherd scopes all look the same. They're 3.5–10x variables with 40mm adjustable objectives and matte-black 1-inch tubes of aircraft aluminum. Inside you get a choice of four front reticles. They differ in circle spacing so the folks at Shepherd can fit spacing to your load.

You zero a Shepherd at 100 yards by adjusting the crosswire to cover point of impact. Then you adjust the front reticles (circles) so they're in line with the vertical wire and your bullets land in the middle of the 200-yard circle at 200 yards. If you have the right reticle for your load, your bullet will thread the other circles well beyond the range most hunters shoot.

How far is that? "Three of our range-finding reticles provide circles that bracket a deer's chest out to 1,000 yards," says Dan Shepherd. "The fourth reaches to 1,000 meters. They're etched on the glass, so when you move one circle, you move them all. We've calculated trajectories for 30-caliber bullets at muzzle velocities of 2,500, 2,700, 2,950, and 3,300 fps. You pick the one that most closely matches your load." He concedes that downrange curves can differ among bullets starting at the same speed, depending on air density and ballistic coefficient. "But out to 400, even 500 yards, you'll hit very close to center."

Shepherd scopes are manufactured at Light Optical in Japan, a prestigious firm supplying glass as well as finished instruments to several American firms. All Shepherd lenses are fully multi-coated. Forward knobs have quarter-minute clicks. Tolerance for impact shift through the power range is half a minute, or less than at least one German maker allows. Because the circles are fixed in the first focal plane, you can't get impact shift there at all.

Leupold is another scope manufacturer known for its innovation. Four range-finding scopes on the Vari-X III optical system have 30mm tubes to give the erector assemblies more room to move. That means extra elevation adjustment for faraway targets. The 4.5–14x, 6.5–20x, and 8.5–25x come with 50mm objective lenses and target-style knobs with quarter-minute graduations. The 3.5–10x40 has

Leupold's M3 military-style knobs. All the Long Range scopes feature a turret-mounted dial for parallax adjustment, first used on the Mark IV scope.

Introduced during the mid-1980s as the military Ultra, the Mark IV got its present name in 1990. It looks like a Long Range scope, but the tube is thicker to meet military specifications, and it's made only in fixed powers: 10x and 16x. Actually, there are two 10x Mark IVs, identical except for the elevation and windage adjustments.

"The M1 adjustments are tall, target-style knobs with quarter-minute clicks," says Leupold's Garth Kendig. "The M3 knobs are shorter but still finger-adjustable. They're calibrated in one-minute clicks vertically, half-minute clicks horizontally. Army specs called for a dial that could keep sightline and point of impact together from 100 to 1,000 yards throughout one revolution of the dial. To make the adjustment that quick, we had to make it coarser."

The illuminated reticle and M1 turret dials, plus a parallax adjustment, make this Leupold a bulky scope appropriate for long shooting.

The M1 Mark IV 10x still sells to some military units. The Mark IV 16x is available only with the M1 knobs. "It's very popular with 50-caliber shooters," says Garth. "It has 140 minutes of elevation adjustment. You can dial into the next area code." With its 90 minutes of vertical movement, the M1 10x can take a .30–06 out to 1,000 yards. The M3 has 70 minutes of lift in its single revolution, "but there are more under the knob," Garth points out. "When zeroing, you can reset the knob to get more distance." Unlike the 3.5–10x Long Range scope, the M3 Mark IV does not have a minute-of-angle scale on its bullet-drop compensator stem. A scope with a "BDC" system, incidentally, differs from a range-finding reticle by incorporating a range-*compensating* mechanism that puts the reticle where it should be for a dead-on hold once the range is known and cranked into the scope. A BDC device must be calibrated for a specific load, of course, because rate of drop influences the correct holdover at long range. A scope set up for a .257 Weatherby won't be of much help on a .35 Whelen.

I'm not keen on BDC scopes. Some work very well, but I don't shoot at extreme range, and I prefer simple, lightweight sights. I dislike complex reticles, certainly any that fill a field with lines, dots, bars, posts, circles, and numbers. A reticle's primary function is to help you aim. Clutter impairs aiming, as does any reticle obscuring your target.

In a laudable move to give shooters a better look at what they want to hit, Burris re-introduced a reticle that I noticed years ago on a Redfield scope. The Peep Plex has a tiny, open circle in the middle of a plex reticle. The idea is to keep the reticle from blocking out targets like prairie dogs. It takes some getting used to because most of us have grown up aiming with a sight that goes right where we want the bullet to go instead of encircling that point. A fine crosshair or small dot is less ambiguous and just as effective on small animals. Shooting quickly at big game, you'll ignore the Peep Plex hole anyway.

But Burris came up with a real winner, in my opinion, when it announced the Ballistic Plex, designed to help shooters not only find the range but correct for bullet drop. It's simpler than the mil-dot. It's essentially a plex with an abbreviated bottom post, the bottom wire crossed by three short horizontal bars below the reticle's intersection. These are like stadia wires: marks or tics calibrated to bracket an object of known dimensions at known distances. But they aren't really stadia wires, because the spaces between them (all of different size) don't correspond to any particular target measure.

The bars are spaced to reflect the trajectory of most modern big game bullets when the scope is set at 9x. (Magnification matters because the reticle lies in the rear focal plane, where most U.S. hunters prefer it; the reticle's apparent dimensions stay constant throughout the scope's power range.) If you adjust your scope for point-blank bullseyes at 200 yards with 130-grain .270 bullets, or 150-grain 7mm Remington Magnum bullets, or 180-grain spitzers from a .300 Winchester Magnum, you'll hit using the top short bar

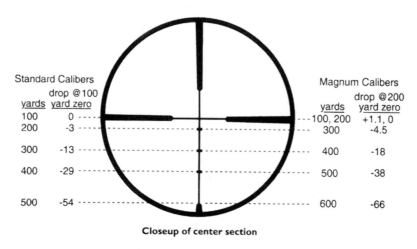

Closeup of center section

The Burris Ballistic Plex is a simple reticle that, with practice, can be used to accurately determine range as far as you're likely to shoot. The author likes the clean, practical design. He used this reticle to kill a pronghorn buck at 394 yards.

at 300 yards and the second bar at 400. The third bar or tic will put you in the vitals at 500. If the target is 600 yards away, you aim with the top of the bottom post.

What if you shoot a .30–06? "You can't change the bars," says Burris's Pat Beckett. "But you can easily find out where your bullet's trajectory crosses those points and zero accordingly." At 100 yards, subtention from center to the first tic is 3.1 inches, to the second tic 4.5, to the third 7.5. To the top of the lower post the thin wire spans 11.1 inches. Naturally, at longer range, you multiply the subtensions by the yardage. At 400 yards, the section of wire above the second bar covers 18 inches (4x4.5), or about the chest depth of a mule deer buck. With a cartridge that doesn't shoot laser-flat, you'll want to zero so your first bar marks the bullet impact at 200 yards, not 300. You could zero a .30–06 with heavy bullets at 100 yards so the top two bars mark the bullet path at 200 and 300 yards instead of 300 and 400. And you can use the scope at another magnification, if you like. You just have to do some shooting with your load at various ranges to check subtention and bullet impact relative to the bars.

Incidentally, the bars are also handy for bracketing game at long, unknown ranges to come up with accurate estimates of distance.

Burris could have put more into this reticle—dots, bars, stadia wires, numbers, all the garbage that's so often thrown into scopes to help you determine precisely how far the target is and where to hold while the animal decides to move out of your field of view. I'm pleased the Ballistic Plex is simple.

Europeans have had a long love affair with posts, partly because a lot of shooting there is done as the stars come out. Besides the American-style post (#2 to the Germans), there's a three-pronged reticle about as heavy as the thick section of a plex. The lower prong ends in the middle of the scope, the two horizontal prongs just shy of center. This reticle is known as the #1 or, if the horizontal prongs leave more space in the middle, #1A. European

#4 and #4A reticles are the same, save for the addition of thin wires in the center, the vertical one extending up as a fourth prong. America's plex reticle is so named in Swarovski's catalog, which shows the similar #7A with its more open center. Schmidt & Bender calls the plex a #8. Adding to the confusion, Zeiss calls its plex reticle the Z-Plex and the more open European design a #8. A crosshair is a #6 in the Zeiss literature, which shows a heavy, tapered-prong version of the #1 as a #11. There's also a #25: a dot on a thin horizontal wire.

Typically, European dual-thickness reticles have a square step where the thin wire gets thick. The heavy end of American plex reticles tapers to the thin section. I actually prefer the squared-off juncture because it gives me a cleaner terminus for rangefinding.

Because European reticles are typically set in front of the erector tube, they must be finer than rear-mounted reticles. Otherwise, they'd appear too bulky even at the low end of a variable's power range. Making mechanical reticles slender enough is difficult, so some European firms etch the reticle on glass. The problem with this is that it introduces another drain on light within the scope.

Electronically illuminated reticles have become modestly popular, as modest numbers of shooters will always have to own the most sophisticated optics available. Zeiss offers one. So does Swarovski and Kahles and Schmidt & Bender. You can get one at lower cost in a Bushnell or Burris scope. The industry leader in lighted reticles, though, is Lightforce. I've used its huge, Japanese-built, high-power variables. The reticles are slim and Spartan variations of Europe's three-pronged #1. They float in the middle instead of extending to the periphery. They look a bit like the artificial horizon on an airplane instrument panel. They're good aiming devices.

Before you can get the most out of a reticle, you must bring it into focus. To do that with traditional fine-thread ocular housings (eyepieces), back the housing out almost as far as it will go. Then point the rifle at the northern sky (not toward the sun!) and screw in the housing until the reticle comes into focus. Close your eyes to rest them for a few seconds, then throw the rifle up quickly, again skyward so nothing but the reticle draws your eye. If the reticle doesn't appear sharp immediately, adjust the ocular bell. Repeat until the reticle is tack-sharp the instant you see it. Then tighten the lock ring. Don't stare! Given even a second or two, your eyes will try to sharpen images that are out of focus, and you'll get a misleading read. European-style eyepieces, with helical threads, are faster to focus, but this is not something you should have to do very often, and the old lock ring arrangement ensures that the eyepiece won't move accidentally.

Lighted reticles in scopes and red-dot sights have rheostats so you can vary brightness. In dark conditions you need *less* illumination for the reticle to show up. Brilliant sunshine floods out the glow of all but the strongest lighted reticles. Using more illumination than you need obscures the target, as does a coarse reticle.

Illuminated reticles are more visible in dim light, but they don't make your target more visible.

Traditional red-dot sights like the Aimpoint, with Bushnell's Holosite and the Tasco 2000, are typically used on handguns, shotguns, and short-range rifles. They lack the precision of standard reticles but will give you accurate shot placement to 200 yards—far enough for most big game hunting. Their chief advantages: You can see them even if your eye isn't lined up with the sight and can aim accurately even if the dot doesn't appear centered. Like any scope, they make the reticle and target seem as if they're in the same plane. They also absolve you of having to focus on two sights at different distances from your eye.

I'm surely old-fashioned, but it seems to me that with two reticles I'd be well equipped for all the shooting I'm likely to do. A standard plex (or European #7A or #8) will outperform anything else for big game hunting. A fine crosswire is hard to beat for target shooting, hunting squirrels with rimfires, or sniping at small rodents far away. Both reticles are quick and easy for my eye to comprehend; they put nothing unnecessary between me and the target.

If you'd rather have something exotic, write Dick Thomas at Premier Reticle, 175 Commonwealth Court, Winchester, Virginia 22602. Could be there's still a Dixie cup with a spider in it on the bench.

15

LOOKING
THROUGH IRON

Not long ago I hunted pronghorns on a ranch that had already been heavily shot. Sixteen-inch bucks with cantilever prongs had been chasing around in my head for weeks, but here a goat with even 14-inch horns was hard to find. The hunt became memorable when I left my scoped .270 behind and took instead a Browning 1885 single-shot, with iron sights, chambered for a pistol cartridge.

Sneaking about the prairie trying to get a 100-yard shot, I found even unremarkable bucks a challenge. At last I managed to creep close to a pronghorn, thumb the hammer back, and settle the bead on a rib. The Nosler drove through the off lung, and the buck died soon after. What would have been a ho-hum event at great distance had ended as an adventure.

Surely, using irons can cost you opportunity. Once, hunting with Barry Taylor from his Arctic Safaris camp north of Yellowknife, I spotted and stalked a magnificent bull caribou. But the animal moved just beyond my self-imposed limit of 175 yards. Cows and calves between us prevented a closer approach. Rather than risk a crippling hit or losing sight of the bull, I signaled for my partner to shoot. He tagged the bull with his Ultra Light .30–06.

Regrets? None.

I started deer hunting about the time Americans started advising the South Vietnamese Army. You could buy a Ford Mustang for $2,750, and nobody used foul language on television. Scopes had been in common use among Michigan deer hunters for years by then, but relatively few locals in our farm community had them. Land sakes, a 4x Leupold cost nearly $60, and even Weaver's K4 set you back as much as a pair of penny loafers. Lots of bucks fell to shotgun slugs and cut shells (shotshells with hulls scored to separate and funnel the charge down the bore like a slug and test the structural integrity of Uncle Bob's Ithaca pump).

My surplus SMLE ranked among the proletariat of rifledom, which included mostly lever-action .30–30s, with some Krags and Springfields in various stages of conversion. Landed gentry used .300 Savages.

Pedestrian my .303 may have been; but it wore good sights. I'd replaced the issue iron with a Williams set. Adjustable for windage and elevation, the rear block featured a very shallow V notch with no distracting ears. When the rifle hit my shoulder, the gold button on the ramp up front flew into that notch like a shotgun bead landing on a barrel rib. It was and is one of the fastest open sights around. With it, I nailed my first whitetail as it sped through dense poplars. I poked the gold button at a narrow opening and yanked the trigger when the deer's nose appeared.

OK, I had as much help there from Lady Luck as from the Williams boys. But I might not have made that shot with a scope. Nor would my rifle have as quickly decked a buck that sprang from a pine thicket and spun to dash straight away. In both cases I needed all the field I could get. In both I fired as if at a grouse.

Not all iron sights are fast. A buckhorn open sight leaves you hunting for the target behind the big ears on either side of the V. Receiver sights with the apertures suited to black-bullseye competition don't work well in the woods, where light is often limited and shots are taken quickly from unorthodox positions. "Globe" or aperture front sights are likewise inappropriate on big game rifles.

There are a few more things to consider if you're looking for "hunting irons." Front sights should be big enough to catch your eye right away, even at the expense of precision. There's no magic bead size, because barrel length affects *apparent* size and target subtention. There's no perfect bead material or color, either. I prefer ivory except in snow. Gold works well against a variety of backgrounds. Fluorescent beads won't black out when backlit, but under bright conditions they scatter light and can vanish in a halo of brightness. Spherical bead faces are bad business because they reflect light most strongly to the light source, shifting the bead's apparent position and causing you to miss. A bead should be flat-faced and angled toward the sky to catch the light.

You don't need a round bead. Redfield's old Sourdough featured a square-cornered red insert. You could use it as a bead or with a six o'clock hold as a post. A standard black steel post will suffice up front, but even heavy versions get lost in shadow. Also, a post thick enough to catch your eye in lodgepoles when light fades *mandates* a six o'clock hold—fine for black bullseyes on white paper but much less precise on game and slower than a bead you can slap directly against your target.

Sight hoods protect the bead or blade and shade it. But they also clutter your field of view and can obscure a piece of the target. I prefer to hunt without them.

Beads, blades, and posts all work with an open rear sight, though each should match the notch profile. A bead sinks nicely

Williams Gunsight Company makes a wide selection of lightweight alloy sights. This one has a U notch; the author prefers the super-shallow V.

into the shallow V the Williams Gunsight Company called its "African" model. A bead also serves in a traditional V or a U notch, the U properly cradling the bead as a sort of aperture open at the top end. If you want a better view, use a bead with a flat-topped rear sight that has no notch at all, simply a white line or triangle indicating the center. It's fast and sufficiently accurate. It covers less of the target than any other open rear sight.

A blade sight seems to me best suited to a U-notch sight; again, flat on top. A blade, like a post, works well with six o'clock hold. A post needs a square-notch rear sight. As with the blade, you must have enough daylight on either side of the post for quick centering, but not so much that you lose precision. I prefer a sliver of air about half the width of a blade and a quarter the width of a post on either side.

It's fashionable these days for expensive bolt rifles to wear Express sights: a bank of open sights differing slightly in height and mounted on a long block or quarter-rib. ("Express" was coined by Purdey long ago to describe his British Cordite cartridges that hit game "like an express train.") Fetching in profile, especially on British doubles and magazine rifles, Express sights have limited utility. All but one leaf must be hinged to fold when using a lower sight, and on rifles of heavy recoil, a single fixed leaf is more dependable. And adequate. There's hardly a pressing need for a 300-yard sight or, to my mind, for multiple-leaf sights of any sort if you're hunting animals with vitals the size of a swamp cooler. The reason it's hard to shoot far with open sights is that we can't see the target well or align the sights properly. Bullet drop becomes a factor at distances beyond those practical for shooting with open sights.

A receiver sight with a big aperture, mounted close to the eye, is as fast as an open sight and more accurate. It absolves your eye of having to focus on three objects at different distances: you simply look *through* the aperture, *past* the front sight, *at* the target. Many clever aperture sights have been built, most for mounting on rifle receivers. The "Little Blue Peep," an auxiliary rear sight, was fastened to the rear of a Redfield scope base. Winchester's Model 71 could be ordered with a "bolt peep," and between the world wars many hunters preferred aperture sights perched on a bolt rifle's cocking piece. Because it comes close to the eye, a cocking piece sight is

The tang sight on this Marlin is a new Marble's. Close to your eye and far from the front sight, it's amazingly accurate when used with a small aperture.

very fast. Because there's some "play" in any striker, it is not the most accurate of aperture sights.

Tang-mounted folding peep sights date back to black powder times. They offer the greatest possible sight radius on hunting rifles. They're so close to your eye, in fact, that on rifles of heavy recoil they can be dangerous. One well-known huntress lost an eye to her tang sight as she fired at an animal steeply uphill. Other disadvantages of tang sights: They're relatively fragile, and they get in the way of your right hand.

While an aperture sight gives you a windshield's worth of field, you must still center the target with the front sight. A front sight big enough to catch quick aim at deer in the woods can be a nuisance if you're shooting far at small targets. Beyond 100 yards or so you want to peek around it to see what you're shooting at. Even a modest bead can hide the target. Distant shots requiring holdover may obscure it entirely. Make the bead smaller and you lose speed up close. One way to ensure clear view of the target is to use an aperture in a globe front sight. Heavy and even more prominent than a sight hood, the tube of a globe sight enables you to suspend the aperture. You can choose a circular steel insert or colored plastic disc with the center bored out to corral the target. An inverted post that comes in from the top lets you hold over without hiding anything.

For many years in smallbore competition, I used a globe sight with an orange disc, the beveled edge of the center hole appearing black around a ring of white paper and the black bullseye. The flared rear end of the globe blocked peripheral light. This sight was easy on my eyes and very precise. Outdoors at 50 yards, that rimfire rifle stuck many quarter-inch groups in the middle. In fact, my iron-sight scores often matched those I shot with my 20x Redfield scope. The only thing hard to do with irons was shade. With a scope's fine crosswire quartering the X-ring, I could nudge the intersection this way and that if a group was forming just off center. Trying to do that with iron sights was like trying to arc-weld a gum wrapper: There was no way to move *just enough*. Good grief, in the front aperture, the entire bundle of black scoring rings appeared as a dot to my naked eye.

The human eye readily puts round targets in the middle of a circular frame and will signal the slightest loss of concentricity. It is not nearly so adept at holding an off-center picture because it *wants* the dots and circles to line up. Besides, your brain first must tell your eye just how an off-center image should appear. Without magnification, your eye can't register a quarter-inch adjustment at 50 meters. Your brain may specify a quarter-inch, but that's like a truck driver easing back on the throttle to cut engine rpms from 2,500 to 2,499. The tachometer and throttle linkage aren't built for such precision. Neither is the driver's foot capable of holding engine speed within one rpm.

Plastic discs in globe sights eventually lost favor with winning shooters, who came to advocate instead a large steel aperture suspended in the globe by arms at 3 and 9 o'clock. The steel proved a good sight in dim light, but to my eye, bright conditions caused the target to swim behind it. Reducing aperture size helped somewhat. I've never seen a hunter using a globe front sight for big game, though a colored disk with a thin bevel encircling a large center should work well. One reason such a sight does not appear in hunting camps is that it is expensive and bulky.

Bob Fulton of Glenrock, Wyoming has experimented with globe sights on hunting rifles. His Ruger Number One in .411 Hawk has a clear plastic insert for a trim globe sight. The insert features a crosswire. The rear sight is a much-modified Krag. At the end of the 27-inch barrel the flared rear end of the globe sight fits almost perfectly in the aperture of the rear sight. There's a very thin ring of daylight around the globe so I can tell instantly if it's out of center. But there's not so much peripheral light that it pulls my eye from the intersection of the crosswire.

"I've made lots of money betting this rifle against scoped varmint artillery out to a couple of hundred yards. Here." He handed me the Ruger. "Aim at that stop sign."

Dropping the lever and making sure there were no cars crossing at the end of the gravel road, I hoisted the single-shot. The crosswire muscled its way into the red and stayed there, held by the weight of the barrel with just a little encouragement from my arm.

"That's 375 yards," Bob said. "Think you could hit it?"

Neither he nor I had any inclination to perforate stop signs. But he'd made his point. The crosswire did not obscure the sign. He went on to tell me it was especially useful against mottled backgrounds because, unlike a blade sight, the reticle cut across the entire field, vertical and horizontal wires capturing the target from four directions.

Bob has also fashioned barrel-mounted rear aperture sights. Long ago, living in the Desert Southwest, he and a colleague bought Model 1895 Winchesters in .30–06 so they could shoot surplus military ammo. The rear sight on Bob's 95 (he still has it) has a platinum-lined ring arcing over the factory notch.

"That's the fastest sight I've ever used," Bob told me. "It's accounted for hundreds of jackrabbits, many on the run." I shouldered the rifle and had to agree that despite my long-held belief that Model 95s were developed by a tractor company, the sights jumped into alignment right away.

Among the few commercial aperture sights for hunting, a clever peep by Ashley Emerson, an entrepreneur from Texas, tops my list. I talked with this tall, rough-hewn rifleman at an outdoors show a few years ago when his product appeared and quickly discovered he was quite capable of doing all the talking himself. Enthusiastic not only about his sights, but about guns, hunting, and life in general, Ashley handed me a Marlin lever rifle with a machined-steel sight perched on the receiver. A ring with a stem threaded into a small block served as the sight. The small block dovetailed into a

The Ashley front sight features a flat-faced blade with a white line that shows up well in shadow.

larger base block and moved across it for lateral adjustment. To raise or lower the sight you simply screwed the ring out or in. The sight looked eerily like something out of my dreams. I'd envisioned such a sight years ago but lacked the engineering skills to make it happen.

"It's small, sturdy, and accurate," boomed Ashley, launching into one of his pig-hunting stories. An Ashley Emerson pig hunt always ends badly for the pigs, mainly because Ashley "gets after it" in the bush and does a lot of shooting. Of course, he credits the sight. "Lookee here how that blade shows up. Porkers haven't got a snowball's chance, friend."

The front sight, a steel blade angled like a Sourdough, has a white line down its middle. Front-lit, that white line leads your eye to the target. Backlit, or in snow, the sight becomes black. The rear aperture is picture-window big. Ashley Emerson is no longer with Ashley Outdoors, but the company has grown substantially and now offers a broad selection of iron sights, mountable on just about any rifle you might want to equip with irons.

Precision shooting with iron sights depends on good lighting, and savvy competition shooters stretch a black elastic band between sight bases to deflect the mirage rising from a hot barrel. Unlike mirage downrange, which helps indicate wind direction and speed, barrel mirage serves no useful purpose. Hunting rifle barrels seldom get hot from shooting, so, except in prairie dog towns, barrel mirage is seldom an issue. Long tubes on globe sights and rear cups on receiver apertures to block sidelight and deliver a "tunnel" image are likewise superfluous on hunting rifles. For slight improvements in the sight picture, you must abide higher cost, more weight and bulk, and a slower target acquisition.

While many hunters would now feel handicapped by iron sights, I don't. Most of the game I've killed has been with scoped rifles, but at ranges that would have allowed use of iron sights. A few years ago, I hunted moose and Dall sheep armed only with an iron-sighted Springfield. My guide and I spotted the first rams far away — but even a hunter with a powerful rifle scope would have had to stalk them. We just had to get a little bit closer. The approach took a couple of hours, but we managed to maneuver above the rams without alerting them. Suddenly, all seven of them popped out from behind a rock outcropping and lined out across the slide below.

I swung the .30–06 and fired. The rear animal lurched, then struggled after his companions, now bounding over the rocks. But my 165-grain Winchester softpoint had done too much damage. He stopped again. At my second shot he spun and collapsed.

The next day I watched another hunter shoot a ram across a canyon. Frank bellied into the grass at ridgeline, laid his scoped Remington 700 across his pack and arced two bullets 400 yards into the ram's lungs. My Redfield receiver sight wouldn't have been up to that shot. And in that case, no other shot was possible. When you use irons, you accept a handicap. But it's not as severe a handicap as most hunters imagine.

Weeks later, I was on the Little Delta River with outfitter Fred Soreson and industrialist Henry Budney, who had bought a moose camp here in 1969. The Super Cub had not landed; it had alighted like some giant insect on a stretch of river cobble that passed as

The author killed this Alaska-Yukon moose with one .30–06 bullet from an iron-sighted Springfield.

gravel only in comparison to boulders. We ferried my duffel to a modified Bombardier crawler, its diesel pulsating lazily. The airplane revved a few octaves higher as Art crowded the stumps and other debris on the west end of the bar. The fat tires bounced three times in a sprint as short as a grocery aisle, and the wings caught air.

"Iron sights?" Henry and Fred looked at each other. Henry shrugged.

Above the tundra, where two tent camps on the skirt of the Alaska Range augment the Little Delta cabins, I glimpsed snow-crowned mountains—and then, incredibly, the sheer white spires of three 14,000-foot peaks. "That one's Deborah," Fred told me, pointing. "It's the only major peak in North America that hasn't been climbed." It and the two flanking peaks seemed to hang from the sky, with no connection to the ground. Clouds obscured their midsections behind the lesser mountains. "No moose up there," he grinned. That was fine with me.

By the second evening we'd seen lots of moose. I'd passed up a shot at a 55-inch bull at close range. Henry had closed on a bigger bull, only to have the wind shift. Low fog delayed glassing the third morning. As it lifted, I followed it up a hill and, from the crest, immediately spied a couple of white specks in a burn about two miles away. I brought Fred up for a look, and we confirmed a bull with the spotting scope. "He's wide. Let's go shoot him."

Easy to say. Two hours of tough stalking later, we were bellied in the wet hummocks at least 300 yards from the bedded bull. The companion cows we'd spotted were not to be seen. They had bedded, too. A minefield.

"How close do you have to get?" Fred asked in a whisper.

"About half this far."

He looked at me and shook his head. "We'll never make it. There's no cover, and those cows will blow up."

"I can't see his vitals from here. Besides, I want to be as close as possible."

Fred sighed and lifted his glasses for another look. I tightened the Latigo sling and duck-waddled forward. The cow that burst from a tangle of spruce debris could have gone in any other direction. But she trotted straight away, toward the bull, literally kicking him out of bed. Then she flanked him as they quartered north and vanished. Other cows began popping up, confused. The strong crosswind prevailed, but they knew something was amiss.

Sure that I'd missed my only chance, I held still, hoping. After long minutes, I was astonished to see the bull reappear, trotting through the scattered spruce. My little gold bead hung motionless in a tiny opening. It seemed the bull would never get there. But eventually his black bulk filled the alley, and he stopped. A military trigger never took so long to pull, but when the Springfield jumped, so did the moose. A *thuk* floated back. He ran as I cycled the bolt. Within thirty yards, however, he slowed. Then he stopped, swayed, and collapsed.

16

THE SUREFIRE ZERO

To be of any use, a rifle must shoot where you look. The most gifted and practiced marksman won't hit if the rifle shoots where he's not looking. That's why it's important to zero a rifle. Zeroing, or sighting in, is aligning the sights with the bullet path, so the bullet goes where you look. You can't change where the bullet goes in relation to the barrel; you can only change your line of sight.

Rifles with iron sights are typically given a rough zero at the factory. That is, you'll probably be able to hit the side of a washing machine at 50 yards without touching the sights. But if you want bullets to land in a smaller target, you'll likely have to adjust. Some open sights have only a step elevator to move impact vertically. Shifting point of impact to the side is a job for a drift punch. Move the rear sight in the direction you want the bullet to go.

Receiver sights and tang sights make you more accurate (they give you a longer sight radius than the open rear sight) and faster (they're closer to your eye and obscure less of the target). Almost all of them allow for precise adjustments. Target models give you knobs with click detents like the windage and elevation dials on scopes.

Excepting external knobs on target scopes, you move a scope's aiming axis by turning the dials on the turret with a coin or screwdriver. Newer dials have raised ribs or knurled knobs for finger adjustment. Dial "clicks" or graduations correspond to point of impact shift at 100 yards, in inches or minutes of angle. One minute of angle, or m.o.a., equals an inch (actually 1.047 inches) at 100 yards. At 200 yards one minute is 2 inches, at 300 it's 3 inches and so on. Scope adjustments with quarter-minute clicks should move point of impact an inch every four clicks at 100 yards, 2 inches every four clicks at 200. A target scope may have adjustment graduations as fine as ⅛ minute, but most hunting scopes feature half- or quarter-minute clicks.

Zeroing your rifle is really zeroing your scope. Start by making sure the scope is mounted firmly, the base screws tight, and the rings secured to the base. Before you snug up the rings, make certain they are aligned. Don't use your scope for this! Dovetail rings are best turned into alignment with a 1-inch dowel. When the scope drops easily into the belly of the rings, slip the tops of the rings over the tube, but don't snug them. Shoulder the rifle to see that the reticle is square with the world and you have the proper eye relief. You should see a full field of view when your face rests naturally on the comb. I like the scope just a little farther forward than most shooters for two reasons: First, when I cheek the rifle quickly, I want the field to open up as I thrust my head forward. I don't want to waste time pulling it back to see more through the scope. Second, I want some room between the ocular bell and my eye should I have to shoot uphill or from the sit. I've been bitten many times during recoil by scopes set too far to the rear for a stock-crawler like me. My rule of thumb is to start with the ocular lens directly over the rear guard screw on a bolt rifle; then I move the scope back and forth incrementally to fine-tune its position.

Bore sighting is not necessary before zeroing, but it saves ammunition and time at the range. Try it this way: After you lock the scope in place by cinching the ring screws (alternately, as you would tighten the wheel on an automobile hub), remove the bolt from your rifle and set the rifle in a cleaning cradle or on a couple of sandbags. Look through the bore at a distant object. I use a rock half a mile away on a hill. Make the rifle secure, the "target" centered in the bore. Now take a peek through the scope. If the crosswire is not quartering the target, turn windage and elevation dials until it does. If you want the crosswire to move right, turn the dial left—opposite the direction you'd turn it to move bullet impact. When the reticle is spot on, check to see that your target is still centered in the bore. Then replace the bolt. Your rifle is now bore-sighted, and you should hit near point of aim out to 100 yards. If Ol' Betsy is a muzzleloader, or a lever, pump, or autoloading rifle, you won't be able to see through the breech. So you'll use a collimator—a device that attaches to the muzzle and puts an optical grid in front of your scope. Just adjust the scope to center the grid.

Before zeroing, bore-sight the rifle by adjusting the reticle onto a target you centered in the bore. The Gunhorse, by Storehorse, is a lightweight, cleverly-designed shooting rest and workbench.

You still must shoot. Don't believe anyone who tells you a bore-sighted rifle is ready for the hunt. Or that he has zeroed the rifle so you don't have to. *Always* follow your bore sighting with shots on paper. *Always* check the zero of borrowed or secondhand rifles, again with live fire. Even if the previous owner was meticulous in adjusting a scope, you may view the sight picture differently. And you may want a different zero range.

Because a bullet travels in a parabolic arc while your line of sight is straight, the two are never parallel. They remain close only for relatively short distances. Your line of sight can be adjusted to meet a bullet path tangentially, some distance from the muzzle. But a single juncture robs you of hits at long range. It's better to adjust the sightline to cross the bullet's arc twice—once quite close to the rifle and again at some distance downrange. Between these two points the bullet will strike above your line of sight. That doesn't mean the bullet rises; your sightline has just cut through its trajectory. Diagrams of bullet arcs can confuse shooters by making the arc appear to rise above the line of bore. It never does. The bullet starts dropping as soon as it leaves the muzzle and continues to drop at an accelerating rate as it loses speed.

Zero range is the second meeting of sightline and bullet path. You can make it almost any range you want with a twist of your scope's elevation dial. But remember that the farther you push your zero, the higher the bullet will strike at midrange. For example, if you zero a 150-grain .30–06 load at 150 yards, it will strike about ¾-inch above sightline at 75 yards. Move zero range to 200 yards, and at 100 steps your bullet hits an inch and a half high. For big game rifles, an inch and a half is still small potatoes. Ignore it. That 200-yard zero increases the distance at which your bullet stays *reasonably* close to sightline. A 300-yard zero, however, boosts midrange arc 5 inches over sightline, which is too much to ignore.

A rule of thumb for big game rifles is to zero as far out as you can without putting the bullet more than 2½ inches above your line of sight. For many modern rifles, a sensible zero falls between 200 and 250 yards, depending on the load. Your "point-blank range" on big game (the maximum range at which you can ignore bullet drop and hold spot on) will be from 240 to 320 yards, depending on the load. If you tolerate more bullet drop than I do, point-blank range may be longer still. Flat-shooting cartridges let you push zero farther out. Rounds like the .30–30 and .358 Winchester, with heavy-bullet loads in the .300 Savage, .308, and .35 Whelen, might call for a 150-yard zero. The .45–70 and .444 Marlin are best zeroed at 100 steps; so too sabot shotgun slugs. Flat-flying bullets from the likes of the .22–250 and .220 Swift could be zeroed at 300 yards, with the 7 STW and 7mm Dakota, the .300 Ultra Mag, and .300 Weatherby. But the hot .22s are not for big game. They're called upon to hit little rodents—targets the size of soup can lids. A deviation that doesn't matter in a big game rifle can be excessive in a varmint rifle. So many prairie dog shooters use scopes with target adjustments that they can change during the day to keep zero near the range at which most shooting occurs. The competitive rifleman zeroes at precisely the yardages he's to shoot, changing scope settings for different stages in a match.

A precise zero is never wasted. The author shot this Wyoming buck at 60 yards—but had to stretch to shoot another with the same rifle at 300.

It's best to zero on a calm day. If you must shoot in the wind, allow for bullet drift and check the scope with a group when the wind isn't blowing. It's a good idea to practice shooting in wind; however, a windless zero makes correcting for drift easier on the hunt.

Your zero is best refined at the bench, with the rifle on a soft but firm rest. You'll want to remove as much human error as possible. Don't shoot only at short range. I once worked hard to get a client within killing range of a terrific bull elk, only to see him miss. Another fellow had zeroed the rifle "3 inches high at 100 yards." But my companion hadn't checked it farther out. The flat-shooting Weatherby cartridge showed me a 330-yard zero when I fired the rifle later. At midrange, between 150 and 250 yards, where a lot of game is killed, it tossed bullets several inches high. A high hold on the bull's shoulder nudged the unfortunate hunter's shot over the top.

This man's scope mounts were part of his problem. The rings were extra high to ensure that a 50mm objective bell cleared the barrel. The higher the rings, the steeper the angle between sightline and line of bore. A scope in low mounts will have a shorter zero range (and less bullet "rise" midrange) than a scope in high rings, if both are adjusted so bullets hit, say, 3 inches high at 100 yards.

I recall a hunter whose .300 Winchester was zeroed for 286 yards. At least, that's what he told me. He must have pulled that figure from a ballistics table, because he had not shot the Browning autoloader at targets that far away. I spied a small band of elk on a canyon wall, and we made a successful stalk to a ridge about 250 yards from the animals. He hit with the first shot, but three more bullets had no effect. The stricken elk finally died. In awe, the hunter remarked: "That's the longest shot I've made in my life."

My question: Why did he zero for 286 yards when all the shots he'd taken at game had been under 250? It's best to zero for the range at which you expect to do most of your shooting. I once hunted with an ex-Army sniper who'd claimed a kill at 1,100 yards in 1971 in the land of rice paddies. Yet he zeroed his elk rifle at 100 steps.

When zeroing, remove all the human error you can with sandbags or an adjustable shooting rest. This rifle is from Virgin Valley Arms, on a Thompson/Center Encore action. Chambering: 7 STW.

When zeroing, bear the following in mind:

1. Changing bullet type can change bullet path, even if starting velocity is the same.
2. The height of the scope mount affects the relationship of sight-line to boreline.
3. Shooting uphill or downhill extends point-blank range (hold for the *horizontal* distance to the target).
4. Elevation (air density) has little effect on bullet impact except at extreme ranges or elevations.
5. Range estimation becomes more critical far away, where it also becomes more difficult.
6. Groups at long range may improve (3 inches at 200 yards, say, when 100-yard groups measure 2 inches) because the bullets "settle down" as they travel, as a top "goes to sleep" during a spin.
7. Resting the barrel against anything hard can cause it to bounce away from a rest and throw the shot wild. Rest only the forend,

and pad it with a jacket, your pack, or your hand.

8. Wood stocks can "walk" over time, changing pressure in the barrel channel and affecting point of impact.

9. An annual zero check makes sense—but not in camp where it can spook game and give anyone nearby an excuse to crown you with the heaviest frying pan in reach.

10. Shots from a clean, cold barrel are the shots that matter most in the field; subsequent shots may not land in the same place. Save one target for a cold-barrel group—a series of first shots from a cold barrel.

Before you take your rifle hunting, check zero from hunting positions. The bench rest won't hunt with you. When you leave it, you leave the firm support that helped guide your bullets when you zeroed. Fire a few groups offhand, and from sitting, kneeling, and prone. You need the practice anyway. If you use a bipod on the

After zeroing at the bench, fire from hunting position. Sling tension and the way you hold the rifle can affect point of impact.

hunt, shoot from the bipod at the range to see if it has any effect on point of impact. I favor a tight sling for field shooting, but I've found that sling tension can pull bullets as much as 9 inches below a bench group at 200 yards. A barrel that's not allowed to swing up-ward away from a support during recoil but is instead tugged to seven o'clock by an unyielding strap gives you, in effect, another zero. Expect 3 or 4 inches at 200 yards. If the difference is greater, think about changing your bench zero. More and more I've come to refine my zero from a sling-assisted sit, a position I use a lot when hunting. It won't give minute-of-angle groups, but I'd rather see a 6-inch cluster around my point of aim at 200 yards than get a tight clump in the wrong place. Your first shot at game must be close to where you look.

It's important to check zero after traveling to camp as well. Some time ago I sat with a couple of hunters on a hill overlooking a basin with a beaver pond in the middle. Above the pond on the op-posite hill, a handful of cow elk drifted along the edge of timber. The herd bull's raspy voice boomed from its depths. There was little light left.

The cows spread out into stunted aspens that had looked wispy through the glasses but now hid the big animals almost completely. We studied the yardage: 400 to the forest, 350 to the scarred log above the second-growth, 300 to the top of the ravine below those as-pens. We hoped the elk, bull in tow, would make it that far.

I caught glimpses of antler periodically as the bull paced back and forth behind the trees and purple shadows slid farther up distant hills. The cows fed too slowly downhill.

Just as we despaired of getting the drop on this bull, he stalked out of the woods to run off a young six-pointer that had slipped to-ward the cows. That accomplished, he moved past the scarred log.

"I can shoot him," said the hunter. His Sako looked steady, rest-ing on my spotting scope. I'd had plenty of time to adjust the tripod.

But 350 steps is a long shot. I gambled. "We'll wait till he's at the top of the ravine." We almost lost him. The young bull made another sweep, and the aspens swallowed both elk for several minutes. When he appeared again, he was still well above the ravine.

"Take him when you're comfortable with the hold," I said. "Figure seven or eight inches drop."

Blam! The bull dropped instantly, but with his head up. "Again!" I hissed. A dark spot had appeared high on his shoulder. "Hold center!"

The next bullet from the .300 Winchester missed. And the next. And the next. The elk was moving uphill now. I had no idea where the bullets were going. My 10x50 Swarovskis showed everything in detail—except the Noslers that sped into the foliage. The man reloaded as the bull stopped in second-growth.

Three rounds later I heard a bullet strike. The animal fell but didn't stay down. Six additional shots, four from his partner's rifle, at last dropped the curtain.

Next day I returned with both rifles, a rangefinder, and a big piece of cardboard, which I taped to a small tree above the bull's carcass. I climbed the hill and ranged the forest at an even 400 yards. The scarred log was 357, the bull 320. We'd had the distance pegged. I fired from the sit with the hunter's rifle, holding center, high, low, and to both sides. Only one hole appeared in the target, a foot high. I retired the Sako and loaded the other, a Remington reworked by Brown Precision. Two careful shots from the sit printed 2 inches apart, 7 inches low. Perfect.

We'd been lucky the evening before to kill a bull with a rifle that wouldn't have hit a minibus at 300 meters. The rifle was not zeroed where the hunter thought it was, and after a few misses he had no confidence either in it or in his own ability. Had not the first shot committed us, I would have insisted he stop shooting.

A precise zero not only ensures predictability in your bullet's path; it gives you great confidence that your rifle will shoot where you look. And that, friends, helps you shoot better.

Part IV:
The Makings
of a Shot

17

WHAT IS GOOD SHOOTING?

The first step in sifting out exceptional performance is setting a standard for ordinary performance. In competition, this happens by itself as shooters try to out-do each other. The superior marksman emerges as we make the target smaller, increase the distance, reduce the time allowed for each shot, impose restrictions on sights, rifle weight, triggers and artificial support, and require more shooting.

Any measure of marksmanship must include position; you can hit much more easily from the bench than from offhand. Less obvious is the influence of conditions. That's why smallbore prone shooters are concerned about their place on the line and their relay scheduling. A range with usually calm conditions first thing in the morning can give you fits later as wind picks up. The lee end of a firing line, or one sheltered by a berm, can protect you from wind that robs points from other shooters. Other variables, some capricious and beyond the control of shooter or official, also influence scores.

"Black-bullseye" competition is probably the best way to assess your marksmanship because the targets show bullet strike precisely, and most courses of fire specify enough shots to minimize the effect of luck. You'll know how you compare with other shooters, who must share conditions with you on the same range on the same day(s). Targets are scored by the same people. Match rules dictate rifle and ammunition, sometimes very specifically. If you choose a cheap autoloading .22 to shoot against marksmen using Anschutz position rifles—betting your open sights against the competition-quality aperture sights of your compatriots, and assuming your discount-store ammo will stand up to Eley Tenex—well, you're sealing your own fate. You may be a fine marksman, but in this black-bulls-eye match, you'll finish at the back of the field because your equipment isn't the equal of what's allowed.

Marksmen who shoot at the top levels of international competition demonstrate precision that ordinary hunters can hardly imagine, mainly because these marksmen have committed years to building their skill. On the other hand, they're using equipment and shooting under conditions you won't see on a big game hunt. Hunters who'd shoot abysmal scores in registered competition can be passable game shots, because the demands in the field are different. While competitive shooters with stellar records typically shoot sporting rifles well, they may come up short when a whitetail catches them out of position, or when they must muscle a heavy trigger with cold fingers.

In 1972, at a range in Mishawaka, Indiana, I uncased my Anschutz 1413 for a go at a spot on the U.S. Olympic Team. Actually, this was a preliminary tryout; I'd have to shoot another if I made the cut. The English Match is an iron-sight prone event that can be fired outdoors or on an indoor range. The indoor target we were shooting is tough, the 10 a dot inside a 9-ring smaller in diameter than our .22 bullets. Of course, I couldn't see what I wanted to hit; the entire black scoring area, several rings out from the 10, appeared as a dot in the aperture. Centering that black in the sight, I had to as-

Bench accuracy and hunting accuracy are different. On the bench, accurate rifles and loads carry the day. On the hunt, or in competition off the bench, shooting skill is what matters most.

sume that my precisely zeroed rifle and its super-accurate ammunition would deliver a center hit. A course of fire in the English Match is 60 shots, for a possible score of 600. I managed 591. It was a very good score for me—good enough to ensure me a place in Phoenix for the final competition. It showed I could put 60 consecutive bullets on top of each other at 50 feet with iron sights.

At the same time, I couldn't hit a pumpkin with that rifle offhand. Nor could I hit a pheasant with a shotgun. In my training, I'd focused on my strengths.

Since then, I've become a bit more competent shooting offhand and have downed a few pheasants. My prone shooting held up long enough to deliver a couple of state championships. But I've not shot as much lately, and no doubt I'd be soundly waxed in a prone match were it held tomorrow. Shooting of any kind helps you develop muscles and techniques useful in all types of shooting, but the only way to excel in any event or shooting sport is to focus your training.

Many hunters will tell you they're deadly game shots but can't hit bullseyes. Mostly, these characters are full of prunes. If you can't hit a paper target, with its well-defined aiming point, how can you expect to hit a target you can't easily define in the sight? Add in all the variables that make field shooting difficult—unknown distance and wind, excitement, fatigue, urgency, perhaps hard breathing and cold or mittened fingers, plus uneven terrain, maybe a difficult shot angle—and there's little chance you'll shoot better on the hunt. The reason mediocre marksmen kill a lot of game is that animals are big, and those that die are seldom as far away as the hunter thinks. Montana outfitter and booking agent Jack Atcheson, Sr., who has seen a great deal of shooting afield, and lots of carcasses, once told me that he'd counted more bullet holes behind the vitals than in them. Animals often die from follow-up shots and from hits far from the hunter's intended point of aim. Bullets that miss are easily forgotten when hunters talk about their kills.

In Utah, just before elk season a few years ago, I spent a day at the Salt Lake City rifle range. Hunters with cow tags were zeroing their rifles, then qualifying with them to meet a marksmanship standard imposed by a local landowner to reduce crippling loss on his property. A passing score was two shots out of three in a piece of typing paper at 100 yards. Any position was allowed, except a rest over sandbags. The hunters could use a sling, bipod, even a post. A low standard indeed, but some shooters still didn't qualify. The rare equipment failure showed up, but most misses were attributable to the shooters. They couldn't hold the rifles still, and they jerked their triggers. Several insisted on qualifying before they checked zeros, only to find that their rifles were not shooting anywhere near where the sights indicated. The session must have been sobering even for shooters who made the grade with their first volley. After they pulled those sheets of typing paper, I didn't hear much about 500-yard shooting at elk. (To be fair, I must note that some astounding groups showed up. A few of these hunters were truly marksmen, clustering three shots inside two inches from solid positions.)

The Utah elk hunters were given a crack at one more test before they left the range. I hung a larger target sheet at 100 yards, with a circle the size of a deer's vitals plainly visible, and asked for volunteers to fire one shot offhand at the circle. Dozens of hunters obliged. About half hit the paper. Fewer than 20 percent hit the circle.

No doubt many of these hunters killed deer and elk that year.

The penchant of most shooters these days to rely on a rest to steady their rifle, and on powerful optics to deliver precision, has impaired their ability to shoot. Marksmanship is like horsemanship; you need the rifle and the horse, but neither can make you an expert. While, partly because of equipment, we see the best shooting ever in

Good group? Depends on the distance and the shooting position. Fired at 200 yards from the sit, it's quite good. At half that distance, it's very mediocre. Before hunting, you should do better than this.

black-bullseye competition, only a few talented, dedicated shooters deserve credit. Most riflemen are big game hunters, and the level of marksmanship in that crowd has not matched the accomplishments of earlier shooters. Certainly it doesn't approach the accomplishments of the men and women who *inspired* earlier shooters.

Men like Ad Topperwein. Women like Annie Oakley.

Oakley came first. Born Phoebe Ann Moses in a log cabin in Darke County, Ohio in August 1860, she was soon called Annie by her four older sisters. Later, she would change her last name to Mozee. After her father died in 1866, her mother could not keep the family intact. Annie was sent to another home, only to be mistreated. She ran away and walked 40 miles back to her family but was not allowed to stay. Reunited when her mother remarried a Civil War veteran named Joseph Shaw, the Moses family struggled financially. But Annie's home life was again happy.

She first shot a rifle at age eight. A squirrel had run through the nearby orchard and stopped at a fence to get a hickory nut. Annie had to stand on a chair to reach the rifle, but when she fired, the squirrel fell, headshot. She didn't shoot again for eight months, in deference to her mother's orders. But eventually she began hunting in earnest. The meat not used at home went to Charles Ketzenberger, who owned a general store in Greenville. From there it was sold to a Cincinnati hotel owner, Jack Frost.

Annie was getting very good with her rifle and with shotguns. When quail no longer presented a challenge, she would whirl in a circle after the flush, to handicap herself—and drop the bird anyway. Then she started shooting birds on the wing with a rifle. At turkey shoots, she was an odds-on favorite. At one of these matches she met Frank Butler, a fabled marksman. The exhibitions of Butler & Company, a traveling theatrical troupe, included trick shooting. Jack Frost, well aware of Annie's skill, arranged a Thanksgiving Day match between the two shooters. Frank Butler, by most accounts, did not know beforehand that his opponent was a 15-year-old girl. She beat him. A year later she married him.

Under the stage name Annie Oakley, Mrs. Butler traveled with her husband's group, at one point performing before Sitting Bull, the Sioux chieftain. Sitting Bull called the diminutive sharpshooter *Watanya cicilia*, or "Little Sure-Shot." Frank and Annie moved to other venues. When Captain A. H. Bogardus, an exhibition shotgunner, left Buffalo Bill's Wild West Show, they immediately asked to replace him. Though the show had just lost much of its property in a riverboat accident and was short on funds, Annie's marksmanship got them both a job. Using a mirror, she fired over her shoulder at glass balls Frank threw in the air. She didn't often miss.

Petite at 100 pounds, quiet and sweet-tempered, Annie became an audience favorite. She charmed the people she worked with, as well as visiting dignitaries. The German crown prince, later to become Kaiser Wilhelm II, asked her to shoot a cigarette from his lips. She obliged—allowing in the wake of World War I that she should have cranked in a little windage. Annie shot coins from Frank's fingers and split playing cards edgewise with bullets. In 1884, using a Stevens .22 rifle at an exhibition in Tiffin, Ohio, she broke 943 glass balls out of 1,000 tossed. A year later she hit 4,772 out of 5,000 with a shotgun, loading by herself and finishing the series in nine hours. Annie once took a bet that she couldn't hit 40 out of 50 live pigeons rising at 30 yards. She downed 49. She could make one ragged hole in the middle of a playing card, shooting 25 shots in 25 seconds with a .22 rifle. Another fast-fire stunt was to release two clay birds from a trap, then sprint, leap over a table, grab a shotgun, and break both birds. Johnny Baker, a fellow shooter in the Wild West Show, tried for 17 years to outshoot Annie, and never did. "She wouldn't throw a match," he said. "Not even for the good of the show. You had to *beat* her, and she wasn't beatable."

Apparently the Butlers' tenure with Buffalo Bill was a happy one, though not unbroken. Annie spoke highly of him and returned in 1889 for a tour of Europe. In her free time, Annie did needlework.

Accidents would plague Annie in mid-life. Once, just before a shooting match, a target trap spring tore open her hand. Undaunted, Annie shot with one hand, breaking 24 of 25 birds to tie the match. Then, in 1901, a train crash that killed more than 100 of the show's horses put Annie in the hospital for months with internal injuries. The inspiration for the Broadway musical *Annie Get Your Gun*, Little Sure-Shot herself performed in the melodrama *The Western Girl* in 1902 and 1903. She and Frank toured miltary camps and even ran a small shooting school in North Carolina.

Tragically, an automobile accident in 1921 permanently crippled Annie Oakley. Despite her injuries, at age 62, she could still hit with a rifle every one of 25 pennies tossed in the air.

This Marlin 1897 is a modern rendition of the rifle Annie Oakley favored in some of her shooting routines. It's accurate, but few shooters can make it perform like it did in Annie's hands.

Phoebe Ann Moses died in November of 1926, followed twenty days later by her husband Frank. She was possibly the best female shooter ever to draw a bead.

Ad Topperwein, a contemporary of Annie Oakley, was born on a farm near New Braunfels, Texas not long after his father settled there in 1869. Herr Topperwein, a Scheutzenfest shooter, organized the area's Bavarian farmers into a rifle club. He also sold a rifle patent to Winchester, delighting young Ad, who was keen to hunt as soon as he was able. The family's 40-caliber muzzleloader was soon replaced by a Winchester 1873. Then Ad got a Winchester 1890, a .22 pump. With this rifle, the gifted young marksman became so skilled as to amaze his friends and neighbors.

Ad liked to shoot aerial targets. He apparently drifted away from hunting and had no compulsion to shoot holes in paper. But anything that could be tossed immediately became a target. As he progressed, he replaced the 1890 with a Winchester 1903 autoloader, then with its successor, a Model 63.

The young Texan was also interested in art. In 1887, at age 18, he left Leon Springs to work in San Antonio, eventually landing a job as a cartoonist. But he shot during off-hours, honing his incredible talent. His time with the rifle was rewarded when the Sells-Floto Circus asked him to demonstrate. He did with a rifle what the man then shooting for the circus did with a shotgun. Ironically, Ad was forced to use .22 shot cartridges to prevent bullets from perforating the Big Top! Still, Ad got better.

In 1894, with bullets, he broke 955 of 1,000 clay disks tossed in the air. Each disk measured just 2¼ inches in diameter. Dissatisfied, he repeated the stunt twice, shattering 987 and 989. Standard clay shotgun targets proved too easy for Ad; he broke 1,500 straight, the first 1,000 from 30 feet, the last 500 from 40. Now in his late twenties, Ad was also polishing his showmanship. A great entertainer, he'd fire at a steel washer. When it returned to the ground with nary a mark, he'd tell the audience that the bullet went through the middle. Immediately challenged by the audience, Ad would stick a postage stamp over the hole for another toss, and perforate the stamp. He could nail the bullet of an airborne .32–20 cartridge without hitting the case.

Winchester hired Ad Topperwein when the tall, slim, blue-eyed young man was about 27. He would shoot for Winchester for 55 years. Initially, "Top" shot without question all the ammunition Winchester supplied, but soon he was asking for inspection rights on each lot. Turns out that he was mostly interested in Elizabeth Servaty, who worked in Winchester's ballistics lab. He married her in 1903. To audiences thereafter, she was known as "Plinky." She not only supported Ad in his exhibitions; she proved herself a gifted shot as well. In fact, some historians rank her second only to Annie Oakley. In 1916 Plinky broke 1,952 of 2,000 clay targets with a Model 12 shotgun. She once ran 280 straight.

Ad handled a shotgun well, too. One of his stunts was to turn his back to target traps holding five clays. On his signal, the traps would launch their birds. Ad would do a backflip, grab his shotgun, and break all five.

Still a rifleman at heart, Ad didn't seem to need a shotgun to hit tough targets. Holding a Model 63 with the ejection port up, he'd fire a round, then swing the rifle up and hit the airborne empty. If anyone thought of betting against Ad Topperwein, they surely changed their minds after *that* routine. He brought his uncanny skill to bear with handguns, too: Holding a single-action .44 revolver in his right hand, he'd toss a 2-inch wooden block with his left, then hit it twice. That second shot, with the block spinning crazily in an unpredictable direction and the revolver needing to be cocked, must have been one of the hardest Ad ever attempted.

He was ever dreaming up new stunts. Using two revolvers, one pointed over his shoulder and aimed with a mirror, Ad would fire both at once, hitting two tin cans. With a .22 rifle, he nailed five airborne cans before any hit the ground. I believe it was Top who came up with the idea of drawing Indian heads on tin with bullets. Certainly he was the master, firing 350 to 450 rounds per profile, at the headlong rate of one shot a second. The tins became souvenirs, then collectors' items.

Topperwein was the clear target for wannabes of the day who fancied themselves expert marksmen. Some were indeed very good. Doc Carver (a shooter with no medical background) was among the

Exhibition shooters used simple, factory-issue rifles to do extraordinary things, like hitting coins tossed in the air.

most ambitious, shooting 11 Model 1890 Winchesters over the course of 10 days, 12 hours a day, to break more than 55,000 of 60,000 tossed glass balls, 2½ inches in diameter. He repeated this marathon, missing only 650.

But B. A. Bartlett, another gifted shooter, was quick to demolish Carver's record. Firing 144 hours, he shattered 59,720 of 60,000 balls.

Ad Topperwein responded to the challenge in 1907 at the San Antonio Fair Grounds. He had 10 Winchester 1903 rifles and 50,000 rounds of ammunition, plus 50,000 wooden blocks cut 2¼ x 2¼ inches. Top ran out of blocks and ammunition, then, when resupplied with .22 cartridges, started shooting blocks a second time. He stopped after 120 hours, 72,500 tosses. He'd missed 9 targets. During one period he ran 14,500 straight. His record would stand until after World War II, when Remington salesman (not an exhibition shooter!) Tom Frye diced up 100,000 wooden blocks and started shooting. Firing Nylon 66 autoloaders, Frye missed only two of the first 43,725 targets. He wound up with a score of 100,004 out of 100,010. Ad Topperwein, then an old man, wrote to congratulate him.

Plinky died unexpectedly in 1945, about the time Ad, with failing eyesight, retired from shooting. He lived for 17 more years. The shooting world lost its most versatile and talented exhibition shooter at the age of 93.

When I get complacent and tell myself that I shoot well enough, I try to remember the exploits of Annie Oakley and Ad Topperwein. Humility is good. It makes you work harder.

18

YOUR BODY, THE SHOOTING PLATFORM

It was so easy. The elk stood 80 yards below me, partially hidden by the curve of the hill but clear of the Douglas fir. Only the lower third of the ribs lay behind the yellowed grass. I stuck the crosswire on the crease behind the shoulder and pulled the trigger.

Actually, I *yanked* the trigger, and the reticle dived into the hillside before the bullet left.

The elk stood. I cycled the action and sent another bullet on its way. Again I hurried and the shot broke high. A drumroll of hooves told me I'd get no third chance.

Sad to say, I've missed a lot of easy shots at game. I have never missed because the scope was off or because a mount screw or action screw was loose. I have never missed because the air was too cold or too warm, or because I forgot to consider the elevation, the barometric pressure, or my horoscope. I *have* misjudged the wind and range on occasion, and in 35 years of hunting probably hit two or three branches with bullets. But almost all my bad shots have resulted from poor shot execution.

It is very easy to miss. Nobody is born a marksman. The mental and physical routines necessary for good shooting are hard-won by disciplined practice. You may be blessed with fine vision, quick reflexes, and extraordinary hand-eye coordination. You may have built great muscles and excelled in other sports. You still must learn how to hold and aim a rifle and control your breathing and trigger squeeze.

Compared to some athletic endeavors, shooting is a simple game. The fundamentals are few. You don't have to be very bright to learn them or in top physical shape to practice them. You don't have to think about teammates because shooting is a solitary effort. The reason you don't know many really good marksmen is that really good shooting comes only after many hours of repetitive practice. A crack shot is not someone who manages to kill game consistently (animals are big targets) or who gives one impressive performance (anyone can get lucky) or who gets the smallest groups from the bench (save your applause for the bench). The deadliest riflemen are those who whittle group sizes down on paper targets from hunting positions, in time eliminating "fliers." These shooters take extra care with their positions and technique. They know that firing with sloppy form amounts to practicing bad habits.

The foundation of every shot is body position. Your body is your shooting platform, and if it is not as solid as you can make it, you'll not shoot as well as you could. The key to a solid platform is bone structure. Bones, not muscles, should support you and the rifle. Muscles are elastic, and they tire. Muscles contain blood vessels that pulse and nerves that twitch. Bones are like bricks, and if you can align them so your muscles don't have to work to keep joints from slipping, you'll build with bones a platform that's as still as the human body can be. The other thing to remember about body position is that it must allow the rifle to point naturally at the target. If you force the rifle on target with your muscles, you'll have the same problems as if you depended on your muscles to support your body's weight. As soon as the trigger breaks, your body wants to relax. If it is already relaxed, the rifle stays on target. If you have muscled the rifle where it doesn't want to go, it will come off target at the shot.

In any position, check for the rifle's natural point of aim by closing your eyes as soon as the rifle is at your shoulder. Take a deep breath and relax. Now open your eyes. If that crosswire isn't still on the bullseye, adjust your position *from the ground up*. Don't just move the rifle with your arms!

The most stable position is prone, mainly because it is the lowest. It gives you the most ground contact and puts your center of gravity just inches above the earth. Your left arm should be almost directly underneath the rifle, to support most of its weight. Your left

A bald Montana knob, stiff wind, and short grass: an ideal situation for prone. Prone is the steadiest position because it's the lowest and gives you the most ground contact.

This shooter shows good form in a solid sitting position.

leg should be straight, but it's a good idea to bend or cock the right leg to roll yourself slightly off your stomach. Reducing stomach contact with the ground helps reduce pulse-bounce.

Sitting is not quite as steady as prone but is more versatile when you're hunting because it puts your muzzle above the grass and low brush, and it allows you to follow a moving animal with your sight. It is also much more forgiving of steep or uneven terrain. I shoot often from sitting, my legs tent-like in front of me, heels dug into the ground. It's important to lean well forward, the rear flat surfaces of your elbows against the fronts of your knees. Muscles in the small of your back will stretch in this position; hold the elbows against the knees. Alternative sitting positions are the crossed-leg and crossed-ankle variations, both popular with competitive shooters. However, they're not as useful on uneven ground. They also put the rifle on a lower plane, which can fill your sight picture with tall grass and brush. The crossed-leg position pulls hard on the muscles in your thighs. Though crossed-leg sitting can give you the best results on paper, it requires lots of practice to perfect.

Kneeling is faster than sitting, but because it is higher it gives you a bit more wobble, typically in an elliptical pattern from 9 and 10 o'clock to 3 and 4. In competition, the best kneeling shooters keep their backs straight, torso weight centered on the tailbone. Sitting squarely on the heel of the right foot, bent underneath, you'll find this an uncomfortable position for extended strings of fire. Practice conditions your foot. The ball and toes of the right foot should bear half your weight. Keep your left shin vertical, supporting the rifle as your left elbow rests just in front of your left knee. Again, "flat-on-flat" is the rule. As with sitting, if you put the point of your elbow on your kneecap, you'll get enough wobble to make you seasick. To minimize horizontal sway in kneeling, turn your left foot parallel with your right leg, which is comfortably off to the side, bearing little weight as it braces your position. Put the rifle butt high on your clavicle, so your face looks directly forward. Don't hunch or lean forward.

In prone, sitting, and kneeling, a shooting sling is a huge assist. I don't mean a strap, which, when you flip it over your arm, tugs at

Proper kneeling form: keep your back straight, half your weight on your tailbone, left shin vertical, elbow just in front of the left knee.

both front and rear swivels, twisting the rifle. A shooting sling like Brownell's Latigo has an adjustable loop that pulls taut between your upper left arm and the front swivel, *while the rear of the sling remains slack.* Result: Sling tension pulls the rifle into your right shoulder and reduces wobble.

Offhand, or standing, is the position of last resort, because your center of gravity is so high and you have so little ground contact. Because your left arm is unsupported by your leg, a sling is of little use in offhand—there's nothing to brace your arm against its tension. Good offhand shooters are rare because proficiency demands more practice than most of us are willing to commit. Though unsteady, offhand is the most-used position for quick shots at running game. It's useful when there's too much tall brush for a steadier shot, or when trying to assume another position might spook the animal. Good offhand shooting starts at ground level. Place your feet shoulder-width apart, weight evenly distributed, with a line through your toes at about a 30-degree angle to sight-line. The importance of a good offhand foundation is hard to overstate. The 30-degree foot angle works for me; you may need to adjust. To find out, put several targets close together horizontally on a wall. With the idea of shooting the center target, eyes closed, shoulder the unloaded rifle. Relax. Now open your eyes. Note where the sight is. Do it again. Again. You may find that the sight wants to hang not on the center target, but near another. Change foot position until when you open your eyes the sight is pointed at that middle bullseye. Your weight should be evenly distributed on both feet. I prefer slight forward pressure on the balls of my feet. My knees are straight but not locked.

Getting the right vertical alignment is not just a matter of raising the barrel with your left arm. To make the most of bone support, you'll have some "lean" built into your torso. Adjust that lean to fine-tune elevation, keeping your center of gravity over your feet.

"Most successful shooters lean back and slightly right to counter the weight of the rifle," says Gary Anderson, an Olympic shooter who has won two gold medals in the 300-meter free rifle event. "They support their left arm by bracing it against their ribs." Try that with a heavy rifle, and you'll agree with Gary. But hunting rifles lack the mass to stay still with the left hand supporting the forend far to the rear. Wind and a wild heartbeat can rob you of muzzle control when you rest your triceps against your chest. You'll get better results by holding the forend near midpoint, where you can actively direct it and steady it against the wind and your pulse. You may find that, even without rib support, a slight right-hand twist in your back helps stabilize your torso.

Stand upright. Lones Wigger, another Olympic double-gold medalist, stands as straight as a new corner-post when he shoots. He says that hunching over the rifle puts you off balance and adds tension to back muscles. Keep your head upright too, even if the rifle's butt projects above your shoulder. You see best when you look straight ahead. With the rifle in shooting position, your right elbow should be horizontal, putting a pocket in your shoulder where the butt rests. Let your left elbow support the rifle from underneath, not out to the side, which strains your shoulder muscles. My left elbow falls directly forward of that shoulder, my wrist angled comfortably to the forend. Grip the forend lightly but with full hand contact. Pull the stock more firmly with your right hand.

When you get a quick shot in the field, point your feet before you point the rifle. Bring it up smoothly to your cheek (not cheek to the rifle) as you breathe deeply to bring oxygenated air to your brain and eyes. Shoot with both eyes open if you can, pressuring the trigger as you let your second breath out slowly. Keep applying pressure if the sight stays on target. The rifle should fire when your lungs are emptied but not purged. Usually, you have time to hold pressure if the sight jiggles off-target. Increase pressure again when it's lined

To shoot offhand, stand straight, left elbow almost under the rifle, right elbow horizontal. Your feet should be shoulder-width apart, toes in a line roughly 30 degrees from sightline. Keep your head erect and look straight through the sight.

up. Don't jerk. You'll disturb the rifle if you try to fire quickly as the sight dives toward center.

Because offhand is the toughest shooting position, you won't always like the results. It's easier on the ego to shoot little groups from the bench. But to shoot well standing (and boost your hunting success), you must shoot standing often, doing everything right, every time. Use bone structure, heed your rifle's natural point of aim, control breathing and trigger squeeze. Though you should commit lots of practice time to offhand, use it in the field only when you must. I recall watching one young fellow fire three shots at a sheet of typing paper at 100 yards back at that "qualifying" test at the Salt Lake City rifle range. He could have used a prone or sitting position, or braced himself, kneeling, against the bench. He could have used a sling. According to the rules, he could have done anything with that rifle to steady it except lay it on sandbags. He chose to stand up, leaning his hip against the bench. His first shot made it into the paper, but his second just nipped the edge. "Better check your ammo," said his companion.

The real problem here was the lad's position. Fussing over ammunition was like checking the tire pressure on a car hitting on half its cylinders. From a solid position he probably could have put all three rounds near center, no matter the load. He simply couldn't hold the rifle still. It's worth mentioning that with a rifle against your shoulder but solidly sandbagged on a bench, heartbeat alone will move point of impact 4 inches at 300 yards. The bobbing caused by twitchy nerves and muscles crying for relief from offhand can throw shots all over the backstop.

A common question from rookie shooters in any position is "Do I hold my breath?" Well, no. But you *do* stop breathing, if only momentarily. I generally take three deep breaths (or one, if time is short) as I raise my rifle and align the sight. Getting oxygenated blood to your head improves your vision. I let the last breath out as I take up trigger slack, but I don't purge my lungs. Some accomplished riflemen suggest letting half the air from your lungs as you start to squeeze the trigger, then locking them. The idea is to eliminate chest movement for the shot while keeping enough oxygen in your body to maintain a sharp sight picture and, if the shot comes late, to prevent oxygen starvation. Holding your breath, as you might when diving to the bottom of a swimming pool, increases the intensity of your pulse, which bounces the rifle.

Even the steadiest position will show you some reticle movement. You can't guarantee that your shot will break when the crosswire is dead-center on your target, so the next best thing is to try to

A slight backward lean is popular with competitive shooters, as it helps bring the rifle's weight over your feet and takes strain off your back muscles.

make the bullet leave when it is *near* center. This means applying pressure to the trigger when the reticle is where you want it and maintaining pressure when it wanders away from that place. Eventually the rifle will fire. When you become familiar with a trigger, you'll come to know when the shot will go. But anticipating the shot can get you into trouble. There's a temptation to snatch a bullseye as the reticle dances through it. A quick tap on the trigger, alas, is hardly ever quick enough. And most of the time it disturbs the rifle, putting the reticle farther from center just as the bullet leaves. Get into this habit, and you'll soon be jerking the trigger, a cardinal sin. Discipline yourself to squeeze, and only when the reticle is where you want it. If you get tired before a shot happens and the sight picture shows increasing wobble, lower your rifle and start over. Soon you'll be able to front-load your squeeze so only a few ounces are left, speeding the shot without jerking.

As with any athletic movement, follow-through is important in shooting. Keep your eye glued to the target during recoil. Your body will move with the recoil, but if you've accommodated the rifle's natural point of aim, your body and rifle should come right back on target. When shooting at game, you may be tempted to look outside the scope to see the animal's reaction to a shot. Don't. Look *through* the scope, your face on the comb. Follow-through enables you to tell where the sight was when the rifle fired, so even if you can't see bullet impact, you'll "call the shot" (predict where the bullet hit based on the sight picture at the instant of firing). Calling a shot should be easy. If you don't know where the reticle was when your rifle jumped, you're shooting with your eyes closed, losing concentration, or jerking the trigger.

The reticle won't show where the bullet will hit if the muzzle is moving when the bullet leaves. "Slinging" a bullet toward the mark often results in a worse shot than you anticipate. That's why a smooth trigger pull is crucial. A trigger jerk seldom gives you as much grace as you expect. As the barrel dips it pulls the bullet off its intended path by more than the displacement obvious in the scope. If you rested the rifle and fired with the reticle in the same place but motionless the bullet would hit point of aim.

Once you know how to *make* a good shot, there's only one way to *become* a good shot. Practice. You don't have to burn a lot of expensive, hard-kicking ammunition. A .22 rifle costs pennies to shoot, and it doesn't make you flinch. Another route is dry-firing. You can do this at home, with a black thumbtack on a wall. Convenient— and there's no noise. After double-checking to be sure the rifle is empty, squeeze off ten carefully aimed "shots" from each position. Call each shot. When you make a bad shot, penalize yourself by shooting it over. A daily dry-fire routine like this will make you a better game shot. Guaranteed. And no, dry firing does not harm bolt-action centerfire rifles. Avoid it with single-shots like the Dakota 10, and with rimfire rifles. If you're in doubt about dry-firing your pet rifle, ask the manufacturer.

Good shooting doesn't just happen. It's the predictable result of a solid position and a sound shooting routine—both well practiced.

19

MAKING YOUR RIFLE HOLD STILL

A deer rifle that spits bullets 3,500 feet per second is like a race car without a steering wheel if you can't hold it still. I was reminded of that not in deer country, but in Alaska. The hunter in front of me had a Remington Model 700 in .300 Ultra Mag—plenty of rifle for a grizzly. But here we were, less than 100 yards from a big silvertip, and he couldn't steady his rifle. Tall grass precluded a low sit, so the best he could do was wait for the rifle to settle.

About that time I felt a puff of wind on my ear. The bear faced us, suddenly alert. Then it was gone.

There's a sequel. I spied that bear later, and we looped crosswind to get within range. My partner crawled to a small spruce about 80 yards from the bear. Through my binocular I watched as a sapling swayed under the weight of the rifle. The sway became a quiver. Then the tree was still. And the grizzly bear died.

Taking a rest makes sense whenever you can do it. But some rests are better than others, and often you have no chance for a rest. Here are some devices and techniques for steadying that rifle.

1. Choose a horizontal rest over a vertical support. The rifle will bounce away from a rest before the bullet leaves the muzzle, and the bounce affects bullet flight. The most predictable bounce—the one most like the bounce you got zeroing—is upward off a horizontal rest. A rifle jumping sideways will put its bullets elsewhere.

2. Pad the rest with something soft: your hand, a glove, or a day pack. A hard contact point accentuates the rifle's bounce.

3. Never rest the barrel; rest only the forend. Barrel contact can affect natural barrel vibration during the bullet's travel up the bore. Result: a shot gone astray.

4. When you rest a rifle against a young tree, consider holding the tree instead of the forend, steadying the forend with index finger and thumb as it rests across the web of your hand. Press forward on the tree to load it with tension. The tension will eliminate most small wobbles.

5. Get your body as low as you can, whatever rest you use. A forend support steadies only the front of the rifle. If the buttstock and receiver move, the rest is just a pivot point. That's why a rear sandbag is so important on a bench. Make your body and the rear of the rifle as steady as possible.

6. Plan for the times you don't have a rest. If you hunt mainly in open country and do limited hiking, a bipod makes sense. The Harris is among the best available. It has leg extensions so you can use it sitting as well as prone and a pivoting cradle that allows you to tip the rifle slightly to eliminate cant on a slope.

7. Buffalo hunters used crossed shooting sticks to steady heavy Sharps rifles. Fiberglass versions are lighter and handier. Stoney Point's Steady Stix and taller Safari Stix collapse for carry in a belt sheath (P.O. Box 238, New Ulm, MN 56073). From the sit or kneeling, plant the stick legs well in front of the rifle's forend and pull the intersection toward you as you push

forward with the rifle. The rifle pushes the legs more firmly into the ground as your hand (or a binding of some sort) keeps the sticks at a constant angle to each other. It's a remarkably steady way to shoot.

8. A monopod does not work nearly as well as crossed sticks, in my view. You can't easily control left-right wobble. The single staff *will* help you brace a rifle for offhand shooting, though it yields to even moderate breeze. Mainly, it keeps your left arm from getting tired.

Stumps not only hide you, they help you shoot.

9. My favorite brace is a sling—not a carrying strap, but a leather shooting sling with an adjustable loop. The loop lets you tighten the sling from the forend to your left triceps without putting tension on the buttstock. The pull of the loop transfers rifle weight from your left arm to your left shoulder while snugging the butt into your right shoulder. If you just wrap a strap around your arm (a "hasty sling"), you are countering the pull on the forend with a tug on the buttstock because the strap is as tight behind your triceps as in front. Furthermore, the tug on the butt is to the side, pulling your rifle into a cant. This skewed relationship of the bore to line of sight will affect your shot.

SLINGS

The sling David used to kill Goliath was apparently a leather pouch with straps. Whirling the loaded pouch in a lariat-like manner imparted centrifugal force that became directional speed when the stone was released. Later, slingshots used elastic bands instead of centrifugal motion to launch stones through forked sticks. By the time I got interested in shooting things, at around age 10, the slingshot had gone commercial. I remember the Wrist Rocket, a magnum model that hurled ball bearings far enough to be dangerous. The optional arrow rest allowed you to fire feathered missiles. These were less popular among urchins who shot them where retrieval could mean a spanking.

It wasn't until later that I discovered the rifle sling, later still that I tried it as a shooting aid.

A neighbor had a problem with rats in his barn, and I would perch on a rail fence outside with a .22 rifle and shoot them as they scampered between burrows in the manure pack that pushed the rotted boards out at the hem of the old building. Though most shots came at roughly 30 feet, I missed often. An older rifleman suggested

I try a sling. "To shoot with," he added. "A proper sling is for shooting, not carrying."

He demonstrated with a target rifle. I was amazed at how that rifle stopped bouncing around when the sling drew tight. It was my initiation into competitive smallbore shooting. After some months I could keep most of my bullets in the middle and had all but forgotten that a sling could also serve as a carrying strap.

Slings date to early times, if you count the ropes and straps attached as handles on heavy muzzleloaders. The first rifle matches were offhand events in which slings had no part. After military-style slings boosted the battlefield accuracy of soldiers in World War I, hunters began using them. Competitive marksmen became skilled in their use. But many hunters now view slings mainly as carrying devices.

The one-piece sling, whatever its shape, is all but useless for shooting when conventionally installed. Some hunters would argue that it can be twisted around the arm to steady the rifle—the "hasty sling" maneuver. But this puts tension on both the front and rear swivels, pulling the stock toe to the left and forcing a cant.

A word on the hasty sling: it's not really a sling at all, rather a technique for using a strap to steady a rifle in the offhand position. (You can, of course, use a shooting sling as well, sans loop.) Poke your left arm between the strap and rifle, then wrap your left wrist once around the strap's front end. The hasty sling puts tension on the rifle, deadening jiggles. It won't prevent the rifle from dipping and bobbing offhand because your arm is still without support. The hasty sling works within a narrow range of strap lengths. If the strap is too long, it will not snug up unless you cock your arm out to the side or grab the strap up front instead of gripping the forend. This takes energy that could better be used to support the rifle. If the strap is too short, you'll find a hasty sling anything but hasty as you worm your left arm around the strap while attempting a natural bend in your elbow. With a too-short strap, you may have to forgo a front wrap altogether, simply using the strap as a brace. Except in windy conditions, I can shoot about as well standing without a hasty sling as with it.

Kneeling, sitting, or prone, a sling with a shooting loop is far superior to a carrying strap. Instead of wrapping your arm around the strap and tightening it front to back by cocking your arm, you slip your arm through the loop of the forward section. As your left hand comes over the sling to grasp the forend and the butt meets your shoulder, the sling pulls taut against your upper arm. That tension hauls the front swivel (and the rifle) back toward you. The rear section of the sling is loose; there's no tension on the rear swivel. Naturally, the loop length and overall length of the sling must be pre-adjusted.

Some shooters eschew an adjustable sling because they think it awkward and slow to use. Actually, a sling can speed up a shot by steadying the rifle sooner than would be the case if you tried to sub-

A hasty sling is a technique, not a product. It's fast, but because your torso has no brace, it is not nearly as effective in steadying a rifle as a shooting sling applied in other positions.

due those wobbles by hand or tried to wait them out. Adjusting a sling takes less time than changing the oil in your pickup, and most likely you'll do it only once. Most slings on my hunting rifles have been set the same for years. I don't change a setting unless I switch the sling from one rifle to another with a substantially different stud spacing. If you hunt in Mexico and the Far North with one rifle, you might also have to adjust your sling to accommodate changes in clothing bulk.

During my first years on the competitive smallbore circuit, I experimented with different sling settings. It seemed that what worked for sitting didn't for kneeling—and that neither of those adjustments sufficed in prone. I also moved the forend stop and buttplate. Later, with an Anschutz 1413, I got more adjustments and had more fun playing with them. But my scores didn't improve until I learned that no matter how sophisticated the rifle, I still had to hold it still, control my breathing and the trigger, and call my shots. Gradually I reduced the number of sling and rifle adjustments between positions. Now, I make no changes between positions.

Because the sling on my smallbore competition rifle is never used to carry it, there's no need for a rear swivel attachment, other than to keep the sling from flopping around. No tension ever reaches the rear swivel. Bulk is no problem at a match, so this sling has a wide leather cuff that helps prevent slippage on my shooting coat sleeve and spreads the tension over a big area. It makes shooting more comfortable and reduces the pulse throb caused by the bite of a narrow strap. On a hunting rifle, a sling cuff would be a liability, interfering with the carry and slowing the aim. For the woods, you'll want something simple and slim.

The military-style sling with two double-claw hooks, leather keepers, and long rows of holes is familiar to a lot of shooters who never used it in the armed services. Designed to help soldiers shoot as well as carry their rifles, it is fully adjustable for loop and overall length. The only liabilities of the military sling are its weight and the dual claws that can bang against the rifle stock.

A derivative of the military sling, the Whelen sling has only one hook. The other fastener is a leather thong that you tie. I have only one Whelen sling, but I like it very much. I remember shooting a bighorn ram with a .270 on a Mauser action stocked by the late Iver Henricksen. That was in Oregon's Steens Mountains on a hot day when rocks and ram both looked oven-baked. The Whelen sling helped deaden my jackhammer pulse as I braced my back against a boulder and peered through the 6x Pecar scope. The Nosler found its mark 300 yards distant.

I've lost no enthusiasm over the years for the Whelen sling, but for many hunting seasons my favorite has been the Latigo, a sling marketed by Brownell's, the gunsmith supply company of Montezuma, Iowa. The Latigo has no hooks, no laces. It is a one-inch sling with one brass button that adjusts loop and overall length, and a brass ring that controls front and rear sections.

Properly installed, neither ring nor button can easily touch the rifle stock. This sling is lightweight and trim, quick to adjust and deploy. As with any hunting sling, all you do is flip the loop a half turn out and slip your arm through it. Then you bring the loop up high on your arm, between bulges of shoulder and triceps, and run the keeper down to snug it there. Flip your hand over the sling and grab the forend. The flat of the sling follows the contours of your left hand as you apply tension by shouldering the rifle.

To my mind, the only suitable sling material is leather. Synthetics are strong and lighter; synthetic fittings are lighter, quieter, and less obtrusive than brass. But nothing will grip your jacket sleeve like rough leather. Its weight, thickness, and stiffness make it easier to handle when you must get a shot off quickly. Besides, leather is a natural material. Synthetic slings have all the esthetic appeal of plastic quarter-ribs.

Sling width varies. An inch has become standard for sporting rifles. It's about as narrow as you'll want for shoulder carry. Some slings (my Whelen, for instance) are inch-and-a-quarter. These require wider swivels than are normally furnished. I like this width and will put up with a little extra sling weight for the broader contact surface on my shoulder and arm. A wide sling doesn't look quite as good as the one-inch on a slender rifle.

Why would anyone put something other than a Whelen or Latigo sling on a sporting rifle?

Well, I don't know. But the most prevalent sling these days seems to be a carrying strap with a wide front end: the cobra-style sling. Its great width not only distributes the rifle's weight for easier times on the trail; it also provides a canvas for leather-workers. Big bucks with outlandish antlers are standard fare. You could no doubt special-order Mermaids or Holsteins to grace your sling, in color if you like. Fleece on the reverse side reminds me of an automobile seat cover, but many shooters buy their slings so equipped. Some come with cartridge loops.

While the cobra strap helps you carry a rifle comfortably, it is an abomination when you must shoot. There's no way to make a hasty sling of that great paddle of leather. If you ignore it—just let it hang—it may retaliate.

Not long ago I was hunting mule deer with two friends. We'd covered many acres over the course of several hours and found nothing. I asked them to post themselves a few yards apart on the lip of a brushy canyon while I circled to its head and pushed through the aspens in its depths.

As I climbed toward my partners, a deer thrashed out of the second-growth. Seconds later the flat crack of a rifle told me it was a buck. But when I found my friend, he only shook his head.

"Fine deer, but this cockeyed sling got in the way." When he'd shouldered the rifle, his coat cuff caught the sling and flipped it onto the barrel, where it blocked his view through the scope. "All I could see was black."

Granted, a comfortable sling on the shoulder helps you hunt longer. But so does a rifle that weighs less than an empty bird-feeder. Without the ability to deliver one accurate shot, you have no reason to hunt. When comfort on the trail costs you a kill, it is expensive luxury indeed.

Now, a cobra-style strap does have some utility. It is probably your best bet if you use a bipod.

For long shooting in open country, bipods like the popular Harris make sense. Across sage flats and canyons, a bipod gives you the stability of a natural rest, with the flexibility to put that rest just where you want it. The price is maneuverability in brush and extra bulk and weight. A wide sling won't make your rifle less sluggish on the mount, but it will help you bear up under the bipod on the trail. Because the bipod serves the same purpose as a shooting sling, nothing is lost if your carrying strap has no loop.

Brian Schuetz from Olympic Arms shoots prairie dogs with one of his .223 autoloaders—assisted by a long-legged Harris bipod.

The other application of a cobra-style strap is on a "scout rifle" designed to be used with either iron sights or a forward-mounted, quick-detachable scope. The rear swivel stud is not in the butt, but forward of the triggerguard (the rifle is meant to be carried muzzle down). A loop on a scout rifle sling would serve no purpose because the rear stud is ahead of your left upper arm. A shooting sling adjusted for an ordinary rifle would be much too long. The cobra strap is installed "backward" on a scout rifle, so the wide part not only contacts your shoulder during the carry but grips your triceps when you shoot. Because the rear swivel is forward, *both* ends of the sling pull the rifle to the rear. You need only adjust overall sling length to get the proper tension when you're in a shooting position. Scout rifles so equipped can be even faster to shoot than a conventional rifle with a Whelen or Latigo sling.

Learning to use a sling is about as easy as learning to use a seatbelt, and you'll see more accurate shooting almost immediately. Not that a sling is a panacea. You must still hold the rifle, control the trigger and breathing, and aim in the right place. But I feel at a disadvantage when for some reason I shoot without a sling in the field. I was certainly pleased to feel its tug on the last day of Montana's deer season, after a buck I'd stalked across an open hillside suddenly decided to move away. The range was about 250 yards, and there wasn't much time. I squirmed into a sit, steadied the crosswire of the Sightron scope, and touched off the Lazzeroni rifle. The buck dropped dead. Without the sling, I'd have been wobbling too much to justify a shot.

One morning many years ago, I was glassing a rocky knoll from a ledge well above it. Suddenly I spied a buck mule deer. I dropped below the ledge and crawled forward in the basalt until I came to a cliff. With no way to get closer, I slipped my arm in the sling, curled into salamander prone and locked the reticle on the deer. The animal looked very small. I felt the wind coming hard from ten o'clock. The reticle crawled up and left. I fired and missed at five o'clock. The buck turned to face me. I favored more to the left and higher, and the bullet bit closer. By now it seemed to me this deer had earned a reprieve. I thought about that for a long moment and would have quit had I not seen the hits so clearly. I favored boldly at eleven o'clock and triggered my last round. The deer sprinted into an old burn and out of sight. It took me some time to reach him. I was pleased to find the .270 bullet had driven through the heart. The sling made small adjustments in aim possible. (Yes, killing with the third shot bothered me. I have not since fired at game so far away.)

Slings are as appropriate for single-shot rifles as for bolt guns. They're not as useful on lever-action carbines designed for short, fast offhand shooting in the woods. Slings installed on lever rifles should be left very loose so as not to interfere with the cycling. Slings belong on slide-actions and autoloaders—slug-shooting shotguns as well as rifles. Swivel studs designed for magazine caps, and for barrels and magazine tubes, make installation easy. My Browning A-5 Buck Special wears a sling when I take it afield.

In my view, barrel-mounted sling swivel studs are not ideal because a tight sling can pull the barrel down and affect point of impact. (I shoot with a very tight sling and have found even a forend-mounted sling, by relieving up-pressure on the barrel, can depress bullet strikes as much as four minutes of angle!) Despite this drawback, barrel-mounted swivel studs make esthetic and practical sense on rifles with extra-short forends like Ruger's Number One "A." They're also useful on heavy-recoiling rifles that might mutilate your hand with a forend stud. Thick-walled barrels mitigate the effect of sling tension, and big-bore rifles built for dangerous game get most of their work close to the muzzle where changes in bullet strikes (and their effects) are minimal.

Many hunters who pack long-barreled pistols now equip them with slings, for both shooting and carrying. No loop is necessary. The sling is adjusted to fit around the back of the shooter's neck so that as he straightens his arms in a two-hand hold it snugs the pistol into his palms. It steadies his arms by pulling them back toward his torso.

On a rifle, a properly-adjusted sling is hardly an accessory. In fact, some manufacturers have supplied slings with their top-of-the-line rifles. Once, when my eyes were younger and sharp, I told a hunting partner I'd choose a rifle with a sling and a receiver sight over a scoped rifle with no sling. Iron sights blur for me now, but there's no doubt my choice would be the same.

20

HOW THE CHAMPS SHOOT

Most of us who like to shoot like to think we shoot well. Most of us don't. But we could if we practice the way a handful of serious marksmen practice.

"Most people have no idea about what it takes to shoot at the top levels of competition," says Lones Wigger. He should know. Lones has won two Olympic gold medals for his shooting (smallbore rifle, position in 1964, and 300-meter free rifle in 1972). He also took a silver medal (smallbore, prone in 1964) and has set 29 world records with a rifle (16 in team events, 13 as an individual). No shooter in the world has taken more than two individual gold medals, and probably none can match Lones Wigger's lifetime achievements on the international shooting circuit. In the Pan American Games and the World Championships, the Championships of the Americas and the Olympics (the four competitions in which international records are acknowledged), Lones has shot his way to 111 medals. It's hard to think of anyone with better credentials as a shooting instructor.

"I don't put a lot of stock in psychoanalysis," he says frankly. "Some of what I've read seems to me 90 percent baloney. Getting yourself ready for a shot is largely a matter of building your confidence, and that comes only through practice. Nothing can take the place of practice. If you've shot enough good scores in practice, you'll be confident of shooting a good score at a match. Same goes for hunters. You must be confident. If you have doubts, you'll make mistakes."

Lones concedes that some mental games can help you shoot better when the tension is high, whether you're on the line to win or on the mountain shooting an elk. He says it's good to visualize the shot before you take it, to see in your mind's eye the center hit or the animal falling. "And you must learn to relax. You can't shoot well if you're uptight. I used to yawn a lot on the mat—found out later that it's a recommended relaxation technique. Now I'm thinking about yawning." He laughs. "I can't say whether a conscious yawn is more or less effective. The idea is to put yourself at ease. Think about settling a fly line on a placid lake—anything to get your mind off the pressure to make a center shot. If you've practiced enough, your body will take care of the rifle, and you'll still have the focus to coordinate a good hold, proper breathing, and a clean let-off at the right time."

Pressure is something you can't duplicate well in practice, according to Wigger, who has competed often under the most intense pressure. "I used to say that once you learn to shoot winning scores in practice, you're three years away from winning. An important match, or a moment of truth in hunting, demands your best effort while all but preventing you from delivering it. You learn to handle pressure the same way you learn to shoot: by repetition. To shoot better when it counts, go to all the matches you can, and put yourself onto game as often as you can."

As a young man, Lones had more opportunities to practice than most shooters. A Montana boy, he proved an able marksman early enough to earn a spot in the U.S. Army Marksmanship Training Unit at Fort Benning, Georgia. There, "my job was to shoot. I practiced three or four days a week, up to four hours a day." A four-hour session might give him 150 to 200 shots. "After that, I had to quit. The mental effort of making every shot good left me completely drained. It's easy to shoot. But it's not easy to shoot a good shot. Real practice—the kind that will help you shoot better—is disciplined practice. You must focus on each aspect of the shot: position, breathing, sight picture, trigger control, follow-through." He chuckles. "It's arduous. It tests your work ethic. Sure, shooting is fun. But when you do it to advance your skills, it is also hard work."

Despite his job description, Lones says that in the early days he wanted and needed to shoot more often than he was scheduled. So he shot on weekends and days off. "You can't get good enough to win at the Olympic level, or even in national competition, unless you can shoot full-time," he adds. "That doesn't mean you have to

Lones Wigger, twice Olympic gold medallist, says that nothing can take the place of practice. Confidence comes from disciplined repetition.

shoot every day. But you must have the time for a rigorous practice schedule. Few shooters do." Lones notes that as he became more proficient, and after winning on the international circuit, he reduced his practice time. "I didn't shoot as often, but I knew better what to work on and how to practice, and each session was more beneficial. Just before a big match, practice again became a priority. I not only shot; I practiced holding the rifle."

Training your body to be a shooting platform is a big part of training it to make a good shot, and Lones admits to working harder for a steady hold than some of his colleagues. "The MTU had many fine shooters when I was at the top of my form," Lones recalls. "Gary Anderson also won two gold medals—in 300-meter free rifle, 1964 and '68—and shoots much like I do. So does Margaret Murdock. We take plenty of time for the shot. John Foster, Jack Writer, and Lanny Bassham shot faster. They seemed to get the rifle locked on center quickly and saw no need to delay the shot. I think a slow cadence helped me, because I often shot better in matches than in practice." He agrees with me that quick let-offs can get you in trouble when the pressure is on and your rifle doesn't settle.

Lones says he dry-fired very little to prepare himself. "But that's because I had ready access to the best ranges and unlimited ammunition. If you don't, dry-firing is a good idea. You strengthen the muscles that hold the rifle, as I did in my holding exercises, and you get practice with breathing and trigger control. Whether you're shooting a match or hunting, you want the confidence that comes from knowing you did all you could to prepare."

Scheduling practice is important, according to Lones, who recommends that you set aside specific hours. "Write them down, and stick to them. Also, you must set goals. Try to make them realistic but challenging. Say you want to learn to shoot better standing. If you're a competitive shooter, you might set a goal of consecutive targets with a score of at least 95. If your average is now 92, that's an attainable but challenging goal. If you're shooting in the high 80s, 95 is too ambitious. Get there in stages, so you can measure your progress." Hunters can do the same thing, he points out, with home-fashioned targets or by measuring group sizes. A 4-inch three-shot group at 100 yards shows that you mastered the fundamentals of off-hand shooting—three times. To prove yourself, you need more holes in the target. That's why competitive events require so many record rounds—160 per day in a smallbore prone match.

How does competitive rifle shooting translate to field shooting? "I think the fundamentals learned in one can help prepare you for the other," says Lones. "But with a hunting rifle, or a lightweight match rifle like the .243 I use in metallic silhouette competition, you must take more control. You don't have the advantage of a shooting jacket or a super-light trigger. The trigger on my position rifle and 300-meter rifle break at about an ounce. The trigger on the .243 is legal at just over two pounds. Couple that with a rifle weight of just 8 pounds, add a little wind, and shooting offhand becomes a real challenge. I still try to keep my left side relaxed, though my left arm must actively hold the forend. My right hand pulls the stock firmly into my shoulder. I'm careful not to disturb the rifle when I trigger a shot—it's so easy to jerk when that reticle is bouncing around!" Lones, who uses the first joint of his trigger finger, says silhouette targets can make him complacent because they're big, and he emphasizes the importance of keeping the reticle in the center—good advice for hunters who commonly miss when they think the animal is too big to miss.

Shooting silhouettes, Lones uses a 6–20x Leupold set at 20x. In smallbore matches, he prefers a 36x scope. "It doesn't matter what scope you like, as long as it helps you hold in the middle." Olympic competition requires iron sights. "An adjustable iris makes sense then, so you can keep the hole as small as available light will allow." A little aperture increases depth of focus, bringing the target and front sight almost into the same plane, sharpening their relationship. Opening the rear aperture, as is often (and properly) recommended for hunters, you get a brighter sight picture and faster target acquisition but reduced depth of focus.

Gary Anderson, a Nebraska farm boy with the grit to practice shooting until he won Olympic gold, is among the most accomplished of American riflemen. At age 20, after just two years of competitive shooting, he won a place on the prestigious Army (USAMTU) team. That same year, 1959, he also made the U.S. team for the Pan American Games and came home with silver and gold medals. He shot in the 1960 Olympics and won his first National Championship a year later. In 1963, he took both the smallbore and centerfire gold medals at the Pan American Games. The next year Gary set a new world record winning his first Olympic gold in 300-meter free rifle competition. In 1968 he again took the gold in that event. Gary has won twelve Na-

If you're shooting a heavy rifle under still conditions, bracing your triceps on your ribs while you balance the rifle on your fingers may help you hold. In wind, or with a light rifle, hold the rifle lightly with your left hand forward. You'll have better muzzle control.

tional Championships and seven World Championships and set six world records with the rifle. His small book, *Marksmanship*, offers a clear synopsis of his rifle shooting technique. The chapter titles reflect his priorities: Aiming Correctly, Trigger Control, Breath Control, Using The Sling, Bone Support, Balance, Relaxation, Head Position, Holding and Firing, Hitting Where You Aim. It's worth noting that the first 9 of these 10 "Secrets of Shooting" have nothing at all to do with equipment (save the sling). They have to do with how the shooter positions and controls his body. The last chapter deals with zero.

Like Lones, Gary stresses the importance of solid, well-thought-out positions, and practice that makes them so comfortable that almost no effort is required to sustain them. Balance and relaxation are linked: a position that puts your muscles at ease is one that is naturally well balanced. If you must work to keep your body from falling, buckling, or otherwise collapsing out of position, you introduce muscle tension that both tires you out and causes tremors that move your rifle. He advocates a smooth trigger pull at all costs, pointing out that if your position is good, the movement you see in the sight won't deny you a good score.

Gary is a left-handed shooter but has practiced enough with right-handed bolt guns to shoot very fast with them. "Practice makes just about anything possible," he smiles. Legend has it that as a youngster he dry-fired his .22 rifle so much that the peening made the chamber unusable. I can't claim such dedication, but when in college I did get my muscles used to shooting positions by studying and watching television sitting and kneeling, swathed in my leather shooting jacket and supporting the weight of my Anschutz 1413. I've since made a practice of dry-firing at a black thumbtack on my living room wall. A few careful "shots" at a thumbtack every day take little time and no ammunition. The benefits are huge.

Gary hunts with a Remington .308. It wears an aperture rear sight. Though he's shot small groups with irons at 300 meters in competition, Gary considers any shot at game over 200 yards to be quite long, and he won't fire at any animal beyond 300. "Too big a chance for a crippling hit," he says.

Shooting black bullseyes gave Gary Anderson and Lones Wigger their fame, and it's still the best way to develop and monitor marksmanship. But it's not the most exciting thing to watch. Tom Knapp, another gifted shooter, turned early to other targets. Now he does shotgun exhibitions for Benelli, explaining all about guns and shooting in a relaxed southern drawl while blasting all manner of airborne objects to pieces. He prepares coleslaw by mincing a cabbage, then "slices and dices" as fast as he can toss other vegetables. He hits 'em with the shotgun held behind his back, too.

Tom combines naturally quick reflexes and extraordinary hand-eye coordination with a discipline to practice familiar to any champion. His feats on camera are astonishing.

To become an expert with your hunting rifle, buy a high-quality air rifle of roughly the same size and weight and shoot it a lot, minding the fundamentals on each shot.

Tom has broken nine clay targets, tossed at once, before any hit the ground. He broke them all without any misses or double hits, using one Benelli autoloader with an extended magazine.

Tom can shatter seven hand-tossed targets with Benelli's Nova pump, and he follows that routine by hitting ejected empties as he runs through another full magazine. He seems as effective holding this gun upside down. "I *should* be familiar with the Nova," laughs Tom. "I fired 60,000 rounds testing it. Proofed it for function with turkey loads, too. I had to give up on those after 3,800 shots because my wrists hurt too bad."

What does Tom Knapp's shotgunning have to do with rifle shooting? He's also a deadeye with a rifle. In fact, where conditions permit, Tom uses a rifle in exhibitions. "I really like the .22 Magnum (WMR); those hollowpoints blow things apart!" With a .22, he's hit a tossed golf ball as many as three times before it landed, clipping it low to keep it aloft. He's shot 13 consecutive hand-tossed aspirins. And he's shot BBs.

"I can see the BB; unfortunately, the audience can't. But when a .22 bullet hits a steel BB, the bullet whines as it is deformed and deflected. You can hear that. BBs are hard to hit, but if you shoot enough, you can do it."

Tom's exploits with a shotgun actually require rifle-like accuracy. "I prefer an Improved Cylinder choke for clay bird shows," he says. "An unchoked barrel would give me a bigger pattern, but those targets fall close to each other, and hitting two targets with one shell doesn't count. Actually, the shot cloud is only about as big in diameter as a clay bird at the distance I'm shooting them. I once had to hold for the bottom half of a bird when it fell close to another. You see that in the slow-motion footage." (Tom has demonstrated his skills on the television program, *The American Shooter*, a TNN series, and on *Benelli's American Bird Hunter*, courtesy of The Outdoor Channel.)

In front of an audience, Tom says he feels pressure to shoot fast. So did his predecessors: Annie Oakley, Ad Topperwein, Tom Frye, and Herb Parsons. The brisk pace of their performances left audiences slack-jawed with wonder before television made the impossible easy with fake imagery.

While exhibition shooting has little in common with the shooting most hunters do at big game, the ability to handle a rifle deftly and to shoot right away with confidence is crucial in both cases. Quick shooting on a big game hunt is sometimes the only shooting you'll get. A buck on the way out won't give you much time. Many hunters lose precious half-seconds getting their rifle up and the sight aligned because they haven't practiced. They haven't practiced getting their feet pointed right instantly in thick brush. They haven't practiced shooting when they're out of breath, or through tiny alleys, or with gloves on. Most significantly, they've not shot enough *without* time limits to have mastered shooting fundamentals. To shoot well fast, you have to shoot well first.

Whatever your target, your ability to hit depends mostly on how often you've hit targets in the past. Repetition builds skill and confidence. You need both to shoot well, either on the range or on the mountain.

21

DOCUMENTING SKILL

The targets came with pasters clustered, black on black, in the paper's broad center. The group measured just under 6 inches. Rick Freudenberg had told me the group was good. Rick has built dozens of very accurate rifles in his Everett, Washington shop.

Shortly thereafter, I was at the bench firing a prototype Browning A-Bolt bored for the .270 Winchester Short Magnum cartridge. My best group measured an inch and a half. . . .

On an airplane weeks later, I chatted up a young man returning from a hunt. He'd nailed a buck at 250 yards. "Hit right where I aimed." Not surprisingly, he implied, given that *his* Browning A-Bolt shot half-minute groups.

Hunters covet accurate rifles—though accurate hunters are in much shorter supply. But neither the rifles nor the hunters come with accuracy ratings. Indeed, assessing accuracy is tricky. Group sizes don't tell the whole story. For example, which of the rifles just described is most accurate?

Well?

You're right. There's not enough information here to tell. In fact, they're all accurate. The Freudenberg rifle delivered the most complete picture with a 20-shot group. At the bench, few hunters fire even five at a time; three is typical. Groups can get a lot bigger as you add bullets. Luck doesn't stick around for extended strings of fire. Now, you say, a 6-inch group hardly shines, no matter how many shots it holds. But these 20 rounds from Rick's 6mm/308 Improved weren't fired at 100 yards. The target was 500 yards away. That's essentially minute-of-angle accuracy twice as far as I've ever shot an elk!

The A-Bolt in .270 WSM was accurate too, because I got my inch-and-a-half group at 300 yards. Checking the zero before a hunt, I punched one oval hole at 200 yards with two factory-loaded 140-grain Fail Safe bullets.

The deer hunter's Browning may have been accurate as well, though a one-shot kill is hardly solid evidence. Animals are big targets, with no aiming points. A bullet can land inches from where the rifle was pointing and still put out the lights. Besides, accuracy is a form of repeatability. Only repetition establishes accuracy or disproves it. To document rifle accuracy, you must shoot paper enough times that chance can't skew results. Fortunately for those of us shooting ordinary hardware, target-rifle precision is no requisite for big game hunting. A rifle that puts bullets where we remember aiming is a deadly hunting rifle, whether it's accurate or not.

"Accuracy won't help you find game," a veteran hunter once observed. "Finding is 90 percent of hunting." After that, he added, all you need is a rifle that shoots its bullets into a target the size of a gallon jug. "Rifles don't run out of accuracy nearly as fast as hunters run out of skill."

Which is why I was so enamored of the 6-inch group delivered by the 6mm/308 Improved. Gary Rasmussen, a crack marksman on the U.S. Palma team, didn't fire Rick's rifle from a bench. He shot that coffee-can-lid group at 500 yards *from prone without a rest*.

The main reason hunters miss is that the sight is somewhere else when the rifle fires. Zero almost any rifle at 200 yards, and a dead-on hold will kill any deer out to at least 250. That's a pretty long shot. A rifle that shoots only 4-inch groups at 100 yards will still keep its bullets inside a 10-inch circle at 250—near the middle of that garbage can lid. Half-minute rifles are superfluous, though they do boost our confidence.

Whether your rifle is a nail-driver or has a musket's wanderlust, you won't know if you can kill big game with it until you document your shooting skill. Without skill, the most accurate rifle is useless as soon as you lift it off the sandbags. A skilled marksman can make even a musket lethal.

Repetition tests marksmanship just as it does accuracy. The place to start repeating your hits, oddly enough, is on the bench. There you can refine your breathing and trigger squeeze and learn

Wayne fired four Barnes X bullets from a .280 Remington into this deer's shoulder from prone at 400 yards. A fifth shot leaked a bit high. The target shows less holdover is needed. Still, this group is a confidence builder.

to read the wind. You'll learn to call shots there, too—"freeze framing" the sight picture at the instant of firing to accurately predict where your bullet will land. Bench groups will be small, engendering confidence and encouraging you to shoot more. If this exercise seems elementary and beneath your dignity, skip it. I still find it useful. You can do this with any rifle, but one that's very accurate and doesn't kick hard is best. You must know that the rifle will shoot where you point it.

Not long ago I fired a series of five-shot groups using a Remington 40x rimfire target rifle and match ammo. I tried to make each group a little smaller than the last. Trigger and breath control were all that mattered; the bench held the rifle. On average, the groups ran a little over .60. The best, my last, measured about .40. You don't have to shoot groups that tight, because not all rifles and cartridges will. But deliver enough shots into a group and replicate the group often enough, and you'll soon figure out which marginal shots resulted from your incompetence. Give yourself plenty of time with this exercise. I had to mind a gusty wind—something you'll find unnecessary with a centerfire cartridge at short range. Then again, with the .22, I didn't have to stop to rest my shoulder or to let the barrel cool.

Next, shoot from a bipod or an improvised rest (not a bench) with your hunting rifle at 100 yards. Shoot half a dozen five-shot groups. They'll be bigger than those you shot from the bench, but if you control the trigger, not *that* much bigger. Wild shots are bad news here. If they happen, dry-fire until they don't, taking care to make each "shot" a good one. Call each, and score yourself.

The last step in documenting your skill is tough, because it forces you to *hold* the rifle and take responsibility for all errant shots. You know the rifle will shoot into, say, three minutes of angle. Shots outside that perimeter can't be blamed on the rifle or ammunition. From 100 yards, fire six groups, two each from sitting, kneeling, and offhand. A sling is OK here, but no bipods, stumps, posts, packs, or other supports that may be unavailable when you see game.

If results here fall short of appalling, you deserve a milkshake. Mine usually point out the need for dry-firing. Whatever the outcome, you'll know how far you can shoot effectively from field positions. Toss out your worst shot from each position, then take the average spread of each pair of groups (one four-shot and one five-shot from each position) and divide that figure into 16. Multiply by 100, and you get maximum effective range.

For example, say that, from kneeling, you print two 6-inch groups. Deleting your worst shot, you come up with one 6-inch group and one that now measures just 4 inches. Average group size: 5 inches. Divide 5 into 16, and you get 3.2. Multiply by 100 and you get 320, the maximum distance in yards at which you should be able to plant 9 of 10 shots inside the 16-inch vitals of an elk. Yes, a big

This .35–404 by Oregon gunsmith Kevin Wyatt dumps a lot of recoil; so dry-firing makes sense between range sessions.

bull can measure 28 inches deep in the chest, but you're aiming for the lungs, which are not in the vertical center of the chest. Realistically, your target offers 8 inches of forgiveness. If you assume a 28-inch target, you could miss or cripple if you hold for the center of the lungs and hit 14 inches low or to one side. Deer vitals are smaller. To get maximum effective range for, say, a 10-inch target, divide the average spread of the groups into 10. So 5 inches average dispersion gives you 2 x 100 = a 200-yard distance limit.

This formula gives you a *maximum* practical limit, because on a hunt many things conspire to make shooting more difficult. Wind, for example. Dope it wrong at long range, and you're in deep trouble. You won't know actual range, either—a real problem beyond the 250-yard point-blank range of most big game rifles. Shivering or panting, you'll make the rifle shake, sending bullets all over the hill. Get excited, or hurry because time is short, and even if you don't jerk the trigger, your pulse and nerves can throw the bullet off target. That's why I'm reluctant to shoot game beyond 300 yards, even from a sling-assisted sit that gives me tight groups. On the mountain, shooting is often twice as hard as at the local range.

A 1936 newspaper article detailing L. S. Chadwick's British Columbia hunt, on which he took the magnificent ram that still tops the Boone and Crockett list of Stone sheep, noted that he killed one at "the almost unbelievable distance of half a mile." Well, to hunters who shoot a lot, killing at half a mile is hardly unbelievable. Modern bullets travel that far with lethal energy. A 2-minute rifle will hit sheep vitals at 900 yards about every other shot, given ordinary dispersion. What's truly unbelievable is that anyone could dope the wind and estimate the range so precisely and hold the rifle and execute the shot so perfectly as to hit game even occasionally that far away. Or assume that he could.

A savvy hunter put it this way: "If you can't be sure of a first-round hit, there's no point in shooting." Don't count on backup from the magazine. Those bullets are as ignorant as the first, and no more able to overcome your inadequacies.

Once I fancied myself a pretty good shot. I'd won a couple of state championships and managed a fine score during an Olympic tryout. Then, in the rugged canyon country separating Oregon and Idaho, I spotted a deer. It wasn't a big buck, but big enough that late in the season. I sat down, cinched up the sling on my .300 Winchester and found the buck in my 4x scope. He looked to be 350 yards off. The crosswire came to rest on his back. I fired.

Six or seven shots later the buck lost his footing and rolled down the hill. I collected him at the bottom of a very steep canyon and had to backpack the meat to the top. That grind was fitting. I shouldn't have shot at the deer at all. The misses and poor hits proved I was incapable of getting it right the first time—or the second or third. If you aren't sure of a lethal first shot, it's best to hold

A dead elk is evidence that your bullet hit a vital spot, but it may not have been the spot you wanted to hit. Learn from bad shots instead of bragging about kills.

your fire. It's better to continue hunting with a clean rifle than to miss, or worse, cripple game.

Shoot when you're sure. Decline when you have doubts. Before the hunt, document your skill so you know what you can and can't do with that rifle. By the time you've determined your limits, you'll probably have extended them. Getting your own measure gives you invaluable practice as you concentrate on fundamentals that make you deadly in the field.

Replicating shots from a bench, we know a rifle is accurate. Replicating shots without support, we confirm our skill. On the hunt, rifle accuracy matters a lot less than marksmanship.

Part V: Special Considerations

22

CARRY

I had the rifle in the crook of my arm, muzzle down, when the buck rocketed out from tall grass in the swale at my feet. In a couple of seconds, the deer was at full throttle and yards closer to timber. Meanwhile, my rifle was coming up with all the snap of a truck bed full of topsoil. I got a shot off at last, and missed. Manipulating the bolt was another slow-motion exercise. The deer was dodging through saplings when my second bullet found him.

It was a lucky hit, but not a good hit. I lost the deer. That episode happened a long time ago. For an eight-second slice of life, it left a big mark in my memory.

The problem here wasn't the errant second or third shots (though perhaps I shouldn't have fired them). The problem was my first shot. It was a bad shot mainly because I was cold and my arms were stiff and slow when I tried to mount the rifle. The rifle's weight hanging from my arm had tightened the already-stiff muscles I needed to get my rifle into action. There was no fluidity in my movements, and they were so slow as to give the deer a head start. That delay allowed the buck to accelerate and put him farther from the rifle.

What might I have done differently?

First, I could have stayed warm or gotten warm before moving where deer might force a quick shot. No matter how you dress, really cold weather can send a stiffening chill through your muscles. If you're sitting or still-hunting, it's a good idea to boost your heart rate periodically with calisthenics. No need to follow the routines you learned to hate in 8th-grade gym class; you can get blood moving with some pull-ups on a tree branch or pushups on a deadfall. Maybe you'd prefer sprinting up a steep slope. Really. It's foolish to hunt deer when your body isn't ready to shoot them.

A cradle carry is the author's choice in the woods. A slight swivel of the torso brings the rifle through brush easily.

The second thing I could have done to make a better first shot on that hunt was to cradle my rifle at the ready, folded left arm supporting it across my front, right hand on the grip.

To cradle a rifle, lay the balance point on your left forearm and wrap your left thumb over the grip. If you expect a shot, place your right hand on the grip, your left over it. Horizontal just above waist level, the rifle is now near your center of gravity so its weight won't affect your balance. It responds instantly to a swivel of your hips. When game appears, twist your body slightly to the right. Your left arm lifts naturally, bumping the muzzle in the direction of aim. If a buck is watching you, turn your left hip toward him and ease your left arm up in line with your body so your elbow supports the forend as you take aim. The deer will see little movement.

Once, still-hunting in heavy cover, I spotted the ears of a doe close by. The rut was on, so I glassed slowly into the brush near her, careful not to make any sudden movements. After what seemed like a long time, I spied the curve of an antler among the branches. Both deer were staring right at me. Slowly I lowered the binocular; slowly I brought the .308 to bear. The hit was beside the left eye, my only aiming point. Because I had my rifle cradled, there was minimal arm movement, most of it in line with my body.

There's enormous pressure to throw the rifle to your shoulder when you know a deer is ready to bolt. If you do, you'll almost surely be too late. And a quick mount likely will end in a hurried, inaccurate shot.

The cradle carry keeps the rifle close to your body's center, so it moves easily with you when you turn. Once, having walked by a big buck that held tight to his cover, I happened to catch the glint of his nose from the corner of my eye. I resisted the urge to spin around and shoot. Instead, I took another couple of steps away from the deer, at the same time turning and lifting my rifle. Another step, almost backwards, put me facing the buck. The crosswire settled on his throat as I stopped. The bullet killed him instantly. To any deer, aggressive movement is a threat, as is the human profile. Make those threats equivocal by moving as if you were neither lethal nor human.

In thickets, where you must snake between trees and step over deadfalls, and perhaps bend over to penetrate dense brush, the cradle carry leaves you in control of your movements. You can swivel the rifle without changing your center of gravity. You can stoop over the rifle to shield it from debris, water, or snow.

There are other useful carries and some not so useful. Slinging the rifle on your shoulder is necessary when you need both hands, and it is a good idea if you're making time in dead country between places you expect to see game. It's not the way to carry a rifle in rain or snow. And you'll struggle getting it into action quickly or unobtrusively. A tip: use a quickly adjustable shooting sling like Brownell's Latigo and keep it long. A long sling permits a low shoulder carry, so the muzzle sinks below the overhead branches. You'll control the butt with your hand.

An alternative sling carry is possible if you have a rifle equipped with both swivels on the forend. This short-coupled arrangement lets you use a cobra-style strap (installed backwards) as a shooting sling. You carry the rifle muzzle down from the right shoulder. It's not as awkward as it sounds. Your body protects the action and scope; light pressure from your right hand controls the muzzle. To bring the rifle up quickly, grasp the balance point of the stock with your right hand and twist the toe of the stock outward as you lift. The sling will pop off your shoulder as the sight comes to the centerline of your body. Now turn slightly to the right of your target and bring your left hand onto the forend. Slide your right hand back to the grip. As with the cradle carry, you can shoulder the rifle without much movement outside the frame of your torso, quickly or slowly.

Slings, by the way, are not bandoleers to be strung across your chest from shoulder to armpit. Getting your rifle into action from this stranglehold will give you ample time to watch deer bound far out of range.

A butt-in-hand, over-the-shoulder carry might be OK for troops on parade, but it's hardly the best way to tote a hunting rifle. Balancing the smokepole on your clavicle, you have almost no control over the muzzle. The barrel moves against an open background away from your body, like a flag signaling the deer that you're coming. It bangs against trees and knocks leaves to the ground. The rifle's center of gravity is high, and it raises yours. To grip the rifle for a shot, you must first lean forward to throw it into your hands. Deer are

For long walks, a cobra-style sling keeps you comfortable by distributing the rifle's weight.

likely to scoot before you get hold of the stock. Teetering on your shoulder, a rifle will go flying if you stumble. Snow, rain, and debris will collect in the action and on the scope's front lens.

The muzzle-forward shoulder carry is a poor choice, too. It gives you more barrel control than a butt-forward carry, but you'll burn even more time getting the rifle aimed, and the butt is an even bigger flag. There's a chance that in swinging the rifle off your shoulder you'll point the muzzle toward you—bad form. Muzzle-forward carry is traditional on African hunts. Like cowboy boots on tourists, it doesn't wear as well as when circumstances gave it real purpose. When gunbearers walked ahead, a muzzle-forward carry allowed the shooter to snatch the rifle from his "boy," who would then drop out of the line of fire. Professional hunters who trudge long miles in open country still find this carry comfortable with muzzle-heavy, broad-beamed double rifles. The barrel of a bolt rifle is harder to control with your hand, and the forend is tougher on your shoulder. The balance point is farther to the rear as well, which makes the rifle dance a bit.

Some rifles just carry more easily than others. As I get older, the lightweight carbines that used to be popular among deer hunters in the East grow more appealing. These little lever guns are well matched with receiver sights or forward-mounted scopes. A clean, slim receiver begs a suitcase carry. I like this carry in brush, where I must thread the rifle through branches in my path. It's also a blessing when climbing in steep places where I might have to shoot quickly—or grab a branch or rock to keep myself on the mountain. Maybe that's why those iron-sighted lever-actions still show up in the hands of veteran hunters in the places deer live.

23

SHOOTING WHERE BULLETS SWIM AND SINK

Most hunters where I live would rather hunt open country than thrash around in the thickets where they can't see. Even when the bucks and bulls keg up in thickets, hunters ply the ridgetops, content to look past the places too dense to afford them a shot.

I've been as frustrated as the next fellow, trying to see game I know is there but unable to stay downwind or to move quietly enough to get a peek before the animals are gone. So I've shot a few animals in the open, where the shooting, ironically, can be even tougher.

It's tougher because it's usually longer, and after its first few yards of flight, the bullet begins to struggle. The forces of wind and gravity tug it off course and slow it down. It leaves your line of sight, causing you to miss. I've missed a lot of shots, enough to write about missing.

Hitting, after all, is really just a botched shot gone sour. If you want to hit, you must first learn how to miss.

I started early, back when you could buy McDonald's hamburgers for 19 cents apiece. It was a raw dawn, raw as only Michigan Novembers can be. The buck had given us the slip the evening before, and I was here alone, in the dark, feeling my way along a fence as the frigid wind sang through its taut wires. I stopped at the edge of the woodlot and waited.

When the heavy sky got gray enough to see the musculature in the clouds, I put the K4 to my eye and scoped a wheatfield, the only area that didn't still look black. To my astonishment, the white stubble had a deer in it. My heart was suddenly beating as fast as a gerbil's, and my mouth was dry. In seconds, the deer brought its head up out of the stubble and showed me a modest set of antlers.

But they didn't look modest to me. Hunting where bucks appeared as infrequently as fairy godmothers, I'd have shot a spike. This rack had *points*; it was spectacular! The deer itself, I reasoned, must be as big as a quarter horse. Quickly, I estimated the range at 350 yards and leveled my Mauser over a fencepost. The hollow crack of the .264 did not bother the deer, which again lowered its head into the stubble. My second shot caused it to look up and momentarily stop chewing. At this point, my gerbil heart found a higher gear. I decided my rifle was not shooting where I was looking, which was over the deer's back. Had I smacked the scope? In desperation, I aimed right at the buck and yanked the trigger. The animal dropped.

Pacing 350 steps, I crossed the stubble, a farm lane, a block of alfalfa, the county line, and enough corn to fill a silo. But no carcass appeared. I decided I'd overestimated the range. Backtracking to just 160 steps from where I'd fired, I found the buck. It was indeed dead, as unlucky a deer as I've ever seen.

Gravity and drag conspire to bring all bullets to earth. The acceleration of gravity, about 32 feet per second per second, brings a traveling bullet down at the same rate as a bullet with no forward

Fast, flat-shooting bullets, like the 150-grain Nosler Ballistic Tip in this 7mm Dakota ammo, help you reach through the soup we call air.

speed. That's why, if you dropped a bullet from your teeth at the exact instant you fired one from a rifle held horizontally, they'd both hit the ground at the same time. The fired bullet would simply land in a different place.

If your sightline were parallel to the bore, a bullet sailing to the target would never cross it because the bullet starts dropping as soon as it leaves the muzzle. But the sights or scope bring our eye across the path of the bullet, so that we look through its arc at short range, and again farther out, where we zero the rifle. Bullet drop in ballistics charts is always predicated on a specific zero range. Change that, and drop changes, because the drop is from line of sight, not line of bore. Drop from line of bore does not change, except as you move the bore off a horizontal plane, so it's of no consequence in aiming. Drop from line of sight matters.

Gravity and drag both have huge effects on a bullet's trajectory. Bullet shape and speed influence drag, or the friction that clutches at every bullet swimming downrange through the soup we call air. Unlike gravity, drag is not constant. It's prudent, once in a while, to think beyond the muzzle and consider the bullet not as a rocket but as a fragment driven by an explosion. This mindless shard of lead, spinning as fast as the crankshaft of an automobile rocketing down the highway, must rip and push its way to the target. To a high-velocity projectile, air is like water. It resists penetration. If you touch the surface of a swimming pool, you feel a little resistance but not much. When you swim, you feel much more resistance. A belly-flop from the 7-meter board shows you more resistance still.

A bullet moves so fast that air can't easily get out of its way. Like water shoved to the side by a diver's body, air cleaved by a bullet saps energy. Its movement generates pressure—pneumatic pressure, as opposed to hydraulic pressure—but pressure nonetheless. There's pressure against the nose and the shank and a vacuum forming behind the heel. This pressure counters the violent thrust of powder gas. As friction overcomes inertia, the bullet slows down, and gravity pushes it to earth. The slower the bullet goes, the more time gravity has to work on it, and the steeper its arc. That's why a bullet travels on a parabolic course, not one shaped like a rainbow. Retardation caused by air resistance is roughly 56 times as strong as the force of gravity on a bullet. In a vacuum, a 150-grain .30–06 bullet launched at a 45-degree angle at the modest velocity of 2,700 fps can travel nearly 43 *miles*. The same bullet shot at the same angle and velocity through our atmosphere exhausts itself in less than two miles.

A fast bullet shoots flatter than a slow bullet not because it is less susceptible to gravity's pull (it isn't), but because its speed carries it a longer distance during the fixed time in which gravity takes it to earth. High velocity, ironically, also ensures a greater rate of deceleration. Doubt that? Hold your hand outside an automobile window as you bring the speedometer needle slowly up to 60 mph. It's no trick to steady your hand while the car moves at 20 mph, but you'll fight to hold it against air rushing by at three times that speed. So slow bullets actually travel more efficiently. We happily sacrifice efficiency for performance, whether it's adding thrust to the engines of a fighter jet or powder in the case of a rifle cartridge. Drag takes more than its share of the extra fuel necessary for high speed.

For any given speed, you'll get flatter flight with a bullet of high ballistic coefficient—essentially a measure of the bullet's ability to maintain its speed as it drives downrange. Ballistic coefficient combines a bullet's sectional density (weight in pounds / the square of the bullet diameter) with its form factor, a mathematical expression of shape. While ballistic coefficient is most accurately measured experimentally because it changes with velocity, you can get an approximation with this formula: $C = w/id2$, where C is the ballistic coefficient, w is weight in pounds, i is a form factor derived from bullet shape, and d is caliber. Modern loading manuals by Hodgdon, Hornady, Nosler, Sierra, and Speer save you the trouble.

Sectional density, by the way, is independent of shape, contributing to flat flight only as it increases inertia. In other words, a bullet that's long for its diameter (one with a high sectional density) maintains its speed better than a short bullet of the same diameter. More energy is needed to thrust a long bullet through the barrel because it is heavier for the bore diameter than a short bullet and generates more friction. But once it gets going it doesn't slow down as quickly, for two reasons. First, the hole it must bore through the air is no bigger than that drilled by a short bullet, so friction on the nose is essentially the same (given the same nose shape and velocity). Second, friction, incrementally greater on the longer bearing surface, is more than offset by the extra mass that acts like the weight of a pendulum against deceleration.

Streamlined bullets, with long, pointed noses and tapered heels or boat-tails, are "slippery" in comparison to roundnose or wadcutter bullets whose front ends dam air rather than slicing easily

From left, the 7mm STW, 7mm Remington, and 7mm Weatherby Magnums. All are flat-shooting cartridges, here loaded with bullets of high ballistic coefficient.

through it. The tapered heel smooths air flow at the rear and reduces the slight vacuum that forms behind any moving object (pulling road dirt up onto the tailgate and rear canopy window of your pickup). Example: Though its starting velocity is roughly 80 percent as high as that of a pointed .30–06 bullet, a .30–30 flatnose bullet drops *more than twice as far* at 500 yards. Why? The .30–30 bullet has a lower ballistic coefficient and decelerates more rapidly. Its 500-yard velocity is only 40 percent of its launch speed. The spitzer from the '06 retains about 60 percent.

A .300 Winchester shooting a pointed 150-grain bullet at 3,290 fps is more potent than the .30–06 but not quite as efficient, retaining roughly 55 percent of its energy at 500 yards. Drop amounts to only 3 inches less than that of the .30–06 bullet. Velocity spread between the two cartridges is 380 fps at the muzzle, only 200 fps at the target. The .300's bullet decelerates at a higher rate. Starting faster, it meets stiffer resistance. So though the .300 retains more speed and energy than the .30–06 out to 500 yards, its initial velocity advantage is moderated by a greater rate of deceleration. It has more "lag"—a popular term for the difference between initial and terminal speeds.

Increasing ballistic coefficient by making bullets longer, with more gradually tapered noses, has its practical limits. Eventually the bullet will be too long to seat in a case or to drive accurately without steepening the rate of rifling twist, which boosts pressures. Increasing sectional density can produce a bullet too heavy to be driven fast enough for flat flight over normal ranges.

How far you can shoot accurately depends partly on the ballistic coefficient of your bullet and partly on its initial velocity, as well as on the inherent accuracy of rifle and load. But mainly it depends on you. Skilled riflemen compete with the .308 Winchester cartridge and iron sights at 600 yards, shooting into black bullseyes smaller than the vitals of a deer. But not many deer are shot at 600, 500, or even 400 yards. In fact, a 300-yard shot is a mighty long poke under field conditions. I don't shoot much beyond that, even with a rest, because at such extreme range the bullet is traveling steeply to its rendezvous with the ground. The competitive shooter can hit the V-ring all day because he's zeroed precisely for that yardage, and the distance doesn't change. On the hunt, you don't get sighting shots; the first must be good.

Long shots come available often in open terrain, tempting hunters who can't shoot well enough to make them—and who, most of the time, could sneak closer. It's always better to shoot short.

Once in a while, though, you get a crack at an animal that won't permit an approach. Then you must decide if a shot is justified. My rule of thumb: If, in practice from this position and under these conditions, I can hit a target that size 9 out of 10 times, I shoot. Otherwise, I don't. It's a hard rule to follow.

In Wyoming some years ago, hunkered on the east side of a sagebrush spine, I watched a small pronghorn buck meander across

The author shot this pronghorn at 394 yards, after calculating proper holdover for his .280 Barnes X bullet. No bullet flies straight; they all drop in a parabolic arc.

a distant draw. Almost too late I spied several bedded does beyond me near ridgeline. One of them was looking directly into my binocular. I slunk back into a wash, then bellied over to the west side of the rim and hiked until I was behind the does. Rifle and rangefinder to my front, I crawled up to a notch in the saddle above them and peeked over. They hadn't moved. Five, six, seven of them. But no bucks. I looked with my 8x42 glass into the valley beyond and picked up four more pronghorns. A couple were bucks, and the biggest impressed me. But with the does in my lap, I couldn't move; and the shot seemed too long to attempt.

Then I reconsidered. I'd spent a day shooting this rifle so I'd be prepared for one long poke. . . .

It had been an unusual opportunity to test not only my equipment, but my skill. Magnum Research had built the rifle on a Sako action. Chambered in .280 Remington, the long barrel comprised a thin steel tube inside a thick, carbon-fiber jacket. The high-power variable Burris scope had a Ballistic Plex reticle. Lifesize deer and antelope targets at 200, 300, then 400 yards taught me where to hold for center hits with the flat-shooting Barnes X-Bullets. After a full day on the range, mostly from hunting positions, I managed to put four bullets into a palm-size group in the shoulder of a paper buck at 400 steps. A fifth shot leaked out. Climbing the hill that morning, I'd been pretty confident that I could kill a pronghorn at 400 yards.

So why was I hesitating? Mainly because the buck looked tiny at what my Leica rangefinder told me was an honest 394 yards. That's farther by half than I normally shoot.

As my pulse settled, I traded the rangefinder for the rifle and got into my sling. Then I wiggled up on top of the saddle, prone with a rock under my left hand. The crosswire was very steady. I felt no wind. Perfect. Pasting the second bar on the buck's lower ribs, I launched an X-Bullet and called a center hit. The buck ran immediately, which pleased me. But there was no *thwup* coming back. That didn't please me. The buck stopped, and I all but decided against another shot. If the first had missed, I didn't know *where*. Hence, I could not correct. If I couldn't correct, there was no point in shooting.

The buck stood, uncertain. "You probably shot low," I chided myself, a fresh round now in the chamber. It would be my last shot, hit or miss. I held the bar higher and carefully sent another 140 Barnes X down the valley. Instantly the buck was on the ground, and the sharp crack that floated back told me the bullet had struck his spine. I cycled the bolt once more and held the crosswire on what little I could see of him. The does and the other buck had rocketed down past him at the first report and were now filing around a distant outcrop. I gathered up my gear and, after marking the buck's position, eased down to him. A finishing shot later, I was lifting that beautiful head and running my fingers over horns that would tape just shy of 16 inches. The promised rain fell in earnest then, soaking me. I gutted the buck, propped him open over a bush, and began the hike out.

Practice had paid off, but even under ideal conditions, my first bullet had gone astray, and the second had hit high. Distance is an enemy.

Overshooting spares lots of deer and not a few pronghorns, both of which are smaller than many hunters think. A big north-woods whitetail may measure 40 inches at the shoulder. If you think it is taller, you will think it is farther, and you will miss over the top. Remember that when you zero a rifle, you adjust the sight so the barrel points above the target. You have already factored in a great deal of bullet drop. For cartridges like the .30–06, a 200-yard zero allows you to forget about trajectory to 250 yards. That's far. A deer looks very small at 250 yards. If you don't know the range, you're wise to aim as if the deer were 50 yards closer than you think.

Unless the range is long enough to give you pause, or your rifle is a Civil War relic, hold the reticle where you want to hit. Shade a few inches high if you think you must, but if you see daylight under that horizontal wire, odds are you'll miss. Through many seasons, I've hit a lot of big game animals in the spine. Two of the three bucks I killed last season were spine-shot. It's very easy to shoot high. In fact, the only time you're likely to shoot low is when you're aiming at a front-lit target across country that is table-top flat. Your tendency under those conditions will likely be to underestimate range.

Range estimation becomes important beyond 250 yards with the '06, beyond 300 with the super-magnums. A 250- or 300-yard zero stretches the flattest shooting of cartridges, but puts your bullet significantly higher at midrange where you'll shoot most of your game. I zero almost everything at 200 and figure a drop of 6 inches at 300 if I'm shooting a .25–06, a .270, or a 7mm or .30 magnum cartridge. Make it 8 inches with a .30–06. All those bullets will get you venison at 300 steps if you hold on the animal's spine. At 350 yards, aim a foot or a little more above where you want the bullet to land. A 400-yard shot delivers your bullet 18 to 24 inches low, depending on the load.

You will, of course, have checked impact points on paper targets before season. You'll also have put your range estimating skills to the test, either by pacing or using a laser rangefinder. If you can stay within 10 percent of the actual yardage, you're pretty adept. Bullet strike error will be insignificant to 300 yards. Any shot farther than that requires a more accurate estimate, as the bullet path gets steeper.

Incidentally, if you're shooting uphill or down, your bullet will hit higher than it would if the shot were taken horizontally. The greater the distance, the greater the effect. So hold low when shooting both uphill and downhill if the range is long and the angle severe. Inside 200 yards, with a gradient of 30 degrees or less, forget about vertical angle. The hold-under at long range is pretty easy to calculate. Pretend you're at one corner of a triangle, the target is at another corner. The third corner is the right angle formed where a horizontal line from your rifle and a vertical line from the target meet. Find or estimate the distance from your corner to the right-angle corner, and hold for that distance. Gravity works parallel to the line from the target to the right angle, and perpendicular to the horizontal line connecting you to the right angle. *Gravity does not work perpendicular to a bullet's path if that path is tilted up or down.* The effect of gravity on the bullet fired at a steep angle is essentially the same as its effect on the horizontal component of that bullet's flight. A bullet traveling at an angle forms the hypotenuse of your imaginary triangle. That's the longest side. Hold for that distance, and you'll hit high, because gravity applies only to the horizontal component, a shorter side of the triangle.

If you have trouble talking yourself into holding low, envision shooting directly up and directly down. The bullet shot skyward flies parallel with gravity's pull, so its path will not be an arc, but, in the

Aim low when shooting steeply uphill or downhill, especially at long range. Gentle angles within zero range (say, to 200 yards) don't require correction if you're hunting big game.

absence of wind, a straight line. Drag (friction on its surfaces) and gravity will cause deceleration and bring the bullet to a stop. Then it will fall, heel-first, straight down. A bullet shot downward, through a pipe that spits the earth on its axis, likewise does not curve in flight. It flies with the force of gravity on its tail. Drag still slows it down, and it will eventually succumb to gravity's effect coming from the opposite side of the earth. Gravity has its greatest effect on a shot fired horizontally, where it acts perpendicular to the flight path. Shots taken at angles between horizontal and vertical show flatter and flatter flight paths as the angles approach vertical.

Fast, flat-shooting bullets demand the least correction. Up to 200 yards, given shot angles of 20 degrees or less, you shouldn't need to compensate for shot angle when you're aiming at big game. As many hunters miss by overshooting game within the point-blank range of their rifles, many more overcorrect when shooting uphill and down. Some "correct" the wrong way. Remember, shade *low* on targets both above and below you, but keep those adjustments slight, save when the angle is very steep or you're shooting low-speed bullets with steep trajectories.

24

SHOOTING WHERE THE WIND BLOWS

The air we shoot through is more like an ocean than a swimming pool. It has currents called wind. Storms whip up invisible waves. You might say that air even has tides—the drift you can't feel but which can be read in mirage.

Unlike gravity, the tug of wind is not constant. It can be gentle or fierce, gusty or steady. Neither does wind follow gravity in bending the bullet's path in only one direction. Wind can come from any direction on a horizontal clock. It can even move your bullet vertically. Figuring out how wind will affect a bullet is part science, part an art. Do the math properly, and you'll hit the target. But getting all the right numbers in your calculations presupposes a wind that can be studied, both at your position and along the bullet's path all the way to the target. Target shooters on manicured ranges do their best with wind flags and vanes on delicate needle bearings, but how do you calculate the net effect of an eight o'clock breeze at the line, countered by a fishtailing wind from three to five o'clock off the adjacent bank at midrange, and gusts that straighten to three o'clock flags at the target butt?

A wind at right angles to the bullet's track is called a "full-value" wind by competitive shooters because it has maximum effect. A quartering wind uses some of its force on the bullet nose or heel, reducing net displacement to the side. For rifles with right-hand rifling twist, a three o'clock wind will move the bullet not only to the left but up to ten o'clock. A nine o'clock wind will depress the bullet as it drifts left. Wind directly from twelve o'clock or six o'clock has little effect unless it is very strong, and then the result may not be what you think. A bullet fired at a distant target across level ground is actually launched slightly nose-up *and remains nose-up.* Surface exposure due to the bullet's in-flight attitude affects shot displacement. Unlike an arrow, a bullet is not heavy at the front and light at the back. It does not "porpoise." So a wind from behind the bullet may actually depress it, while a wind from the front can lift it. Net effect may be high or low, depending on drag. Remember, wind is simply a change in pressure, boosting or reducing air resistance on a bullet's flight path. Of course, a 20-mph wind (moving 30 fps) can't push a bullet zipping along at 3,000 fps. But the change in pressures fore and aft, relative to those on a day with no wind, can affect shot placement. Ordinary wind speeds don't appreciably retard or accelerate bullets; with hunting rifles you'll seldom see any changes in point of impact.

Thermal drift has little physical influence on a bullet, but mirage moving up from a warming earth or rifle barrel can distort or even move the target image. You'll wind up aiming at an imaginary target. That's the bad news. The good news is that mirage shows you wind that's too light to register reliably on other indicators. I've often kept close watch on the mirage that weaves lazily up through my sight picture on a warm day. As long as the current is vertical and my shots are hitting center, I shoot as fast as I can. Such still conditions are not to be squandered. If the mirage flattens out to one side or the other, though, it's time to reassess. Even if you can't feel the breeze,

The .240 Hawk, essentially a 6mm/06 with the shoulder moved forward, can hurl 80-grain bullets over 4,000 fps. They also buck wind better than .22 bullets sent that fast. Fred Zeglin developed the cartridge.

it's there, and if you're shooting a .22 rifle at 100 yards or a centerfire at 600, a wind that barely bends mirage can cost you points by the bushel. Likewise, if I've zeroed for a prevailing wind that taps my bullet into the X-ring from three o'clock, I'm spooked by heat waves that suddenly rise across the bullseye. A let-up will put me out of the middle to the right. It's as deadly as a pick-up in wind speed, which in this case would shove my bullets left.

The worst surprise is a reversal in wind direction, because it's so insidious. Zeroed for a 5-mph breeze from, say, nine o'clock, you'll be hammered by a wind that caroms in at 10 mph from three o'clock. The net effect is a 15-mph blow, a veritable gale if you're trying to thread a .22 bullet into a 1-inch circle the length of a football field away. You'd feel 15-mph wind if it suddenly hit you on the line. But a 10-mph bandit breeze at the backstop is harder to detect. That's why I'm particularly concerned if a prevailing breeze suddenly dies. A let-up often precedes a reversal. The 20x scopes commonly used for any-sight events in rimfire matches will pick this up quickly. If you're shooting with iron sights, seeing the mirage through the spotting scope only between shots, you may catch a reversal too late, after your bullet has made an unpatchable hole in the 8-ring.

Hunting bullets are subject to the same abuse as target bullets, as prairie dog shooters are well aware. But big game is commonly shot at ranges, and with bullets, that don't show the effects of wind so graphically. A .30 magnum slinging a 150-grain Nosler Ballistic Tip bullet at 3,200 fps gives you less than 3 inches of drift at 200 yards in a 10-mph full-value wind or a hard 20-mph wind quartering in. A 5-mph breeze drifts the same bullet from a .30–06 just 3½ inches at 300 yards—as far as I'll likely shoot. You can ignore a lot of wind.

Fast bullets buck wind better than slow ones. Bullet shape can markedly affect drift; Nosler Ballistic Tips show less drift than most hunting bullets. Here are some comparisons of deflection from a 10-mph wind at 90 degrees. (Abbreviations: N = Nosler, H = Hornady, SP = Soft Point, FP = Flat Point, BT = Ballistic Tip, RN = Round Nose.)

range (yards)	0	100	200	300	400	500
.223 Rem., 55-grain NSP						
velocity (fps)	3200					1603
drift (inches)		1.0	4.5	10.8	20.5	34.7
.30–30, 150-grain NFP						
velocity (fps)	2300				1044	
drift (inches)		1.9	8.4	20.4	38.9	63.7
.308 Win., 180-grain NBT						
velocity (fps)	2600					1806
drift (inches)		.6	2.9	6.8	12.4	20.2
.308 Win., 125-grain NBT						
velocity (fps)	3000					1840
drift (inches)		.8	3.4	8.0	14.9	24.4
.30–06, 150-grain NBT						
velocity (fps)	2900				1926	
drift (inches)		.8	3.0	6.9	12.8	20.7
.300 Win., 150-grain NBT						
velocity (fps)	3200					2163
drift (inches)		.6	2.6	6.0	11.0	18.0

Note the differences in velocity spreads between the 180-grain and 125-grain .308 Ballistic Tips. The bullets leave 400 fps apart but at 500 yards are traveling at about the same speed. The 180's higher ballistic coefficient and modest start make it more efficient. Wind drift is the same out to 250 yards, as the greater weight of the 180 offsets the velocity edge of the 125. But beyond 300 yards the heavier bullet stays closer to the sightline. The 125's great rate of deceleration reflects its vulnerability to wind. Weight alone has less effect on a bullet's performance in wind than you might think. Consider the 55-grain .223. This bullet weighs a third as much as the 150-grain .30–30 Flat Nose bullet, but its greater speed and, more importantly, more aerodynamic shape give it an edge. At long range, it drifts only about half as much as the .30–30 FN. A 150-grain Ballistic Tip in a .30–06 doesn't move from the muzzle as fast as the .223 bullet, but at 500 yards its 300 fps deficit has been erased, and it is traveling that much *faster* than the .223 bullet. A higher ballistic coefficient is responsible. The 150-grain .30–06 bullet shows only a third of the wind drift downrange that you must expect from the less aerodynamic .30–30 bullet of the same weight. Some other figures to ponder, again assuming a 10-mph full-value wind:

range (yards)	0	100	200	300	400	500
.300 Wby., 180-grain NBT						
velocity (fps)	3200					2296
drift (inches)		.5	2.2	5.1	9.3	15.0
.375 H&H, 300-grain HRN						
velocity (fps)	2500					1164
drift (inches)		1.6	7.1	17.3	33.2	55.6
.458 Win., 500-grain HRN						
velocity (fps)	2100					1112
drift (inches)		1.7	7.1	17.0	31.8	51.7

A 180-grain bullet from a .300 Weatherby, driven as fast as a 150-grain from the .300 Winchester, drifts 3 inches less at 500 yards, a function of the additional weight and 133 fps less lag at that range.

The improved long-range performance results from a higher ballistic coefficient. Given the same bullet shape and diameter, you reduce deceleration as you add weight. Deceleration rate is part of the reason the 300-grain .375 bullet deviates a bit more from line of bore at long range than the slower bullet from a .458. Terminal velocities are nearly identical, but the .458 loses only about 988 fps en route, while the .375 drops 1,336 fps. (This .375 solid, incidentally, is one of the least aerodynamic of many .375 bullets available.) The ballistic coefficient of the .375 is slightly lower than that of the .458, whose great weight also extends maximum range and reduces wind drift.

Bullet displacement due to wind is most critical at the muzzle because that's the apex of a bullet's angle away from bore line. A tiny shift in course there puts the bullet far off the track far away, just as a bullet nicking a branch near the muzzle will strike farther from center than if the branch were just in front of the target. On the other hand, because the bullet's velocity is highest at the muzzle, it is most resistant to wind there. So, for any given increment of travel, it will be less affected up close than it will downrange when velocity has dropped.

It's important to practice shooting in the wind. Not many hunters do, because wind makes the groups bigger. But just as practice from the bench won't prepare you for shots from hunting positions, so too practice only on calm days is no way to learn wind-doping. To shoot well in the wind, you must have experience reading it, and you must know its effect on the bullet you're shooting. You're also smart to shoot standing when the breeze is up to practice holding and trigger control. A small anemometer like the Kestrel, and a swinging vane-and-propeller arrangement like that used by competitive riflemen will help you learn to judge wind speed. Watching the effects of wind on the grass and leaves also makes sense, because on a hunt you may have to dope wind quickly while shouldering your rifle.

Keep in mind that bullet drift in charts is commonly noted for 10-mph crosswinds, but that in the field you'll seldom get a wind

You'll learn a lot about wind by shooting—and watching a partner shoot—prairie dogs at long range.

perpendicular to your bullet flight. I have a few rules that help me correct for drift with ordinary pointed softpoint bullets (ballistic coefficients .350 to .430): At 200 yards, a 10-mph crosswind drifts a bullet about as much as gravity depresses it (or midrange trajectory, given a 200-yard zero). Ditto at 300 yards. By the time the bullet reaches 400 yards, drift in a 10-mph wind diminishes to 60 to 70 percent of drop. Double the wind speed, and you double the drift. Drift triples between 100 to 200 yards. Drift doubles between 200 and 300, and again between 300 and 400.

My friend Jeff Hoffman at Black Hills Ammunition has more precise formulas. His firm provides the Match ammunition for Army and Marine rifle competition. Accuracy standards are high, and testing at long range, Jeff has to know the effects of wind. "The military formula is too slow to use in the field," says Jeff. "My favorites are lots simpler. One method is to square the range in hundreds of yards, then subtract it, again in hundreds of yards, to get inches of drift. For example, if you're shooting at 600 yards, you multiply 6 times 6 to get 36, then subtract 6 to get your correction, in this case 30 inches. You'll hit close to the middle if you're shooting a .308 Match bullet in a 10-mph crosswind."

Another way to come up with correction is to subtract 1 from the range in hundreds of yards to get minutes of drift. Using the 600-yard range again, you'd subtract 1 from 6. The result, 5, is in minutes, so you must multiply to arrive at inches: 5 x 6 = 30, or the same answer that you got with the first method. Of course, if you use a bullet with markedly different flight characteristics, the formulas don't hold.

It's easy to overestimate the effect of wind on a big game bullet, but shooting prairie dogs or paper targets at long range with smaller bullets, you'll be impressed by the influence of even a small breeze. As with gravity, the longer you subject a bullet to wind, the more pronounced the curve away from your straight line of sight.

25

WHEN THE
TARGET MOVES

The buck catapults through the opening and is gone. You play it again in your mind in slow motion. Your niece could parallel-park a Greyhound where that deer crossed. Why didn't you shoot? If the whitetail had been a ruffed grouse, you could have easily fired both barrels.

Running game is harder to hit than standing game, so I generally pass up running shots. But if you develop skill practicing on moving targets, there's no reason to hold your fire. After all, a running deer is just as big as one standing still. The key is knowing how much to lead, possible only when you know the animal's *apparent speed*—actual speed mitigated by the angle of travel. A deer running 20 mph across your front has an apparent speed of 20 mph, same as its actual speed. If that buck turns at a 45-degree angle, his apparent speed is cut in half, though he's still moving at 20 mph. A deer running directly toward you at 20 mph requires no lead; apparent speed is 0. The other components of your lead equation are range and bullet speed. Say the range is 225 yards and you're shooting a 7mm Remington Magnum. Your 160-grain 7mm bullet leaves the muzzle at 3,000 fps. But wait. That's only *exit* speed. You need to know how long the bullet takes to reach the target, so *average* velocity over 225 yards is the correct figure. That's just shy of 2,800 fps. The target is 675 feet distant, and the bullet arrives in a quarter-second. During that time, the deer moves about 7 feet (20 mph is roughly 29 fps; ¼ x 29 = 7+). Swing the crosswire 6 feet in front of the shoulder and keep swinging as you fire. You'll shred the lungs.

Trouble is, calculations like this only work when you have lots of time to do the math, or to recall where, in practice, you held that sight. Happily, shots that require lots of lead are shots you won't have to take often, because mostly they're the long shots in open country, evidence of stalks gone sour, of inept hunters and shooters who don't hit with the first bullet.

But even up close, lead matters. And though the correct lead may be short, you'll typically have to know it instantly. Forget calculations if your reticle is trying to catch a big buck flagging his way through the thornapples. Good grief, in that wink of time, I couldn't tell you my zip code! And as for those practice shots, they never quite prepare you for what happens on a hunt. They do help you shoot better; but field conditions make each shot a new experience. You have to earn, through experience, a *vision*. The vision comes instantly, and it shows you just where to put the sight.

The vision is most valuable on shots up close, for deer rocketing from cover you could touch with a fly rod, and vanishing so fast that a .410 skeet gun would feel like an irrigation pipe in your hands. There's seldom time to swing smoothly in front of deer or elk jumped in thickets. You must shoot fast.

My first snap-shot happened before I had time to participate. The buck appeared 15 feet away, leaping over a fence and dashing off through the hardwoods. The old SMLE fired itself. It must have been on my shoulder, as I remembered later seeing the bead against the buck. It was such an instant kill that I felt cheated—until later, when I had a chance to repeat.

The author shot this bear as it walked fast, quartering away at 150 yards. The lead? Six inches or so.

This second buck gave me more time. Caught seducing a hot doe in a swale between two woodlots, he sped straight away through tall grass. My fingers were cold, though, and the rifle as sluggish as an Oldsmobile's exhaust pipe. Finally, I found a tail in the K4 and yanked the trigger. Before I could chamber my second round, he'd dodged at right angles. I missed as he melted into the maples.

The next buck bounded out of a swamp and ran up a hill in front of me. It was a crossing shot at 50 yards, and I was prepared. Swinging the .303 smoothly, I fired with the bead passing his brisket. Without so much as a shiver, he continued on out of sight. I followed and, shortly, found him dead.

The difference between pointing a shotgun and aiming a rifle isn't that great. In both cases you must align the barrel with the target. Sights simply help you align it more precisely. Up close, though, precision becomes less important than speed. Hitting the watermelon-size vitals of a deer far away takes time. At 20 yards you should be able to hit a watermelon in no time at all.

In fact, you do it with a shotgun routinely. When you really clobber a grouse or a clay target, the center of your pattern passes within a few inches of the mark.

Snap-shooting a rifle is part art, part science. It is not merely throwing bullets at game and hoping for a hit. It is a high form of marksmanship, fluid but orchestrated, the equivalent of a smooth give-and-go in basketball, the cat-quick snake of a heeler's rope in the rodeo arena. Snap-shooting means taking instant aim with a moving rifle and ticking off a few carefully rehearsed procedures in rapid succession—perhaps in the wink of an eye.

Still-hunting through the woods, stop where you can shoot. Bucks often break cover during a pause in your movement. Pick places where your feet can be quickly placed for a shot and where you have shot alleys in several directions. Have your rifle in hand, not slung on your shoulder. Keep an elastic chest strap on your binocular so there's no interference when you bring the rifle up quickly. In cold weather, wear slitted mitts that free the fingers of your right hand. Keep that hand in a large jacket pocket if the day is especially bitter. You won't have time to shuck a glove when a buck streaks away.

Fast shooting starts with good footwork. Keep your feet shoulder-width apart, your left foot advanced a few inches toward the target. Keep your weight on the balls of your feet, knees and hips relaxed. Think of how you'd shoot a grouse. Keep your right elbow high (to form a pocket in your shoulder), your left hand well forward (to better control the muzzle).

Before the sight and target merge, you'll have committed not only to a shot but to a shooting technique. It's the one you've practiced on rabbits or hand-tossed cans and milk jugs. There are three common options.

Paint the deer out of the picture. Duck hunters pass-shoot this way, bringing the gun up from behind a bird and firing when the muzzle blots it out. The key is to swing faster than the target and keep the swing going after the shot. Proper lead comes after you pull the trigger, the muzzle accelerating out in front as the shot exits. This swing-through method works for deer crossing openings. Deer sprinting through the woods can change direction quickly, and you won't see the tree that catches your bullet. Also, the deer won't be in the scope field for your entire swing, and there's a temptation to keep the reticle on the animal when they come together. Result: You slow your swing as you shoot, and you miss behind.

Tug the deer along on a string. Establishing lead, then sustaining it as you pull the trigger, you don't have to time your shot as precisely as when swinging from behind. Presumably, no matter when you fire, you'll have the correct lead. The problem with sustained lead is that it tempts you to stay with the target too long as you anticipate changes in speed or direction and verify your hold. You won't squeeze the trigger as quickly. A whitetail crossing a stubble field gives you lots of time; deer in the thickets must be shot quickly. Also, a long swing can pull your body into an awkward position, causing you to muscle the rifle and miss.

Map out a hit, then snap-shoot. Imagine a sight picture as soon as a deer appears. Gauge target speed and direction while you position your feet and lift the rifle. Shoot quickly when the sight looks right; you build in the lead before the scope allows you to aim. Snap-shooting, you find shot alleys before the sight gets in the way. The sight picture is really a confirmation of your bullet's path, the shot a conclusion to events already in motion. You can shoot quickly this way when you must or use more time as you lift the muzzle. Though your rifle should move with the deer, you are not committed to a swing. The shot happens where the bullet has its best chance. Snap-shooting makes the most of limited time and tight shooting alleys.

No matter which method you choose, mind your stance. Stay fluid, and anticipate your rifle's movement. Position your feet

When taking a moving shot, stay fluid, knees bent, more weight on the forward foot, your body aimed where you expect the shot to occur. Swing quickly and smoothly. Don't hesitate.

immediately to allow a comfortable swing. Accommodate your rifle's natural point of aim. Remember that you must be spot-on for lead, whereas bird hunters have a broad pattern to help them. A shot string is long, too, with pellets following pellets into the target plane; rear pellets kill when you lead too far. Bullets give you no such latitude. Finally, remind yourself that a deer must be hit in the vitals. If getting a bullet to the lungs looks difficult, pass up the shot!

I like the snap-shot best, partly because an accomplished snap-shooter is so much fun to watch. A snap-shot is to marksmanship as a barrel roll is to aviation. It's evidence of fundamentals long mastered, a flawless melding of procedure and natural rhythm, consummated in triple-time. My snap-shooting is, by most standards, hardly snap-shooting at all because I'm by nature and training a very slow shooter. Exhibition shooters might not only chuckle at my efforts, but deny snap-shooting themselves. Though much faster and more accurate than I am, they feel the time pass slowly, a result of great economy of movement. Only the novice feels rushed. Tom Knapp doesn't look hurried when he breaks nine clay targets, tossed at once, before any hit the ground. He just doesn't waste time. In fact, he points out that because those targets fall so close to one another, he sometimes must pull his shot off center, smashing the edge of the disk to avoid hitting another.

No matter its speed, a snap-shot is still an *aimed* shot. If your sights aren't on target (or properly leading it), you will miss. Rehearse your shooting routine, releasing the safety, shouldering, aiming, and dry-firing at the thumbtack you've stuck on your living room wall. Do it over and over, beginning a smooth trigger squeeze as you cheek the stock. Complete it without hesitation. Your goal is to better direct the sight as the striker is falling, not to time your shot when the sights look good. Dawdle, and you'll miss your chance to shoot. Up close, that rifle must go off by itself. Once you commit to the shot, don't stop until after your follow-through. One exception: If you must abort a shot for safety's sake or because the target made cover or another animal crossed your sightline, abort instantly and without thought to continuation. Indecision, like stalling a trigger squeeze, handicaps you. Don't practice it.

Holding your fire in anticipation of a standing shot is not hesitation. It's procrastination. You haven't given yourself over to the shot. Though the rifle may come to your shoulder, you're waiting. You're also gambling that the animal will stop, or that you'll have time to shoot anyway if it doesn't. In waiting, you relinquish the best moving shot for the possibility of a standing shot—at least, that's what you must assume. Sometimes luck is with you.

I was tripping along toward camp late one afternoon when a bull elk jumped from a waterhole to my right. A quick spin, and I had elk hair in my scope field. But I didn't shoot. Rifle and bull were out of synch, bouncing this way and that. He might stop. . . .

He did, and at 70 yards the shot came easy.

Another time, a herd of elk erupted from the slope across from me, hurtling into the timber. Odds were slim at best that any would stop. I swung the .270 and fired and a spike bull somersaulted. At that instant, the woods held only the echo of hooves. A second's procrastination here would have left me with no shot at all.

In Africa, when a huge eland all but sideswiped me on his way out of a thicket, I fired without thinking about standing shots. Something about the place, the sound, the sight picture told me instantly not to wait. I can't say the demeanor of the animal matters, because when you must shoot right away, you may see nothing but the blur of a scapula in front of your sight. No, there's an intuition born of experience that tells you to shoot fast or wait. It's the same intuition that tells you whether or not you have a shot at all.

26

WHERE TO HIT
BIG GAME

When we shoot at a black bullseye, we shoot for the middle. It's just as important to pick a spot on a game animal. Simply shooting at the animal is like asking Lufthansa for a ticket to the Middle East without specifying a destination airport. To shoot well, you must shoot at something almost too little to hit: an off-color wick of hair, a tiny muscle crease. Archers know the perils of aiming at the whole animal. Riflemen get help from the reticle or sight, but quick kills also depend on picking the *right* spot.

"I shoot 'em in the neck. They drop in their tracks."

Well, animals always drop in their tracks because they can't very well drop anywhere else. But shooting for the neck or the head is bad business. The reason: Neither is a vital organ. The neck and head comprise myriad bones and nerves, muscles and organs, many of which can be lost without preventing escape. The spinal cord in the neck and the brain in the head are vital organs. But they're hard to hit. If you can't hit a grapefruit under hunting conditions, you've no business shooting for the brain. The spinal column is long, but hidden. It lies very low ahead of the shoulders. If you miss the brain or the spine, the bullet can cause the animal great misery. Break the jaw, rip the eyes, shatter the nose, or slice the esophagus or windpipe, and the animal will run off with serious damage that commonly turns septic. I once dispatched a starving deer I found on a forest road. The creature's lower jaw had been shot off by an inept hunter.

Hitting a spinal process (one of the "blades" protruding from the spinal segments) may put the animal down temporarily; but you must destroy the spinal cord or cut the carotid artery or jugular vein for a quick kill. Long hair on elk and the swollen necks of rutting bucks make those nerves and vessels very hard to place. Shooting game in the neck is like shooting at a hose in a clothes-dryer-exhaust tube hidden behind a curtain.

A shattered rear spine disables the rear legs. But the spine is as hard to find in the body as in the neck. I've read of hunters shooting animals at the root of the tail, following up with a shot to the vitals. I hit a Coues deer there once, with a 140-grain bullet from a 6.5x55. It drove forward far enough to kill after shattering the spine. Mostly, I pass up rear-end shots. End-on, the spine's terminus is a tiny target; from the side, it is also obscure. If you miss the spine, the animal will in all likelihood escape with gruesome internal injuries. Long ago in a Michigan swamp, on a dark day that leaked cold rain, I spied a whitetail buck at close range. I was carrying a Marlin 62 in .22 Magnum. The buck was facing away from me. I had only a second, long enough to break the spine at the root of the tail. I aimed, hesitated, declined. At that time I had never killed a deer and wanted one badly. But it was the right decision.

Years later in Zimbabwe, I sneaked up behind a Cape buffalo and hit him with a 300-grain .375 bullet from the rear—not a smart thing to do. The grass and mimosa were thick enough to derail a locomotive, and the buffalo, lots of them, were close enough to interview. "Best you drill the bugger now." The problem was that the big fanny in front of my sight had no aiming point. I couldn't see

This fine Utah bull required several hits because the first was not in the right place.

enough of the animal to know at what angle my bullet would strike. I shouldn't have fired.

When the Model 70 mashed my shoulder, there erupted a great popping of brush, as if the beasts were racing away in heavy boots. Slamming another cartridge home, I pushed forward. A big hairy hand yanked me back. Eager beavers, it told me firmly, become compost. Wait.

Silence settled hot on the gray thorn. Twigs ticked down through the dust. The sweet cattle-smell of buffalo remained. We inched forward. How far had it been? Forty feet? Can't kill a buffalo at forty feet? Wait; there's movement! I poked the muzzle at the black mud suddenly filling the slits between branches. I reloaded and fired again, jamming more solids into the magazine. The death-moan came. And I felt ashamed.

When you must stop an attack, or down a cripple, or kill to eat, shooting to anchor makes sense. But most of us shoot at uninjured animals for sport. There's no good reason to shoot to disable. If you can't thread a bullet to the vitals, best wait until you can. When you shoot at pieces of animal that aren't immediately vital, you're shooting in desperation. Desperation and sport have nothing in common.

Shoulder shots have advocates, because the shoulder is major structure. Smashing it keeps the animal from going far, and the bullet is likely to damage vitals between the shoulders. Each shoulder has two main components: The humerus connects the fused radius-ulna, or top leg bone, to the scapula, or shoulder blade. When I target the shoulder, I aim for the center of the scapula, two-thirds of the way up on the animal's torso so the bullet shatters the spine, too. But because a shoulder shot often requires a follow-up, and because it ruins a lot of meat, I seldom use it.

Occasionally, a shoulder shot excels. Once, hunting elk, a client and I glassed up a fine bull in a basin below. Shadows had flooded the brittle wyethia by the time we'd made our way to the basin floor. The bull bugled from inside the trees, but shooting light had almost left us when at last he appeared—almost 300 yards distant and not coming closer. When he stopped, my companion fired, aiming for the shoulder. Through binoculars I watched the bull collapse. We hurried forward to give it a finisher. Had my partner targeted the lungs instead of the scapula, this huge elk might have run and died far enough into the timber to make recovery difficult that night.

Another time, hunting alone, I spotted a bull elk as it broke cover on the far side of a narrow canyon. It sped through an opening, my only shot alley. I swung a couple of feet in front of its shoulder and triggered my Model 70. The 180-grain Speer struck the point of the shoulder, and the elk cartwheeled just short of timber.

Still, my favorite shot is to the lungs. Assuming the bullet opens as it should, a hit through the "forward slats" is always fatal and generally brings the animal to earth within a few seconds. You lose no meat. Best of all, the lungs are a big target, and they're surrounded by organs and bones that make marginal hits lethal. Miss the lungs high, and you likely shatter the spine. Aim too far forward, and you strike the shoulder, too far back the liver. A low bullet often hits the heart.

The lungs lie between and behind the shoulders. I've been surprised, when opening dead elk from the side to assess the placement of organs, to find that the lungs fill almost half the rib cage. Indeed, they extend from the third rib to the ninth on top, tight to the spine, and from the third to about the sixth along their bottom edge, which lies about even with the visible "elbow" joint of an elk. The lungs are big enough to hit easily.

Here's where to shoot from the side: Divide the near shoulder into fourths vertically, starting at the hump and running your imaginary line to the elbow joint. Mentally cross out the bottom quarter and the top two quarters of this line. Now, in your mind's eye, pivot

The author shot this outstanding caribou in its bed with an iron-sighted .300 Savage, angling the bullet from the rear ribs forward. The bull never got up.

the remaining segment horizontally. You get the equivalent of a crosswire superimposed on the front ribs tight behind the shoulder. Draw a circle around the outer ends of the crosswire. If your bullet lands inside that circle, you'll kill the animal.

I've heard of many failed lung shots. But having seen some animals recovered that had been reported as lung-shot, I suspect that many, if not most, game lost to riflemen were hit somewhere else. Animals commonly run or stagger a short distance after a lung shot. Sometimes they react violently, kicking with their rear feet at their brisket and sprinting. One whitetail, hit with a Speer bullet from my .30–06 Improved, dashed 50 yards and piled up. The exiting bullet sprayed the snow red 19 feet beyond the buck. But you can't count on either blood or theatrics to tell you of a fatal hit. Assume every shot is fatal—otherwise you wouldn't shoot, right? A big animal can absorb a lung shot without responding. Two elk I recall hitting at modest range with heavy, high-speed bullets simply moved off. Both were dead in seconds. If the bullet doesn't exit, you may find no blood on the ground, despite massive internal hemorrhaging. A whitetail I hit with a .300 Savage bullet bolted at the shot. Confident, I marked the spot, evident from hoof-gouges in the earth. Then I followed the track. No blood. I returned to the shot site and looked more carefully, finding two short hairs glued together with a dab of pink tissue the size of goose shot. It was proof of a lung hit. I again took the trail, found blood within 70 yards and the carcass, after a sharp turn, just beyond that.

Bullets needn't destroy both lungs, though a double-lung shot generally gives you quicker results. Of the three elk I shot most recently, two were hit in one lung. Both stayed on their feet, one falling after a dash into timber. The other gave me a chance to shoot again. The third bull took my bullet through both lungs. He ran too, but only after hunching, and it was immediately clear that no second shot was necessary.

Hunters who think the heart a superior target are certainly better marksmen than I am. The heart of an ungulate is less than a quarter the size of the lungs. Besides, it lies low in the chest, where a rough trigger pull or an error in range estimation can mean a broken front leg and a long, fruitless tracking job.

The only lung-shot animal I've failed to recover was a mule deer hit just before dark during a snowstorm. I hit the animal poorly with my first bullet, but got another shot as it scrambled over a small ridge on the hillside. I called a good let-off and heard the strike. But darkness and snowflakes as big as shuttlecocks were obscuring the sky. The woods had turned black. Hurrying to the ridge, I brushed away snow and found blood. The trail led into a thicket impenetrable in the descending darkness. I climbed to continue my search the next morning and found deep snow over everything. No tracks.

My failing in that situation was shooting in the first place. The storm was freakish, but even without snow, a shot taken on the edge of night puts recovery at risk. I'd have been wiser to pass. Last year, much older, if only a bit wiser, I declined a long shot at an outstanding buck in the last hour of daylight. I'd like to have claimed those antlers.

Knowing where you want the bullet to travel inside an animal, you sometimes have to adjust point of impact on the outside because not all your targets will be standing broadside. Hunters who shoot well in the field think in three dimensions. My companion Ron surely was when he triggered a shot a few years back.

They were obscenely big bulls, each bigger than most hunters will ever see during a hunt. And there were seven of them, in sum enough bone to build another antler arch in Jackson Hole's town square. We were above them, within rifle range, and it was hard to tell which animal had the best rack.

It was foolhardy to advance, exposing ourselves to see all the elk under the lip. We should have waited. But we didn't. All those bulls, almost close enough to touch! It affected our brains.

Then one of them saw us and decided to leave. The others followed, sifting through the boulders, climbing to the east where the red hill would hide them. But it was our day. Antlers broad enough to cradle a powerboat, the bull we'd spotted from across the basin finally came into view. He was quartering steeply away. Ron drove a 250-grain Partition into his flank. It was as if the .338's report had triggered a bomb in the basin's belly. Six bulls put the hammer down, trailing dust as they galloped east. The wide bull labored north, straightaway. I heard the bolt shut. "He'll stop," I said. He did. The rifle pounded again, and the elk, broadside at 300 yards, buckled.

The beams taped 50 inches inside and 54 inches long. But I was more interested in the first bullet. I found the entrance hole and tracked the bullet as it had angled through a rumen stuffed to near bursting. A morning in the pasture had packed enough greenery in there to fill a forage wagon. The Nosler had gamely fought its way forward but run out of steam just after punching the diaphragm. Bullet failure? No. Wet hay stops the best bullets. The second Partition had threaded both lungs like a hot nail through Crisco.

Shot presentation matters. Because you don't always get a look at the forward ribs, it makes sense to use a powerful cartridge and a bullet that will drive through a truckload of sugar beets. Doesn't it?

Not necessarily. Most big game is shot from the side. And it's hardly coincidence. Deer and elk don't like to expose their hindquarters to predators. So they position themselves to move right or left. Besides, they can see well to the side, not well to the rear. How many animals, after detecting you, have stood with their hindquarters toward you? Probably not many. When you spot an animal first, there's usually a chance to get a side-to or gently quartering shot. You can either wait or move to give yourself a more favorable angle.

But what if the animal doesn't show you its side? Well, sometimes you'll have to conjure up vitals behind the reticle. They're three-dimensional, essentially a ball whose diameter is one-fourth the depth of the animal's chest. (Really, they're bigger. But give yourself a

Quartering shots can be deadly. But on big animals like elk, don't hit the ham, and even when you angle a bullet into the rear of the rib cage, use a deep-penetrating bullet. Here, hit the off-shoulder. Credit: Chuck and Grace Bartlett

small target, and you'll shoot better.) If the game is quartering away from you, aim for the off-shoulder. The steeper the angle, the farther forward you want the bullet to exit. Threading a bullet from the last rib, aim for the point of the off-shoulder. Assuming your bullet is strong enough to penetrate the paunch, that's a deadly shot.

From the front, you're just reversing the bullet path. An animal quartering steeply toward you can be taken handily with a hit just inside the point of the near shoulder. But a bullet striking that big shoulder knuckle on an elk will have hard sledding. It may not drive through. Even if the shoulder is badly damaged, bullet failure there leaves the animal with all its lights burning. On three legs, a deer or elk will leave you far behind. The trickiest part of shooting animals from the front is keeping your bullet far enough forward while avoiding heavy structure.

I've shot two elk quartering so steeply that, keeping my sight as close as I dared behind the shoulder, I still hit only one lung. The first bullet, a 140-grain .270 Swift A-Frame, stopped in the off-side flank, nicely mushroomed. The second, a 200-grain Nosler Ballistic Tip from a 8.59 Lazzeroni Galaxy, exited from the off-side flank. The first elk died running in a few seconds. The second gave no reaction but allowed me a second shot. Big, sturdy animals can survive a one-lung hit long enough to give you a trailing job.

A straight-on shot gives you a narrow target, but if you can keep the bullet between the shoulders, it's a sure thing. One morning long ago a bull elk sauntered out of the mist in front of me. I put the reticle in the middle of his chest and launched a 180-grain Partition from my .300 Winchester. The impact threw him back, but he recovered and ran off. I followed and found him dead a few yards away. The bullet had driven into the off-ham. On another occasion, I shot a black bear in front with a .308 Winchester. The 165-grain Trophy Bonded bullet penetrated 32 inches, through the paunch. The bear collapsed at the shot.

Given such penetration, animals facing away should be as easy to kill, right? No. A bullet delivers most of its energy and the widest part of its wound channel in the front third of its path, so a back-to-front trip doesn't have the same effect. Also, a bullet driven through the chest encounters less resistance than one hitting the ham; which means it doesn't open as violently. You can't expect a bullet that plows easily from brisket to haunch to get as far starting from the rear. A bullet sliding between the hams has a much easier time of it. Depending on the distance, bullet speed and construction and animal size, a shot below the tail *might* reach the brisket. But there's not much space between the hams, and the pelvic girdle is a formidable barrier. If expansion puts a broad nose on your bullet on entry, drag will likely keep the bullet from driving forward.

Shooting down on an animal is pretty easy. You just make the bullet track between the shoulders. Ditto for shooting up. But be aware that you're not seeing a side view. It's easy to hit low when you're shooting at game above you, and high when you're shooting down, because you're seeing mostly belly and back. Hold in the vertical middle unless the shot angle is so steep and the animal so distant that a low hold is justified. A lot of game that is poorly hit from above and below would have been better shot if the hunter had forgotten about the effect of shot angle on bullet trajectory. With close game at gentle angles, forget it.

Some shots just need to be declined. Alas, most hunters who finally get game in their sights are loath to pass. That amiable campmate who offered you a Snickers bar while telling you about his daughter's piano recital at mid-morning break can become a monster when antlers appear. His eyes glaze over and his lips curl carnivorously. He wants to kill something because something is in front of him and he has a 7mm Magnum in his paws, now hairy and long-nailed. Your noon chat about Thoreau and Leopold, and the shared wonder at autumn's color, is lost on him as he ratchets the bolt to send a hail of bullets toward the horizon.

One man chastised me for writing about 6mms and .25s as elk cartridges, ending his note by claiming that anyone who said they'd decline a shot at a mature bull was a liar. It seems to me anyone with so little self-control as to shoot reflexively is a hazard in the woods.

Any shot that requires a "brush-busting bullet" is best left alone. That's because there are no brush-busting bullets. In tests, I've sent a variety of bullets through sagebrush screens into paper targets and found that branches small enough to snap between your fingers can turn even heavy bullets. Husky 250-grain .35s entered the paper sideways several inches from center—though the paper was mere feet behind the brush. A 12-gauge Foster shotgun slug looks formidable, but it too deflects on twigs. The worst offenders, of course, are fast, lightweight bullets of low sectional density; but when you shoot into brush, you take a chance of deflection with any bullet you throw.

Not long ago, still-hunting elk in Montana, I came upon a bull standing behind a thin screen of dead conifer branches. The bull was only 60 yards away, and for 50 yards my bullet would have had

Short magnum cartridges properly feature bullets built to hold together. Unnecessary for deer (in fact, more frangible bullets give quicker kills on light game), they're best for elk and moose.

clear sailing. I saw no big limbs, just wispy stuff all so close to the elk that any deflection of my big .338 bullet would have been slight indeed. Still, I passed up the shot. The bull left.

Later, on the last day of a deer hunt, I had a crack at a whitetail buck under much the same conditions. I didn't want the whitetail more than I wanted the elk, but the weather had been tough for days, and this would be my only chance. I took it. The slug cut white hairs from the buck's brisket but, happily, didn't hurt him. It was a shot that shouldn't have happened. Penetration is one thing; straight flight is another. Bullets that drive through big trees may still deflect on small branches, resulting in a miss.

In sum, "an animal's life is between its shoulders." A hunter told me that long ago. He's still right. Aim a third of the way up from the elbow on side shots. If you don't have a side shot, wait for one. If you can't wait for one, shoot quartering animals to pass the bullet between the shoulders just below centerline. Take steep quartering-away shots only if your bullet is designed to penetrate. Avoid big bones on the near side. Decline shots through the hams—and shots through brush. And follow up every shot you take, whether or not you see signs of a hit.

27

SECOND CHANCES

Most hunters take pride in a one-shot kill. In truth, many animals must be shot repeatedly before the hunt is over. Because follow-up shots must often be taken quickly, at animals on the move or farther off, they're usually more difficult than first shots. What makes them *really* hard is your own sense of urgency. Or panic.

Some years ago a hunter and I sneaked within 100 yards of a bull elk visible through a gap in the forest. He shot. The bull went down, got back up, and stood still, unsure of where to move. The hunter fired four more times, reloaded and shot another magazine dry without a hit. He was resting the rifle over my spotting scope, but his body shook uncontrollably with excitement. Every miss increased the urgency of the next shot. My efforts to calm him proved fruitless, partly because I was pretty excited myself. Eventually he ran out of ammo. Luck was with us. I raced back over the ridge to fetch a rifle from another hunter in the next drainage. The bull was still standing when I got back.

This man handicapped himself, I believe, by using an autoloading rifle, which can encourage fast, sloppy shooting. While a single-shot rifle hardly guarantees better results, it can make you more deliberate. But the most glaring void in this hunter's kit was a practiced self-discipline. Though no one would want to lose the excitement of the hunt, keeping emotions under control for follow-up shots helps you hit.

One Wyoming autumn in the high country, I spied a bull elk sneaking through a stand of Douglas firs. He paused in an opening and dropped to my shot. But he wasn't dead. Partially visible, he thrashed around in low brush as my partner came up from below to join me. "Shoot again!" he urged. Without a good target, I declined. He got very excited telling me to hit the elk before it got up. It was not bad advice; but I was sitting, wrapped in a sling, with the elk in my scope. I could have shot instantly if the elk had jumped up. Had I fired without a sure target, the elk might have rocketed off while I was working the bolt. I waited a few more seconds, got a look behind the shoulder, and put one more bullet through both lungs.

The best shot you'll get is usually the first. That's not because it's closest (sometimes a hit animal will run toward you). It may not afford you the best presentation or the best light or the clearest view. It is, however, *the shot that gives you the most options*. You can choose to trigger the rifle, wait, or not fire at all. You'll select follow-up shots, too, but after a hit you can't choose not to shoot. That prerogative is yours only with an animal that hasn't been hit. When you draw blood, you're committed and must finish the job.

The first shot is also the best because it is typically at an undisturbed animal. There's no rush. You can find a rest or steady position, double-check the wind and the distance, let your crosswire settle a bit, crush the trigger as if it were an egg and you didn't want to wet your finger.

Still, no matter how confident you are, no matter how easy the shot, things can go wrong. A second-shot routine makes sense for anybody who hunts with more than one cartridge in his rifle. Oddly enough, many hunters who carry enough ammunition to have turned the tables at the Little Bighorn do not practice second shots.

A long second shot put this deer on the ropes after a marginal first hit. It is much better to make that first shot the best shot.

The first rule of second shots is to reload right away, before the echo of the first shot has died. Train yourself to reload automatically, whatever the reaction of the animal and wherever you think the bullet went. Forget about the brass. Don't look at it. Don't even think about it.

If you hit an animal, well or poorly, the best option is to stay where you are, rifle ready, and shoot again as soon as you get a good opportunity. If your quarry is moving away and unlikely to show you its vitals, shoot again as fast as you can with accuracy, aiming for what you can see. (Be sure it is indeed the same animal you hit!) Keep your eye glued to the animal, noting its travel direction and behavior, and that of other animals if it is in a herd. Shoot when you can hit, but decline low-percentage shots.

Several years back I came through a dense stand of conifers at dusk and jumped a herd of elk. They crashed away in all directions. I pivoted toward a flash of antler and put a .338 bullet into the shoulder of a bull. The animal went down but got back up and was in the thickets moving fast. I fired as soon as I saw hide in the scope, then fired again. The last round in my rifle dropped the bull for good. In this case, waiting for a better shot would have meant no follow-up at all.

If you move toward an apparently helpless animal, it may find the energy to bolt. Once a hunter and I jumped a big elk from its bed. It stopped when I chirped on my cow call, then collapsed at the hunter's shot. My companion started forward. I pulled him back. We waited one full minute, then moved toward the motionless form. At less than 10 yards the animal vaulted to its feet and sped off. The hunter stared. "Shoot! Shoot!" I screeched. He did, three times, barely killing the elk before it got out of sight.

This rifleman surprised me with his deft bolt manipulation. Many hunters don't know how to reload quickly because they shoot mostly from a bench, picking out each fired case and leisurely dropping it into an ammo block. In the field, you can't afford to look down. The animal may vanish or change places with another of its kind, leaving you wondering which was hit. Take a tip from National Match shooters who must operate the bolt very fast in the rapid-fire stage of that event: Make up some dummy cartridges (mark them well!) and practice running them through the chamber as you watch television. Some riflemen do that from the shoulder; I prefer dropping the butt slightly. Bulky hunting clothes should be part of your drill.

You can't duplicate in practice the panic you might feel as a big buck or bull sprints away. But you *can* boost your pulse with a burst of exercise before each routine. This will force you to tame the rifle and control the trigger as you aim through a sight picture that looks like news coverage of an 8.5 quake.

Second bullets shouldn't be necessary. Often they are. The hunters who bring home the most game don't all make one-shot kills. But no matter how good they think the first shot was, they're always prepared to shoot again. They start engineering their second hit even when they're sure they won't need it.

Sometimes they do. And so will you.

Your rifle must cycle cartridges smoothly and dependably. Practicing bolt manipulation prepares you for a quick follow-up shot.

FIRST BLOOD

The elk had come out early, in my path. I'd seen her first and had made no mistakes. She was in a draw on a horse trail, nibbling thistle. I'd never shot an elk in such an easy place.

At about 100 yards, the slope fell away to give me a clear shot over the weeds. Kneeling, I pressed the trigger. The elk ran off, vanishing into the belly of the draw to the right. I bolted in another round. It wouldn't be needed though; I'd called a shot through the heart.

A bit low, I remembered. But not *too* low.

Suddenly two elk popped out of the draw to my left and raced through a small opening to the timber beyond. At woods edge, both stopped. Then one lifted a foreleg and limped ahead, halting after a few steps to look back. With the crosswire against her ribs, I hesitated, then. . . .

Last fall a moose hunter and his guide spotted three bull moose and two cows far away. Steep, brushy terrain prevented a stalk. After a while, the animals drifted into the trees to bed. Hunter and guide followed, and after a lot of sneaking and peeking, took a quartering shot. Confident that at least one of his two bullets had struck, the hunter joined his guide on the animal's track.

Suddenly a bull sprinted into view. The hunter swung and fired. Moments later he stood over a mediocre and very dead moose. The bigger bull, still losing blood, reappeared shortly in an opening a few yards ahead of the men who'd resumed their tracking. The hunter took aim and. . . .

What would you have done, seeing an elk limp away from where you'd just shot? How about finishing an animal you knew you'd crippled, after shooting another?

Taking care with a first shot should absolve you of such dilemmas. Follow-up shots are the penalty for poor marksmanship. But even the most careful hunters make bad hits. Then they must decide whether another shot makes sense.

Sometimes it doesn't.

The problem with shooting twice is that you can hit two animals. It happens often, commonly this way: The target vanishes at the shot, then leaps into view again. Here, truly, is a sucker's draw, and hunters who fire hastily show their inexperience. Missed animals almost never disappear instantly; only a bullet is quick enough to erase a target during recoil. The reincarnation is bogus: a second animal that you didn't see. Sadly, many hunters shoot before they think, partly because they haven't enough confidence in their first attempt.

Calling a first shot good should be routine. If the reticle isn't on the vitals when the rifle jumps, you either took a risky shot or failed to hold or squeeze properly. If you can't say where the reticle was, you closed your eyes. Incompetence is easier to identify than to admit.

This fine elk took three hits before collapsing. Even if the first shot is good, hammer elk until you see their undercarriage. But make sure you're shooting at the same elk!

If the sight looked right, though, what then? How much faith should you have if the animal you thought you killed reappears?

I held my shot at the limping elk mentioned above. Despite evidence to the contrary, I was sure my first bullet had struck the vitals. A few minutes later, I was proven wrong. Tracks showed that the elk had dashed right, then doubled back in the draw, emerging to the left with its companion. Kicking myself for poor shooting and for letting that follow-up opportunity slip, I trailed the elk up into the forest until nightfall. Next morning I was back, gaining only a few more yards before the sparse blood stains vanished altogether. Given the nail-head droplets from the off-side only, and a few specks of brisket fat, I concluded the bullet hit lower than my call, nicking but not breaking the left foreleg. The elk had climbed steadily through difficult timber without bedding. I lost the trail at ridgetop.

Too much confidence in my call? You bet. Should I have triggered a second round? Sure. Is a bad call as reprehensible as a bad shot, or a hold so shaky as to preclude an accurate call? You answer that one.

The fellow who shot the wrong moose, on the other hand, assumed his first hit was *not* fatal. The blood trail so indicated. But he was wrong to shoot without making sure. The second shot forced upon him another choice: Finish the big bull and report the boondoggle or let the animal go. After watching that moose join its companions, hunter and guide decided the wound was not lethal. They left the moose, hoping it would heal.

If you shoot as if each shot will be your last, you'll shoot better. Follow-up shots won't be needed. You'll shoot again at elk you know you hit only because every savvy elk hunter says you're smart to keep shooting at elk until you can see their undercarriage. But if you aren't sure which animal took the first bullet, a second shot is risky. Killing two elk won't win you any friends. Killing a second after maiming a first merely underscores your incompetence.

A client of mine once clobbered two elk. I'm not sure which of the five big bulls he was aiming at when the follow-up shot hit a leg. But it wasn't the wounded bull I had in my binocular. "Stop shooting!" I screeched. We got the first elk after a short tracking job and another bullet. The second escaped. Of course, I was partly to blame. Had I directed the hunter more clearly, perhaps a mixup wouldn't have occurred. The "second bull from the left" may have been on the extreme left in his field of view. When it's the last day and yellow rumps are packing six-point racks toward Tulsa, hunters and guides alike make quick assumptions in the interest of a quick shot.

If, in the heat of the moment, an inner voice whispers that you might stop shooting, you're smart to comply. Right away. Sometimes, we don't hear that voice.

In the subarctic a few years back, I chanced upon a small group of caribou. Though I'd already shot a fine bull and had not intended to fill my second tag, the sight of tall antlers flipped a switch. I shadowed the herd. At last the biggest bull moved away from the others. Offhand to clear the brush, I couldn't steady the rifle against the stiff wind. Foolishly, I fired anyway, calling a high shot even as the bullet kicked a small geyser from the lake beyond the caribou. A chase ensued. Three 120-grain Noslers later, the bull was down. Walking toward him, I was astonished to come upon a caribou that looked just like him and appeared equally dead. Concentrating on just one animal, and waiting for clear shots, I'd nonetheless killed a second bull.

On some outfitted hunts, there's a "first blood" rule. Your tag is committed at first evidence of a hit. If you don't find that animal, you go home without one. It's an incentive to shoot carefully and at modest ranges. It's also an incentive to fire follow-up shots. But no rule can tell you what to do when you lose sight of a target momentarily and then see its likeness again. Despite my failure to tag the elk that gave me a second chance, I reserve follow-up shots for animals I can *positively* identify as the initial target—animals that have been in sight all the time or that are so distinctive as to be unmistakable.

It's possible that as much game has been clobbered unintentionally with follow-up rounds as has been lost by hunters too cautious to fire again.

28

YOUTH, SAFETIES, AND COMMANDMENTS THAT DON'T COUNT

These days, you can get in trouble recommending guns for kids. Murder in high schools makes a compelling argument for keeping guns *away* from kids. At least, by current logic.

But that logic is suspect. When I was a kid in the 1950s and early '60s, guns were more accessible than they are now. My parents didn't like guns and didn't own any. But most of my friends had guns at home. We saw them on wall pegs over the fireplace, in glass-fronted cabinets, behind coat racks in mud rooms, under pickup seats, and in closets, bedrooms, and basement workshops. For us youngsters, however, those guns might as well have been on the moon. We didn't touch 'em without permission. If we wanted to shoot, we earned the privilege by obeying the rules of the house.

We all wanted to shoot.

Toy guns enabled us to act out our fantasies. The snap and smoke of cap pistols mesmerized us for awhile, but we eventually tired of them because they didn't launch anything. Water pistols of that day were as potent as pocket tubes of insect repellent. I bought, for three dollars and sixty-seven cents, a plastic rifle and a half-dozen metal cartridges with spring plungers that pushed plastic bullets at paper airplane speed. It was more sophisticated than my slingshot, not nearly so lethal. Its effective range was shorter than that of a paper clip from a rubber band—the silent weaponry we hid in our desks at school until one day in class the preacher's son stung the superintendent with a well-aimed clip fired through an open window. Had he not gawked at the reaction, rubber band dangling, we'd have avoided disarmament a lot longer.

I whittled a submachine gun from a piece of scrap lumber. I tried to make a matchlock with a two-by-four and some black powder poured into the hole I'd bored with a brace and bit. Fortunately, the two-by-four misfired. Next came a pistol with suction darts to shoot empty raisin boxes tossed in the air. My father, an academic, thought this a deplorable waste of time.

As cowboys and Indians, mountain men, and defenders of the Alamo, then as GIs in the Pacific Theater, we urchins handled toy guns with abandon. We pointed them at each other and yelled "rat-tattattatgotcha!" fast enough to make any wooden submachine gun smolder. But there was a line we didn't cross: We never allowed real guns to point at anybody. We knew the difference.

I was a long time wishing for a gun of my own. I visited the local hardware store weekly to stare at a single-shot Winchester .22, dreaming I'd someday have the $16 and permission to buy it. By the time a BB gun came my way, I was practically old enough to shave. Big game hunting seemed far off, indeed.

A lot of hunters these days grew up with much easier access to real guns, but the generation of hunters now graduating high school and college will find them less accessible, and shooting less acceptable. Bullets get a lot of play on television, and they don't come across as good things for kids. What's missing are real-life experiences for children on the target range—chances for children to have fun shooting.

Shooting is not what children these days are led to believe. Television and video-game violence not only makes traditional cowboy-and-Indian games look civil; it is even less realistic. No risk or effort is required for destroying things on screen. You press buttons and all life collapses at your feet. Omnipotence for pennies. And unlike the black-and-white westerns that inspired our play in the

Never allow the muzzle to point at anything you'd regret shooting. And remember: the muzzle is always pointing somewhere.

post-war years, there are no *good* men on screen. Only victors and vanquished. Chilling.

Not long ago I fired a 50-caliber machine gun. Its roar can make you feel the gods themselves are at your trigger thumb's command. Then you think of Verdun and Guadalcanal and Tet. Only children can imagine the power without the consequence. If in growing up they miss the connection, they make the gun into something its designers never intended.

Few young people today have watched an exhibition shooter. That era passed in my youth, as Herb Parsons gave his last demonstrations. He'd lay perhaps a dozen guns on a table. He'd tell the people in the bleachers about gun safety and what guns he had, and how guns worked—and while he was talking he'd throw eggs, potatoes, and cabbages over his shoulder and blow them apart with bullets. It was great fun for one so gifted, an inspiration for those of us determined to practice until we, too, could milk seven rounds from a Model 12 in a burst so fast it sounded like the roll of thunder, leaving only smoke floating where seven clay birds had hung briefly in the air.

The biggest threat to shooting's future may be our inability to fuel a passion for it among the young people doing battle on video screens to the throb of hard rock music. The increasing cost of hunting, with permit quotas and short seasons, discourages beginning hunters. Black-bullseye games are dull compared to what is on-screen and online. Besides, skill with firearms requires both discipline and coaching, both in short supply in single-parent homes.

Oddly enough, equipping young shooters gets more attention than teaching them. We like to talk about rifles, scopes, and cartridges. Equipment has little to do with a youngster's marksmanship or hunting success. Coaching does. Hitting is the point of shooting. A gun by itself is no alternative to the mindless screen games that promote the violence we seem so shocked to find in schools. To get youngsters excited about target shooting or hunting, it's important that they learn to hit—that they see shooting as more than gun ownership or the killing of game. Shooting competition and hunting can demonstrate elements of sportsmanship and valuable life lessons; but they're also fun. Promoting the fun while introducing those other elements of marksmanship is difficult these days. It's still a sound investment in our youth. Coaching tells young shooters not only what to do, but that you're interested in them and in shooting. Children need applause for a hole near the middle of a paper target, and for shots well executed even if they're far off center. Just as they need a nudge toward disciplined practice.

There's little more to say about rifles for young people. Your preference of rifle, cartridge, or scope doesn't matter. Marksmanship matters. The discipline that produces good marksmanship comes largely from the enthusiasm and coaching we bring to the firing line, where we can help youngsters discover guns and hunting for what they are, not for what television and video games imply they are.

It's unfortunate that guns have been painted as dangerous and deadly, because they are neither. The shooter determines whether a firearm is loaded or not, and, always, where it points. Handled intelligently, a rifle is no more dangerous than a lawnmower; statistically you're much more apt to suffer harm in an automobile. A rifle can't do anything alone. People do things with rifles. Rifles respond only to physical cues. So it is that sometimes rifles do not fire when we want them to, and occasionally they fire when we don't want them to.

When accidents happen, it's natural to blame the rifle. The Remington Model 700, for example, has had its share of recriminations. Claims that the safety on this rifle has been responsible for several injuries and deaths afield has left many owners questioning the reliability of their 700s. Is the safety safe?

No—inasmuch as the safety is a mechanical device. Only shooters can be safe or unsafe. A safety is one helpful layer of protection against accidental discharge. Anything mechanical can fail.

The trigger is not a handle. Keep your finger off until you're ready to shoot.

Which is why I seldom use safeties, or encourage their use, on a firing line. In my view, reliance on a safety makes shooters careless. They forget about where the muzzle is pointing. A safety is handy in the woods because it can prevent discharge if brush or clothing snags the trigger. Safeties that block the striker (the 700's does not) can break the firing cycle if your rifle falls and the impact frees the sear. But the safety is not what keeps people from being shot. Muzzle control is the only thing that can do that.

As a youngster, I dutifully learned the ten commandments of shooting safety. I've since jettisoned them—not because they're worthless, but because 10 is too many to remember easily. So many that no single rule stands out as important. I've come to lean on one rule: Never allow a gun to point at anything you'd regret shooting. That's all. Remember that, obey it, and you'll never shoot anyone accidentally. A corollary might be: Keep your finger off the trigger unless you intend to shoot. Resting your finger on the trigger, a common fault, can embarrass you. Still, the shot won't hurt anyone if the muzzle is under control.

Do manufacturers bear any responsibility for accidents? The courts determine that. We'd be quite angry if an automaker installed cardboard brake lines. How irresponsible! But if we accelerate into a sharp corner and say after the rollover that a proven brake system failed, what then?

About four million Remington 700 rifles have been produced since the rifle was announced in 1962. In 1982 the thumb safety was modified to allow bolt cycling with the firing mechanism blocked, a change most shooters welcomed. Some hunters point out that it can also lead to accidental bolt lifts. A bolt out of battery will not permit firing, so a hunter yanking his rifle from the scabbard or off his shoulder for a quick shot might find too late that he needed to tap the bolt shut first.

Debate over the 700's alleged propensity to fire as the safety is released continues. According to one attorney, several hundred such cases have been reported. One "gun expert" was said to have "seen literally hundreds of thousands of customer complaints where people have complained about pushing the safety off and the gun firing through floorboards of pickups, through picture windows, through roofs, you name it." If this expert counts the way I was taught to count in grade school, hunters have a problem — and not only with shoddily-built rifles.

If safety failures were as common as fear-mongerers would have us believe, they wouldn't make headlines. My gun rack holds 11 Model 700 and 78 (an economy-grade Model 700) rifles, in standard and wildcat chamberings from .22–250 to .338. Some are old, some new. Many of the triggers have been adjusted light enough to make any class-action attorney lick his chops. None of those rifles have ever fired accidentally. Sure, by reducing the sear engagement I can make any of them fail to cock. I can do that with the Winchester Model 70s beside them and with just about any other rifle. In 35 years of shooting and being around shooters, I've seen no injury accident caused by a Model 700.

Can releasing the safety on a Model 700 cause the rifle to fire? In my experience, that's possible only if the sear is held out of engagement at the same time. Usually, pressure on the trigger trips the sear. But if the trigger was pulled earlier and for some reason (grit, a weak spring) did not return to its original position, the safety then acts as a trigger. That's probably how Remington engineers were able to "trick" about 1 percent of a sampling of Model 700 rifles to fire by safety manipulation alone.

Wrangling over the merits or shortcomings of rifle mechanisms can't bring a bullet back. Nothing brings bullets back.

When I was growing up, safeties didn't get much press. Every so often a writer with a tight deadline and an empty docket would compare safeties that locked the striker with those blocking trigger movement. Most still agree that for bolt rifles, it's hard to beat the three-position Model 70 Winchester safety that came along in the late 1940s. When "on," it locks the bolt and striker. The center position lets you operate the bolt without unlocking the striker. Still, many fine rifles and aftermarket triggers incorporate safeties that work like the Remington 700's.

They're all easier to use than the hammers whose half-cock notch served as a safety on lever and pump guns like the Marlin 336 and Winchester 94 and 97. I remember a 97's hammer slipping off my wet thumb as I stood to reload after shooting a goose. The unexpected recoil nearly blew me out of the canoe. A single-shot 20-gauge I used on pheasants as a lad had a hammer spring strong enough to use on a half-track suspension. Many a rooster flew off as I struggled with that spur, and once or twice it got away from me. It's a good idea, when thumbing back *any* hammer, to turn the gun slightly so you catch the spur with your knuckle sideways. Pulling straight back with the thumb pad invites slippage.

Safety has become a political issue these days. The firearms industry has largely capitulated to calls for a heightened level of safety in gun storage and use. Shooters get "free" trigger locks, and we are all urged to keep guns under lock, out of sight. Gone, I'm afraid, are the days when you could admire fine rifles and shotguns on the wall or in glass-fronted cabinets. We're told that display openly invites

The Remington 700 safety has had its share of criticism. It's like every other safety: a useful layer of security that is also a mechanical device prone to failure.

theft and plays to adolescent curiosity. Vaults are the rule now, tombs in which we bury fiddleback French walnut and case-hardened Colts, svelte upland doubles and the silvered steel of antique saddle guns—all safe at last from prying eyes.

In the field we're safer because, besides the half-cock notch on the hammers of lever rifles, there's a crossbolt safety. Remington and Sako rifles feature locking bolt shrouds, complete with keys you can lose to make your firearm forever safe. For twitchy fingers, gun companies and their legal advisors have given us triggers that will lift an unabridged dictionary.

Like a dull ax, guns made difficult to use can be *more* dangerous. You have to work harder with a blunt blade; consequently, you lose control. Rely on safeties and heavy triggers, and you'll wield any gun with a heavy hand, paying less attention to the muzzle.

Of course, design flaws that lead to accidental discharge need fixing. But design flaws are usually caught early on in products with high engineering and tool-up costs. I'm not selling my 700s.

Many years ago, bone-tired after a long, cold day hunting ducks, I staggered home, shed my vest on the screened porch, and stowed my 870 pumpgun in a corner just inside. After a late supper, I stumbled toward the bedroom, bleary-eyed but remembering to check the shotgun's chamber. I slid the forend back, peeked in, closed the action and pulled the trigger. The roar of the 20-bore brought the ceiling, shredded by a magnum charge of sixes, raining onto my shoulders.

"Something wrong with the stove?" Alice called from the bedroom.

"Uh, no. Just a gun problem."

Not true. Shooters who leave shells in the magazine as I did are not gun problems. This is hardly a new trick. "Checking" your rifle or shotgun without a deep look into the well can be worse than not checking at all. You take liberties that you wouldn't if you knew there were cartridges inside. A friend of mine, guiding elk hunters, almost lost his hearing when one of the men, riding beside him in his pickup, decided to pull the trigger of his rifle. The rear window disintegrated, the bullet narrowly missing my amigo. Shaking off the concussion of the 7mm Magnum, he rolled both hunters out of the cab and told them quite clearly that he didn't approve.

Never allow a gun to point at anything you'd regret shooting—that's really impossible, of course, unless you store your rifles outside. A firearm is always pointing *somewhere*, and only the sky and earth, among things that come quickly to mind, can be shot without regret. I'd as soon have not shot the ceiling, and I wouldn't have if I had remembered the corollary and kept my finger off the trigger. Probably you've never done something so stupid. Maybe you never will. Impossible or not, the rule is still a good one because it prompts you to think about where the muzzle is. That's what matters. The position of the safety does not. Nor does its design.

INDEX

Note: Page numbers in boldface indicate illustrations.

Y
Yellowstone Park, 63
Young, Arthur, 7
youth and guns, 309–19
   need for coaching, 312–13
   and sportsmanship, 313

Z
Zeglin, Fred, 43, 92

Zeiss, 136, 152, 163
zero check, annual, 186
zeroing, 116–17, 129, 141, 154, 158, 195, 243
   from hunting position, **186**, 196, 243
   tips for surefire, 179–83, **183**, 184–89
   and the wind, 184
zero range, 182–84, 259